GOD AND HISTORY IN THE BOOK OF REVELATION

This is an interdisciplinary study which constructs a dialogue between biblical interpretation and systematic theology. It examines how far a reading of the Book of Revelation might either support or question the work of leading theologians Wolfhart Pannenberg and Jürgen Moltmann on the theology of history, exploring the way in which the author of Revelation uses the dimensions of space and time to make theological points about the relationship between God and history. The book argues that Revelation sets the present earthly experience of the reader in the context of God's ultimate purposes, by disclosing hidden dimensions of reality, both spatial – embracing heaven and earth – and temporal – extending into the ultimate future. Dr Gilbertson offers a detailed assessment of the theologies of history developed by Pannenberg and Moltmann, including their views on the nature of the historical process, and the use of apocalyptic ideas in eschatology.

MICHAEL GILBERTSON took his doctorate at the University of Durham. Ordained in the Church of England, he is now the Vicar of Stranton in Hartlepool, England.

SOCIETY FOR NEW TESTAMENT STUDIES
MONOGRAPH SERIES
General Editor: Richard Bauckham

124

GOD AND HISTORY IN THE BOOK OF REVELATION

God and History in the Book of Revelation

New Testament Studies in Dialogue with
Pannenberg and Moltmann

MICHAEL GILBERTSON

CAMBRIDGE
UNIVERSITY PRESS

PUBLISHED BY THE PRESS SYNDICATE OF THE UNIVERSITY OF CAMBRIDGE
The Pitt Building, Trumpington Street, Cambridge, United Kingdom

CAMBRIDGE UNIVERSITY PRESS
The Edinburgh Building, Cambridge CB2 2RU, UK
40 West 20th Street, New York, NY 10011–4211, USA
477 Williamstown Road, Port Melbourne, VIC 3207, Australia
Ruiz de Alarcón 13, 28014 Madrid, Spain
Dock House, The Waterfront, Cape Town 8001, South Africa

http://www.cambridge.org

First published 2003

Printed in the United Kingdom at the University Press, Cambridge

Typeface Times 10/12 pt.   *System* LaTeX 2_ε [TB]

A catalogue record for this book is available from the British Library

ISBN 0 521 82466 4 hardback

For Jenny

CONTENTS

PREFACE

This interdisciplinary study brings together a reading of the Book of Revelation with an assessment of the work of Wolfhart Pannenberg and Jürgen Moltmann on the theology of history. Although both theologians have been influenced by apocalyptic, there has been no detailed study of their work in the light of Revelation, the most important Christian apocalypse.

Chapter 1 sets Pannenberg and Moltmann in their context, showing the influences which have shaped their work. Chapter 2 examines some of the methodological issues which arise in relating scripture and systematic theology together.

Chapters 3–5 form a detailed study of Revelation, exploring the way in which the author uses the dimensions of space and time to make theological points about the relationship between God and history. This in turn encourages faithfulness to God in the present.

Chapter 6 is a detailed assessment of the theologies of history developed by Pannenberg and Moltmann, including their views on the nature of the historical process, and the use of apocalyptic ideas in eschatology. Their proposals are analysed alongside conclusions from the reading of Revelation in chapters 3–5.

The study therefore constructs a dialogue between biblical interpretation and systematic theology, giving due weight to both disciplines.

ACKNOWLEDGEMENTS

This book is a revised and updated version of a PhD thesis submitted to the University of Durham in 1997. Particular thanks are due to my supervisor, Dr Stephen Barton, for his encouraging support and wise guidance. Other members of staff at Durham also provided welcome advice, including Professor David Brown, Professor James Dunn and Professor Ann Loades of the Department of Theology, and Dr Mark Bonnington of Cranmer Hall. I am most grateful to the examiners of my thesis, Professor Anthony Thiselton of the University of Nottingham and Dr Loren Stuckenbruck of the University of Durham, for their perceptive and helpful comments.

It was most useful to be able, from time to time, to present ideas from the study as 'work in progress', to be discussed and critiqued by colleagues. In this respect, my thanks are due to the members of the Postgraduate New Testament Seminar in the Department of Theology at Durham, to Dr Dennis Stamps and the members of the Bible and Theology Seminar at the annual conference of the Society for the Study of Theology, and to Dr Steve Moyise and the members of the Revelation Seminar at the British New Testament Conference.

I should also like to thank Professor Richard Bauckham, the General Editor of the SNTS Monograph Series, and Kevin Taylor and Jan Chapman at Cambridge University Press for their guidance, patience and courtesy.

Finally, I must thank my wife, Jenny, for her support and patience, when the demands of this project often meant sacrificing time with the family.

ABBREVIATIONS

Unless otherwise indicated, scriptural references are to the Book of Revelation. References to 'Revelation' with an initial capital are to this text, rather than to divine disclosure in general, for which I have used lower case.

Abbreviations for canonical texts and for the Apocrypha follow usual conventions. Abbreviations for texts from the Old Testament pseudepigrapha are based on those used in *The Old Testament Pseudepigrapha*, ed. James H. Charlesworth (2 vols., New York: Doubleday, 1983–85).

Where abbreviations for modern publications appear in the list set out in the *Journal of Biblical Literature* 107 (1988), pp. 579–96, I have followed that guide. Other abbreviations are listed below.

BNTC	Black's New Testament Commentaries
IJPR	*International Journal for the Philosophy of Religion*
JSPSup	Journal for the Study of the Pseudepigrapha, Supplement Series
MTheol	*Modern Theology*
NIDNTT	*The New International Dictionary of New Testament Theology*, ed. C. Brown (3 vols. Exeter: Paternoster, 1975–78).
Theol	*Theology*

1

SETTING THE SCENE: A MODERN DEBATE ABOUT FAITH AND HISTORY

1.1   Introduction

The starting point for this study lies in twentieth-century debates about the relationship between history and faith. These debates are one of the most enduring features of the modern theological scene. As far as New Testament studies are concerned, the debates have most often arisen in the context of the application of the historical-critical method to scripture. The two most obvious examples of this have been the various 'quests' for the historical Jesus, and the continuing discussions about the extent to which the resurrection of Jesus is accessible to the historical-critical method.

However, this study is concerned with a rather different question, which relates not so much to the exercise of the historical-critical method, but rather to some of the underlying assumptions made about the nature and significance of history as such. This more fundamental question is about the relationship between divine reality and the world of historical events. Of course, this question cannot be isolated from issues relating to the application of historical criticism to the biblical record. Three of the main protagonists to whom I refer in this opening chapter – Troeltsch, Bultmann and Pannenberg – have engaged in great depth with both sets of questions, and a major point of Pannenberg's programme is precisely the illegitimacy of dividing the two sets of questions from each other. Nonetheless, the focus in this study will be especially on the debate about the significance of history *per se*.[1]

Two opposing approaches have been particularly influential in the exploration of this question. One approach is marked by a conviction

---

[1]   The distinction I am making between two sets of questions in the theological disciplines is paralleled in history and philosophy by a distinction between 'speculative' philosophy of history, dealing with attempts to discern a meaning in history as a whole, and 'critical' philosophy of history, dealing with methodological questions such as the extent to which the writing of history inevitably entails interpretation as well as the reporting of fact. Walsh (1951) and Dray (1964) give standard accounts of both areas of the philosophy of history.

that there is a fundamental discontinuity between the world of historical events and divine reality. An important proponent of this view has been Rudolf Bultmann. In contrast, other theologians, notably Pannenberg and Moltmann, have reacted against the tendency in dialectical theology to draw this sharp distinction between the realms of faith and history. They have sought to re-emphasize a fundamental unity embracing both the divine and the historically contingent. The approaches adopted by Pannenberg and Moltmann are not identical. Pannenberg stresses underlying continuity in the historical process, which he sees as the self-revelation of God, culminating in the eschaton, at which point the coherence and purpose of history will be manifest. Moltmann stresses the hope of future *transformation* of reality by the inbreaking of the power of God. However, both of these theologians represent a reaction against the epistemological dualism inherent in Bultmann's work. In developing their theological positions, Pannenberg and Moltmann have both made use of ideas from apocalyptic literature. For Pannenberg, the attraction of apocalyptic is the idea of an ultimate eschatological horizon within which the whole of reality might be situated. For Moltmann, the attraction is the apocalyptic theme of the transformation of reality in the dawning of the new age.

The present study is an examination of the extent to which a reading of one particular apocalyptic text, Revelation, might be used to support or question the proposals of Pannenberg and Moltmann, and the extent to which their proposals provide a fruitful starting point for a contemporary interpretation of the text. In chapters 3–5 I shall examine the text of Revelation in detail, and in chapter 6 I shall relate my reading of the text to an analysis of Pannenberg's and Moltmann's theologies of history. The purpose of this opening chapter is to introduce the main contours of the twentieth-century debate about the theological significance of history. This will enable Pannenberg and Moltmann to be placed in context, and give an indication of the issues at stake. I am not offering a comprehensive account of the debate as a whole, but will highlight some of the main questions by describing briefly the work of two key figures, Ernst Troeltsch and Rudolf Bultmann, before considering Pannenberg and Moltmann. I hope to identify in particular some of the longer-term intellectual influences which have shaped the views these writers have expressed, and also the ways in which they relate to one another.

1.2   The challenge of Ernst Troeltsch

The German theologian and philosopher Ernst Troeltsch (1865–1923) saw clearly the challenges which modern historical method posed to traditional theology. Assessments vary as to how well he succeeded in meeting those challenges. But the problems to which he drew attention are enormous and have influenced the work of theologians and biblical scholars ever since.

Troeltsch was convinced of the validity of the historical-critical method, established in the nineteenth century by von Ranke and others. He claimed that the modern idea of history had 'developed into a unique mode of thought and research that has authenticated itself with most brilliant results'.[2] In an important early essay, 'Historical and Dogmatic Method in Theology', published in 1898, he described three important elements of modern historical method.[3] First, he identified the principle of *criticism*, according to which 'in the realm of history there are only judgments of probability' and hence no certainties.[4] This principle applied to the history of religions, including Christianity, as much as to any other history. Second, Troeltsch described the principle of *analogy*: 'Agreement with normal, customary, or at least frequently attested happenings and conditions as we have experienced them is the criterion of probability for all events that historical criticism can recognise as having actually or possibly happened.'[5] Lying behind this second principle was an assumption of the 'basic consistency of the human spirit and its historical manifestations'.[6] Troeltsch's third principle was *correlation*, according to which 'all historical happening is knit together in a permanent relationship...inevitably forming a current in which everything is interconnected and each single event is related to all others'.[7]

These three principles have far-reaching consequences. As Troeltsch himself remarked: 'Give the historical method an inch and it will take a mile. From a strictly orthodox stand-point, therefore, it seems to bear a certain similarity to the devil.'[8] Troeltsch argued that the rigorous application of the historical method (which he regarded as inescapable) was incompatible with traditional dogmatic theology. The principle of criticism opened the Bible up to the thoroughgoing scrutiny which would be applied to any other ancient text. This process was of course already well advanced by the time of Troeltsch. More generally, if historical enquiry was to regard 'facts', even those related in the New Testament, as merely more or less probable, then this struck at the heart of the traditional direct

---

[2] Troeltsch (1972), p. 45. *The Absoluteness of Christianity*, from which this quotation comes, was first published in 1902.

[3] For an assessment of this essay against the theological background of the time, see Drescher (1992), pp. 70–97.

[4] Troeltsch (1991), p. 13. This and the next four references are from 'Historical and Dogmatic Method in Theology', 1898.

[5] Troeltsch (1991), pp. 13–14.   [6] Troeltsch (1991), p. 14.

[7] Troeltsch (1991), p. 14.   [8] Troeltsch (1991), p. 16.

connection between faith and fact. As Van Harvey puts it: 'If the theologian believes on faith that certain events occurred, the historian regards all historical claims as having only a greater or lesser degree of probability, and he regards the attachment of faith to these claims as a corruption of historical judgment.'[9]

The principle of analogy also implied a fundamental reassessment. Instead of taking tradition on trust, historians were bound to apply the criterion of their own experience. If recorded 'facts' such as the resurrection or the ascension did not correspond at all to current experience, then historians were bound to judge them to have been improbable. The whole edifice of external supernatural miraculous warrant, which Troeltsch saw as underpinning traditional Christianity, was at risk.

The principle of correlation meant that all 'facts' had to be seen in the context of other events, traditions and beliefs which surrounded them. It was no longer legitimate to treat Christianity as if it were in a privileged position, isolated from the rest of history. Troeltsch attacked what he termed the 'old dogmatic method' for perpetuating an invalid distinction between sacred and profane history: 'By its principles this method is absolutely opposed to the historical one. Its essence is that it possesses an authority that, by definition, is separate from the total context of history, not analogous to other happenings, and therefore not subject to historical criticism and the uncertainty attaching to its results.'[10]

Despite Troeltsch's hostility to traditional dogmatics, the overall aim of his theological programme as a whole was positive. His objective was not to undermine Christianity, but rather to re-present it in a way which was compatible with the application of historical method. He advocated a 'history-of-religions' approach, which would draw conclusions about Christianity from historical study, rather than from dogmatic preconceptions. He ruled out vigorously all notions of supernatural explanation. In a stance which nowadays appears strange, however, Troeltsch also remained a child of German idealism, accepting the existence of a universal principle, the Absolute, as a spiritual driving force within history. He attempted to reconcile this with his attachment to historical method by seeing the Absolute not as a pre-existent principle which imposed itself on historical events, but rather as a teleological principle, or 'the Goal towards which we are growing'.[11] Deductions about the nature of the Absolute could only be made following detailed historical study, and

[9] Harvey (1967), p. 5.
[10] Troeltsch (1991), p. 20. From 'Historical and Dogmatic Method in Theology', 1898.
[11] Troeltsch (1991), p. 105. From 'The Dogmatics of the History-of-Religions School', 1913.

even then it would not be possible to describe the Absolute clearly. It could not simply be identified with historical Christianity, even though for Troeltsch historical Christianity, of all known religions, came the closest to the Absolute.

At the heart of Troeltsch's theological system was a contradiction, which he found increasingly difficult to reconcile. He was fully committed to the unrestricted application of historical method; yet he sought to maintain the assumption of a universal principle lying behind historical events. Indeed, his examination of the history of religion revealed a picture of such complexity that it became impossible to detect the operation of such a universal principle in any coherent way.

Troeltsch was committed to seeking to bridge the gap between contingent historical events and the work of God; he was opposed to any solution which would resort to a reimposition of a natural/supernatural division. As Coakley argues, he held 'a religious objection to the idea that God has two distinct modes of activity: one relatively unimportant and humdrum, which critical scholarship is allowed to probe, and the other salvifically decisive but sealed off from critical scrutiny'.[12] Yet seeking to avoid such a division was an uncomfortable task. On one side, the 'historical' end of Troeltsch's bridge was eroded: the failure of the historical method *per se* to reveal the workings of God in history meant that Troeltsch had to admit that some element of faith presupposition was essential if divine action was to be identified.[13] At the opposite, metaphysical end of the bridge, a different process of erosion took hold: by the end of his career, the complexity of the historical process had led Troeltsch to doubt whether one single universal principle was at work after all.

For present purposes, the importance of Troeltsch lies in his brilliant yet flawed attempt to use the historical-critical method to trace a universal divine purpose working in history. Holding this programme together coherently was ultimately beyond him, but the challenge he laid down has never been totally answered. In the remaining sections of this chapter I shall examine briefly different responses to that challenge.

1.3   Rudolf Bultmann: a dualistic response

Bultmann's response to the problems exposed by Troeltsch was marked by a series of dualisms.[14] He embraced wholeheartedly the principles of historical investigation set out by Troeltsch, yet sought to protect faith

---

[12] Coakley (1988), p. 83.   [13] Coakley (1988), pp. 86–7.

[14] For a perceptive account of the dualisms at the heart of Bultmann's theology, see Roberts (1977).

from the rigours of such investigation by postulating a fundamental discontinuity between the world of contingent historical events on the one hand and divine reality on the other. Thus, faith could be isolated from the ambiguities and uncertainties of historical criticism.

In this respect, Bultmann's thought needs to be seen as standing in an intellectual tradition stretching back to Kant and Lessing. Each of these thinkers developed views of the relationship between faith and history which assumed a dualistic model of the perception of reality. Kant made a fundamental distinction between the realm of the 'phenomenal' (that which is knowable by being accessible to scientific investigation) and the realm of the 'noumenal' (which includes transcendental concepts relating, for example, to God, and which cannot be 'known'). Since God lies beyond the phenomenal, nothing may be known about him save that he is transcendent. Thus there is an epistemological dualism at the heart of Kantian thought between the phenomenal and the noumenal, the immanent and the transcendent.[15]

Lessing's work assumed a logical dualism between the uncertain and approximate world of historical knowledge and the world of eternal truth. He argued that it was illegitimate to base conclusions relating to eternal truth on the foundations of contingent historical events, formulating the problem most famously in his image of a ditch:

> If no historical truth can be demonstrated then nothing can be demonstrated by means of historical truths. That is: Accidental truths of history can never become the proof of necessary truths of reason ... That, then, is the ugly, broad ditch which I cannot get across, however often and however earnestly I have tried to make the leap.[16]

Lessing's ditch was thus an expression not so much of a *temporal* distance between the Christ event and the modern believer, but rather a *logical* distance between two kinds of truth, contingent and eternal. At one level, this appears to be a major difficulty: how can the realms of history and faith be brought together? However, for Lessing, this difficulty in fact dissolves away. Since the eternal truths of reason cannot in any case be

---

[15] Yovel (1980) has demonstrated how this division works itself out in Kant's philosophy of history. Yovel argues that Kant ultimately failed to explain how his notion of a transcendent reason in the realm of the noumenal interacted with the phenomenal world of events.

[16] This passage appears in 'On the Proof of the Spirit and of Power', published in 1777, reprinted in Lessing (1956), ed. Chadwick, pp. 53, 55.

derived from history, there is no need to bring history and faith together in that sense.

> The point, then, is that Lessing does not have to leap the ditch for which his essay is most famous ... he is in effect rejecting the notion that the truth of authentic religion is dependent upon the occurrence of certain historical events or on the emergence at an identifiable moment in time of a truth not previously available to us.[17]

In effect, history becomes a vehicle for disclosing truth of a non-historical character. A consequence of this line of argument is that religious truth becomes effectively insulated from the scrutiny of historical research. There are clear resonances with certain strands of twentieth-century dialectical theology, with their attempts to safeguard faith from the advance of historical criticism.[18]

These are the long-term intellectual influences against which Bultmann should be seen. More immediately, he was influenced by the Neo-Kantianism of nineteenth-century scholars such as Cohen and Natorp.[19] Their distinctive contribution was to radicalize Kant's epistemology: they argued that not only can we not know 'things-in-themselves', but even the senses through which we experience the world cannot be depended upon. Thiselton argues that in Bultmann's case this development of Kant was fused with a brand of nineteenth-century Lutheranism, which stressed the need to avoid seeking one's security in anything but God. The combination of these two influences led Bultmann not only to dilute the importance of empirical historical enquiry for faith, but to regard any attempt to base faith on historical fact as misguided.[20] This is the source of Bultmann's fundamental mistrust of anything which 'objectifies' faith on the grounds that this will inevitably consist of worldly knowledge rather than genuine encounter with the transcendent. Thiselton comments: 'Bultmann ... accepted the Neo-Kantian assumption that knowledge which objectifies

---

[17] Michalson (1985), p. 38.

[18] Bultmann's approach is also strongly influenced by Kierkegaard's critique of Lessing. Although Kierkegaard kept Lessing's and Kant's distinction between the world of faith and the world of history, he emphasized the importance of the particular moment in the mediation of divine truth to the believer. Eternal truths were inaccessible to fallen human reason without God's initiative at particular moments. See Michalson (1985), pp. 61–92.

[19] See Thiselton (1980), pp. 208–12.

[20] Carnley (1972) argues that Bultmann's radical dilution of the importance of historical events as a foundation for faith is based on a mistaken view of the nature of historical evidence. While it may be true that any particular view of a piece of historical evidence is provisional and open to correction, that does not mean that all historical knowledge is necessarily uncertain in principle.

in accordance with law is a knowledge in which *man* does the shaping and seizes the mastery. Therefore, in the light of his Lutheranism and his dialectical theology, talk of God cannot take this form.'[21]

How does this Neo-Kantian inheritance work itself out in Bultmann's theology? The epistemological dualism between the world of faith and the world of historical research which I noted in the thought of Kant, Lessing and Kierkegaard is also present in Bultmann, albeit expressed in a different way. Bultmann's statement that 'the world which faith wills to grasp is absolutely unattainable by means of scientific research' is a typical summary of his position.[22] At the heart of Bultmann's position is a fundamental dichotomy, which occurs throughout his thought in different contexts. On one plane is the merely actual, the world of empirical history and factual knowledge. On a quite distinct plane is authentically and specifically human existential encounter and the self-understanding of human individuals in their historicity. Nothing in the first plane can claim to have ultimate value, and as long as individuals understand themselves in terms of this plane, their true selves remain in bondage, in inauthentic existence. In his consideration of history, Bultmann expresses this distinction by means of two German words: *Historie*, to represent the world susceptible to historical investigation; and *Geschichte*, to represent the world of authentic existence which cannot be accessed by historical investigation. This accords with Bultmann's theological conviction that we cannot and must not seek knowledge of God from objectified sources (i.e. from data which can be assessed and explained using human reason). For Bultmann, 'God does not stand still and does not put up with being made an object of observation. One cannot *see* God; one can only *hear* God.'[23] Hence his assertion that he actually welcomed negative results of historical criticism, since they discouraged the founding of faith on the wrong premises.

Along with this dichotomy, Bultmann held to a view of history as a closed continuum of events, in effect applying Troeltsch's two principles of analogy and correlation to exclude the idea of special supernatural intervention in history.[24] Unlike Troeltsch, Bultmann did not believe that the results of historical investigation could bear the theological weight of

---

[21] Thiselton (1980), p. 226.   [22] Bultmann (1969), p. 31.

[23] Bultmann (1985), p. 144. From 'Science and Existence', 1955.

[24] Morgan argues that Bultmann's commitment to the thoroughgoing application of the historical-critical method places him in some respects close to Troeltsch. 'Both theologians [Bultmann and Troeltsch] do their history according to modern critical norms, and try to draw out its theological significance. They both stand opposed to Barth, whose theological method resists the autonomy of modern critical history' (1976, p. 60).

presenting the Christian message. However, it is important to understand that Bultmann is *not* saying that God is not active at all; he is merely saying that God's action cannot be seen by empirical observation. It is possible to speak about God's act only in the context of existential encounter. 'God's act is hidden from all eyes other than the eyes of faith.'[25]

Bultmann's most sustained discussion of the nature of history and how it relates to faith and authentic existence comes in his *History and Eschatology*. He traces the development of different ways in which scripture conceives of the relationship between history and faith. He contrasts Old Testament prophecy, which he sees as speaking of the execution of God's judgement within history, with later Jewish apocalyptic, which saw divine judgement bringing about the end of this world and the dissolution of history. For Bultmann, the New Testament draws on both of these views, although the apocalyptic element predominates in the earliest traditions, such as Jesus' proclamation of the inbreaking of the eschatological reign of God. Passages such as Mark 13 and 1 Corinthians 15 also appear to show little interest in any continuing history or divine judgement within it: in effect, history is swallowed up by eschatology in the context of intense expectation of an imminent parousia.

Bultmann interprets Paul in an existential light, as stressing 'the historicity of man, the true historical life of the human being, the history which everyone experiences for himself and by which he gains his real essence'.[26] This concept of the historicity of the individual is vital for Bultmann. It functions almost as a redefinition of what is truly significant in history, once one accepts his contentions that nothing which is objectified is of ultimate value and that authentic existence is glimpsed only in existential encounter. When Bultmann speaks of the 'historicity' of the individual, he therefore means something very different from the world of historical investigation.

For Bultmann, the Fourth Gospel takes this process further and, unlike Paul, dismisses any concept of future eschatology, so that eschatological reality is seen as breaking into the present. (This argument depends of course on Bultmann's ploy of regarding the references to future eschatology which appear in the text as being the work of an 'ecclesiastical redactor'.) Bultmann therefore detects in both Paul and the Fourth Gospel (for him the most important parts of the New Testament) a sense that the present time, swallowed up in eschatology, has a particular character as a 'time-between'. In Paul it is the time between the resurrection and the

---

[25] Bultmann (1985), p. 111. From 'On the Problem of Demythologizing', 1952.
[26] Bultmann (1957), p. 43.

parousia, in John the time between the glorification of Jesus and the death of the individual believer.[27] In each case, the present time is more than merely chronology. For Bultmann this represents a valuable perspective, since eschatological reality and therefore existential possibility are woven into the present.[28]

One senses the tone of regret as Bultmann argues that with the delay of the parousia this view of the present became unsustainable, and a sense of history re-emerged distinct from eschatology, so that eschatological reality came to be understood primarily as anticipation, rather than as current reality. Only with the Romantic reaction against the teleology of the Enlightenment, and with what Bultmann sees as the modern sense of man's historicity, is there a renewed opportunity to glimpse the reality of history as personal encounter and decision:

> the present is the moment of decision, and by the decision taken the yield of the past is gathered in and the meaning of the future is chosen. This is the character of every historical situation; in it the problem and the meaning of past and future are enclosed and are waiting, as it were, to be unveiled by human decisions.[29]

Thus, for Bultmann, meaning in history is to be found in momentary existential encounter in the present moment, rather than by historical investigation. In the believer's experience of Christ, what matters is not whatever can be pieced together about the history of the Christ event, but rather Christ's summons to decision in the present. And Bultmann is strongly opposed to any notion that a meaning is to be found in the broad sweep of history. Schemes such as those developed by Hegel or Marx which depend upon a view of history as a whole are for Bultmann illegitimate because a vantage point from which the whole of history may be seen is unattainable.[30]

Bultmann is representative of one possible response to the challenges laid down by Troeltsch at the beginning of the twentieth century. He accepts Troeltsch's historical-critical agenda, yet, under the influence of his Neo-Kantian inheritance, seeks to preserve a secure zone within which faith might be appropriated, safe from the rigours of historical investigation. This is not, however, the only possible response.

---

[27] Bultmann (1957), p. 49.

[28] In fact, Bultmann's use of scripture can be attacked as arbitrary and selective. As Roberts points out, the New Testament includes a variety of eschatological perspectives, and not merely the realized eschatology detected by Bultmann; see Roberts (1977), ch. 2.

[29] Bultmann (1957), pp. 141–2.

[30] Bultmann (1985), pp. 137–8. From 'Science and Existence', 1955.

1.4   Wolfhart Pannenberg: a unitive response

Wolfhart Pannenberg has responded to Troeltsch's challenge in a way which is fundamentally opposed to that of Bultmann. I shall discuss Pannenberg's proposals (and those of Jürgen Moltmann, whose approach bears key similarities to that of Pannenberg) in more detail in chapter 6. However, at this stage I shall examine some of the salient points of Pannenberg's approach, to set the scene for the chapters which follow.

Whereas Bultmann's thought owes much to the intellectual tradition represented by Kant, Lessing and Kierkegaard, Pannenberg clearly owes a strong debt to Hegel. Although Pannenberg distances himself from Hegel's conclusions at important points, he shares some of Hegel's central concerns. The first of these is Hegel's conviction that reality should be understood in a unitive, rather than a dualistic, way. Plant places this conviction in the context of Hegel's Germany, arguing that political and religious divisions, together with increasing intellectual specialization in the eighteenth century, had led to a sense of social fragmentation, which Hegel sought to overcome.[31] In particular, Hegel reacted strongly against Kant's distinction between the noumenal and the phenomenal, and against Lessing's distinction between accidental and necessary truth, both of which he regarded as fostering ontological and epistemological dualism. The second concern of Hegel of particular importance to Pannenberg is the sense of an unfolding dynamic meaning in history as a whole. For Hegel, life (and therefore history) was characterized by constant dynamic process. Although he believed in the ultimate unity of reality, there was a sense in which this ideal had not been achieved, and history represented a constant struggle to realize it. Hegel argues that the process by which the unity of reality is achieved is dialectical. It contains three movements, which constantly recur. The first phase is that of the concept, existing in unconscious identity: it is characterized by unity, but lacks consciousness of itself. In the second phase, differentiation, the concept is objectified: this is simultaneously both the same in content as the concept and also its utter negation. In the third phase, the objectified form and the concept are united in a way which both reconciles them *and* preserves concept and negation in a greater unity. This logical process is the basis of Hegel's dialectic. In the context of history, Hegel sees the concept as Spirit, and this is the role God plays in his system. Thus, by a constant process of

---

[31] Plant describes Hegel's aim as 'the recreation of a whole man in an integrated, cohesive, political community' (1983, p. 25). Significantly, the intellectual and religious environment into which Hegel was born was partly shaped by apocalyptic thought; see Dickey (1987), pp. 1–137.

objectification of itself in the world and reconciliation back with its own concept, Spirit aims through history to emerge into self-consciousness.[32]

Pannenberg picks up the Hegelian themes of the unity of reality and universal history. This is reflected in the central thesis of *Revelation as History*, which Pannenberg produced with a group of colleagues in 1961. The central argument of the book is an attempt to rehabilitate the idea that divine self-communication comes through historical events, over against the stress, in Bultmann and others, upon a distinction *between* the plane of faith commitment and the plane of historical events.[33]

From the idea of revelation as history come the principal elements of Pannenberg's programme. He rejects the Neo-Kantian division between fact and value which lies at the heart of Bultmann's thought. Events and their meaning are inextricably entwined. He attacks Kähler and Bultmann, for whom reports of historical facts are accompanied by testimony to their revelatory value, which is supplementary to the events in themselves, and which exists for faith alone.[34] Pannenberg expresses a parallel concern in respect of the appropriation of faith by the believer. He rejects the idea that reason and faith should be seen as existing in two separate planes. Rather, the self-revelation of God is in events which are publicly observable: faith must be built on the foundation of history: 'In no case is theology ... in the position of being able to say what was actually the case regarding contents which remain opaque to the historian.'[35] The reverse side of this coin is that faith cannot be insulated from historical criticism. This leads Pannenberg to accept Troeltsch's principles of criticism and correlation.

Pannenberg embraces the historical-critical method highlighted in Troeltsch's first principle, since to seek to insulate Christianity from historical criticism would imply a division in ultimate truth and hence vitiate the principle of unity. At the same time, Pannenberg is aware of the danger that the historical-critical method can itself threaten the unity of truth: he criticizes its anthropocentric tendency, 'which seems apt to exclude all transcendent reality as a matter of course'.[36] He is also in principle prepared to accept Troeltsch's criterion of correlation, since he believes

---

[32] Some of Pannenberg's later writing about the relationship between the infinity of God and finite reality is strongly influenced by Hegelian dialectic (Pannenberg, 1991, pp. 397ff.)

[33] See my discussion, in chapter 6, of the support which Pannenberg derives from scripture for his position, and of the various criticisms which have been made of the idea of revelation as history; although he has refined his position in various respects (see pp. 145–54), he has continued to hold to the basic principle of divine self-revelation in historical events. See Pannenberg (1991), pp. 243–57.

[34] Pannenberg (1970), pp. 85ff.; and (1991), p. 250. Pannenberg is also highly critical of Bultmann's Christology, with its lack of interest in the historical Jesus (Pannenberg, 1968, pp. 21–32).

[35] Pannenberg (1970), p. 50.   [36] Pannenberg (1970), p. 39.

events to be comprehensible ultimately only in relation to the whole of the rest of history:

> It belongs to the full meaning of the Incarnation that God's redemptive deed took place within the universal correlative connections of human history and not in a ghetto of redemptive history, or in a primal history belonging to a dimension which is 'oblique' to ordinary history . . . if, indeed, it has not remained in an archetypal realm above the plane of history.[37]

The best-known application by Pannenberg of this idea is his assertion that the resurrection is in principle accessible to historical investigation.

A further implication of the idea of revelation as history is that, for Pannenberg, history is a universal whole. History has a unity and coherence which form the basis for theology: 'History is the most comprehensive horizon of Christian theology. All theological questions and answers are meaningful only within the framework of the history which God has with humanity and through humanity with his whole creation.'[38] Pannenberg finds support for this position in the prophetic and apocalyptic traditions in scripture. He argues that the early traditions of the fulfilment of divine promise in past events such as the exodus gradually develop into the apocalyptic expectation of the future demonstration of divine glory, in an eschatological perspective. Building on this biblical foundation, Pannenberg outlines a picture of history characterized by dynamic purpose: 'Within the reality characterized by the constantly creative work of God, history arises because God makes promises and fulfils these promises. History is event so suspended in tension between promise and fulfilment that through the promise it is irreversibly pointed toward the goal of future fulfilment.'[39]

At the same time, Pannenberg emphasizes the ultimate sovereignty and freedom of God. God is not constrained by a plan of history which works towards its conclusion regardless. A universal horizon and a fundamental unity of truth must be maintained if God is God. But any attempt to impose a pattern on historical development is illegitimate because, being of human design, it must be finite and cannot take account of the history of the future yet to happen. The only solution for Pannenberg is to hold the idea of universal history together with the idea that history is radically contingent. This is one of the areas in which Pannenberg distances himself most sharply from Hegel. He is concerned that the grand sweep of Hegelian dialectic has the effect of 'flattening out' the

---

[37] Pannenberg (1970), pp. 41–2.   [38] Pannenberg (1970), p. 15.
[39] Pannenberg (1970), p. 18.

particularities of history in order to fit them into the scheme as a whole. Pannenberg concludes that: 'in spite of all [Hegel's] efforts to allow the particular and individual to receive their due...he remained fixed in the primacy of the universal'.[40] For Pannenberg, there *is* a pattern to history, but until the end of history, when all events will be comprehensible in their full context, humans will remain unable to discern the pattern fully. His concern to stress the freedom of God makes him doubtful about Troeltsch's third principle (analogy) because it can be used to limit the openness of the future. He is concerned that this principle will inevitably tend towards anthropocentrism, and skew historical judgement by reinforcing the interpreter's own presuppositions. He argues rather that: 'if the historian keeps his eye on the nonexchangeable individuality and contingency of an event, then he will see that he is dealing with nonhomogeneous things, which cannot be contained without remainder in any analogy'.[41]

Hegel's system, which postulates a universal Absolute gradually realizing itself through history, is essentially evolutionary: what takes place in the future is an organic development from what has already taken place. But this, for Pannenberg, would compromise the freedom of God, who, for all his involvement in the unfolding of history, remains both transcendent and immanent. For Pannenberg, therefore, the dynamic flow of history is not from the past into the future, but rather from an open future into the past.[42] Truth in history can be seen only *in retrospect*, and then only provisionally, since events still in the future will alter the context within which past events are seen. Pannenberg's conclusion is that the one 'earth-shaking objection' to Hegel's philosophy of history is that future truth is excluded from his system.[43]

---

[40] Pannenberg (1971), p. 23. Attempts by Hegel and others to produce an overall theory of historical development, within which all events may be located, have been attacked, notably by Collingwood in *The Idea of History* (1994, especially pp. 263–6: originally published in 1946).

[41] Pannenberg (1970), p. 46. Pannenberg argues that the use of analogy *does* have a proper place in historical method, but that its true value lies *not* in a principle that historical deduction depends on the interpreter being able to identify analogy. Instead, its value is in showing the *limits* of the applicability of analogy to historical events: 'The most fruitful possibility opened up by the discovery of historical analogies consists in the fact that it allows more precise comprehension of the ever-present concrete limitation of what is held in common, the particularity that is present in every case in the phenomena being compared' (1970, p. 47).

[42] See the discussion (in chapter 6, pp. 171–6) of Pannenberg's complex idea that ontology is driven from the future, and Moltmann's parallel arguments in favour of 'anticipation' over 'extrapolation'.

[43] A common criticism levelled at Hegel by historians relates to his apparent belief that history had in a sense reached its end with the rise of the Prussian state. Interestingly,

At the same time, it is a central element in Pannenberg's thinking that in the resurrection of Christ, understood against an apocalyptic background of hope for the general resurrection of the dead, the end of history has been revealed proleptically. Even this, however, is still provisional, since it requires its ultimate vindication by God at the eschaton. Hence, although Pannenberg locates his thought in an apocalyptic framework, it is apocalyptic as transformed in the light of the Christ event.

The key areas of difference between Pannenberg and Bultmann should now be clear. Pannenberg completely rejects the Neo-Kantian division between fact and value which lies at the heart of Bultmann's position. This has three implications. First, there is for Pannenberg no secure realm for faith beyond historical investigation. As Michalson puts it, '[for Pannenberg] the strategies that Lessing, Kierkegaard and such successors of theirs as Herrmann and Bultmann adopt to neutralize historical-critical difficulties are a greater threat to faith than historical criticism itself'.[44] Second, the world of contingent historical events cannot be held to be in some way irrelevant for faith (as Bultmann claims); on the contrary, it is precisely on the self-revelation of God in history that faith must take its stand. Third, as the self-revelation of God, history as a universal whole acquires a fundamental meaning, which will finally be revealed at the eschaton. In Pannenberg's scheme, the whole of the historical process, past, present and future, is a unity. This is fundamentally at odds with Bultmann, who stresses rather the importance of the present moment of decision for the individual.[45]

Thus, Pannenberg represents a third position alongside those of Troeltsch and Bultmann. Like Bultmann, he accepts Troeltsch's principles of criticism and correlation. However, he applies them more radically than Bultmann, since he will not accept a bifurcation between faith and history which would leave the former secure, isolated from historical investigation. Yet that same refusal to divide faith and history leads Pannenberg at another level to part company with Troeltsch, since he is not prepared to reduce historical method to a positivist conception which (on the basis of

recent years have seen the revival, in various different forms, of the idea that history has effectively ended. Although such ideas often take the form of post-modernist reactions against metanarrative, they are to some extent still dependent on detecting grand patterns in history – in this case, the pattern of an end to historical development. See Niethammer (1992) for a helpful survey of this movement.

[44] Michalson (1985), p. 123.

[45] See also Löwith (1949), pp. 252–3, for a similar critique of Bultmann's concentration on the present moment. Pannenberg studied philosophy with Löwith at Heidelberg in the early 1950s.

Troeltsch's principle of analogy) would rule out the possibility of divine intervention in history in ways which burst through the limits of previous experience. As Thiselton comments:

> Pannenberg refuses to accept a dualism from which (with Troeltsch) we abstract facts for the historian but relativize the meaning; or from which (with Kähler and Bultmann) we abstract meaning for the theologian but relativize, as it were, the facts. Pannenberg refuses to allow the wholeness of the tradition to be torn apart, and either the facts or the interpretation to be evaporated.[46]

1.5   Jürgen Moltmann: radical eschatology

Moltmann's approach to the theology of history bears strong similarities to that of Pannenberg, and in many respects stands in the same tradition. Like Pannenberg, Moltmann distances himself from Bultmann. He attacks dialectical theology for its espousal of what he terms 'transcendental subjectivity', which implies a static, ahistorical, view of the historical process. In Bultmann's case, Moltmann argues that this takes the form of the 'transcendental subjectivity of man', with a concentration on the call for decision by the individual in the present moment, at the expense of a truly historical perspective. Moltmann traces the origins of Bultmann's approach back to Kant and a dualism which divorces faith from history.[47]

As with Pannenberg, the influence of Hegel is apparent, although, like Pannenberg, Moltmann is highly critical of Hegel in places. In Moltmann's case, Hegel's ideas are mediated through the work of the Marxist philosopher, Ernst Bloch, in particular Bloch's monumental *The Principle of Hope*.[48] The assumption underlying Bloch's work is that the world is not a settled, stable entity, but is rather in process and unfinished. He is attracted to the idea of eschatological history present in the Old Testament. He also draws heavily on Hegel, although he reorders Hegel's dialectic radically, removing from the picture what he saw as Hegel's false subject (the World Spirit) and Hegel's spiritualized account of the

---

[46] Thiselton (1980), p. 81.

[47] Moltmann (1967), pp. 46ff. He has recently returned to this theme (1996, pp. 19ff.), arguing that Bultmann's position leads to the swallowing up of history by eschatology.

[48] First published in 1959. Pannenberg also acknowledges the importance of Bloch in reawakening interest in eschatology (1971, pp. 191ff.).

process. The process becomes a purely earthly one, with the 'subject' as the working man. Bloch also sought to rehabilitate the concept of utopia, as fundamental to the nature of reality as something unfinished. Like Pannenberg, Bloch argues that Hegel's system is insufficiently open to the future. For Bloch, Hegel's epistemology is backward-looking, restricting knowledge to the knowledge of what has become, while his ontology also looks backward to a mythical first point when all was present in potential. Since Bloch sees the ontological structure of the world as essentially un-settled and unconcluded, he regards any epistemology or ontology based on a backward-looking orientation as deficient. Bloch also uses the con-cept of transcendence, though not in the usual sense of a reality existing 'above' the earthly present, but rather as an immanent, eschatological concept. But the role that utopia plays in relation to the world at hand is not merely eschatological: it is also dialectical. It interacts with the world at hand in a process which includes a role for utopia in judging the inadequacies of the world at hand. This framework becomes highly significant for Moltmann's idea of hope as contradiction of the present, which is one of the most important ways in which his approach differs from that of Pannenberg.

In the introduction to *Theology of Hope*, Moltmann writes that 'from first to last, and not merely in the epilogue, Christianity is eschatology, is hope, forward looking and forward moving, and therefore also revolution-izing and transforming the present'.[49] This statement is a good summary of some of the basic themes in his thought. First, Moltmann's theology has a fundamentally future, eschatological orientation. Eschatology is not simply a branch of Christian doctrine appearing at the end of volumes of systematics: it is fundamental to theology as a whole. Second, this stress on the future means that hope is central to the Christian faith: 'Where the bounds that mark the end of all human hopes are broken through in the raising of the crucified one, there faith can and must expand into hope... in the Christian life, faith has the priority but hope the primacy.'[50] Third, Moltmann emphasizes the role of hope in revolutionizing and transform-ing the present. Hope in the future of Christ is necessarily a contradiction of the sinful world in which the Christian lives.

It is partly this stress on the future which leads Moltmann to distance himself from Bultmann's preoccupation with the present moment. How-ever, Moltmann's emphasis on an open future and the need for future transformation leads him also to differentiate his approach from that of

[49] Moltmann (1967), p. 16.   [50] Moltmann (1967), p. 20

Pannenberg. Moltmann argues that Pannenberg does not go far enough in his criticisms of Troeltsch's principle of analogy. Merely asserting, as Pannenberg does, that there must be room for contingency within history, is insufficient:

> The rediscovery of the category of the contingent does not in it-self necessarily involve the discovery of a theological category. For the raising of Christ involves not the category of the accidentally new, but the expectational category of the eschatologically new ... The resurrection of Christ does not mean a possibility within the world and its history, but a new possibility altogether for the world, for existence and for history.[51]

While Pannenberg responds positively towards Jewish apocalyptic literature because of the universal historical horizon within which he takes it to operate, Moltmann is more ambivalent. He criticizes the apocalyptic genre for propounding a determinist view of history, in which events unfold according to a preordained plan, in an almost deist system. In this system, what matters is the fulfilment of the plan, not the freedom of God to act in new ways. Moltmann therefore argues that the interpretation advanced by Pannenberg, to the effect that apocalyptic represents a cosmological interpretation of eschatological history and therefore is a key source for a view of universal history, is inadequate. Moltmann argues that apocalyptic needs to be seen as the radical historicizing of the cosmos, not the cosmologizing of history; this reflects his concern, following Bloch, for a radical, transforming eschatology and his desire to avoid any move towards a settled view of the nature of the cosmos.[52]

Moltmann's attitude to the concept of universal history neatly encapsulates the similarities and differences between him and Pannenberg. On one level, he agrees with Pannenberg about the need to maintain a universal historical horizon, for example in the interpretation of the New Testament. However, Moltmann parts company with Pannenberg when it comes to defining the *shape* of universal history, and the points on which they differ provide a helpful summary of the more general difference in their overall approaches. Moltmann's argument here is that what links the past and the future is not the *substance* of history but rather the hope which points beyond any given moment. The promise is constantly re-actualized, but it remains promise, and it is this eschatological sense which forms the link between the past and the future. In a criticism aimed

---

[51] Moltmann (1967), p. 179.   [52] Moltmann (1967), pp. 137–8.

partly at Pannenberg, Moltmann declares: 'The theologian is not concerned merely to supply a different *interpretation* of the world, of history and of human nature, but to *transform* them in expectation of a divine transformation.'[53]

1.6   Conclusion

The purpose of this chapter has been to indicate some of the main developments in twentieth-century theology on the subject of the relationship between faith and history, placing the work of Pannenberg and Moltmann in the context of earlier contributions to the debate. I began by outlining the significance of the adoption by Ernst Troeltsch of the three principles of criticism, analogy and correlation, and the challenges which this has posed ever since to attempts to relate faith and history together. One reaction to this challenge, articulated most influentially by Bultmann, has been to assume a fundamental epistemological separation between the planes of faith and history, emphasizing the importance of faith-response in the present moment of decision, and radically diluting the significance for faith of the historical process. Pannenberg and Moltmann represent in their different ways an alternative reaction to Troeltsch's challenge, seeking to keep faith and history together, and to emphasize the coming of God from the future. I shall consider the arguments of Pannenberg and Moltmann in greater detail in chapter 6, in the light of my reading of the Book of Revelation in chapters 3–5. However, exploring the relationship between systematic theology and scripture raises certain important methodological issues, and it is to these that I turn in chapter 2.

---

[53] Moltmann (1967), p. 84. This is an application to theology of Marx's eleventh thesis on Feuerbach: 'The philosophers have only interpreted the world, in various ways; the point, however, is to change it' (Feuer, 1969, p. 286). Moltmann also suggests (1977, pp. 213–15) that Pannenberg's use of the category of universal history has the effect of simply reimposing an authoritarian framework in the vacuum left by his rejection of the authoritarian concept of the Word in Barth and Bultmann. I return in more detail to the views of Pannenberg and Moltmann on universal history in chapter 6, pp. 164–70.

2

RELATING SCRIPTURE AND SYSTEMATIC
THEOLOGY: SOME PRELIMINARY ISSUES

2.1   Introduction

The aim of this study is to assess how far a reading of the Book of
Revelation might be used to support or question recent theological un-
derstandings of the relationship between historical events and divine reality, with particular reference to the work of Pannenberg and Moltmann.
Chapter 1 set the scene by giving an overview of the twentieth-century
debate about the relationship between history and faith, within which
the contributions of Moltmann, Pannenberg and others need to be seen.
Chapters 3–5 will turn in detail to the text of the Book of Revelation, to
explore the way in which the seer conceives of the relationship between
God and human history. In chapter 6 I shall examine some of the conclusions reached by Pannenberg and Moltmann and reflect on these in the
light of my reading of the text of Revelation. But before dealing in detail
with either of the two poles of my subject – the text of Revelation on the
one hand and contemporary systematic reflection on the other – it will
be necessary to cover some foundational questions about how these two
poles might relate to each other. That relationship has been the subject
of prolonged and intensive scholarly discussion over the last two to three
decades.

In this chapter I examine some of the different ways in which the relationship between biblical interpretation and systematic theology has
been understood. Section 2.2 considers the question of the relationship
between the two disciplines of biblical interpretation and systematic theology, as this has been discussed in debates about the definition of biblical
theology. In Section 2.3 I consider the distinct but related question of the
way in which scripture might be used in systematic theology – again,
with reference to some of the recent debates on this subject. The findings
of the chapter, summarized in the short concluding section 2.4, lay down
principles for the more detailed work in chapters 3–6.

2.2 Scripture and theology: the interrelationship of historical and theological disciplines

In chapters 3–6 of this study I consider in some detail the exegesis of the Book of Revelation and relate this to the work of certain contemporary theologians, especially Pannenberg and Moltmann. My concern is to allow the text and contemporary theological reflection to interact, while ensuring that the voice of each is heard appropriately. However, there is an influential school of thought which argues that the two disciplines of exegesis and theological interpretation should be kept separate from each other, so that biblical interpretation becomes a 'two-stage' operation, consisting of two *successive* elements, the first historical and the second theological. In the first part of this chapter I therefore consider this 'two-stage' model, offer an analysis of its strengths and weaknesses, and explain why it is unsatisfactory as a methodological framework. This is not to say, however, that those who promote it do not have valid points to make; and, as I make clear, I have sought in chapters 3–6 to avoid some of the dangers against which they warn.

The 'two-stage' model of biblical interpretation

As a starting-point, I have taken Krister Stendahl's highly influential essay on contemporary biblical theology, which appeared in *The Interpreter's Dictionary of the Bible* in 1962, and which has continued to shape discussions down to the present. Stendahl's aim is to define the nature and role of the discipline of biblical theology. His basic thesis is that the discipline of biblical theology should be regarded as a 'descriptive task', which 'yields the original in its own terms, limiting the interpretation to what it meant in its own setting'.[1] Stendahl is especially concerned with the question of the historical distance between the time of the original text and the present day. He discusses the way in which a renewed sense of historical distance from the text was encouraged by the reaction of Schweitzer and others in the early twentieth century against the liberal quest for timeless values in the text. He does not regard this intensified feeling of historical distance as merely a problem, but rather also as an opportunity, seeing 'experience of the distance and the strangeness of biblical thought as a creative asset, rather than as a destructive and burdensome liability'.[2] But he remains very concerned to do justice to this sense of distance, hence

---

[1] Stendahl (1962), p. 425.   [2] Stendahl (1962), p. 420.

his commitment to the idea of a descriptive task within biblical theology, which is to be kept clear, as far as possible, of the intrusion of contemporary theological questions.[3] The descriptive task of biblical theology is one which may therefore be discharged by believers and agnostics alike: its results should in principle be unaffected by the interpreter's own faith commitment.[4]

Stendahl is aware, however, of some of the dangers which arise if this point is pressed too far. He accepts that no historian can be purely 'objective' and that all scholars bring their own presuppositions to bear on the task. His argument is rather that the inevitable existence of presuppositions should not be seen to rule out the possibility of a biblical theology which is as free as possible from the influence of interpreters' faith commitments. It is important to recognize the exact extent of Stendahl's claims at this point. He is not, as some have been tempted to argue, seeking a naïve return to a positivistic view of history.[5] However, Stendahl's arguments do leave him exposed to the criticism that he is at least *tending* towards adopting a historical method of that kind.[6]

Stendahl goes on to describe a second task, which he terms 'hermeneutical'. This is to be kept clearly distinct from the descriptive task. It concerns the way in which the interpreter is to relate the text to the contemporary world, and hence determine the meaning of the text for today. The activity Stendahl seems to have in mind here is the use of scripture by systematic theology, although he does not label it specifically as such. Stendahl dismisses two opposite and equally unsatisfactory tendencies in the hermeneutical phase of his model. The first, typified for Stendahl by nineteenth-century liberal theology, works with categories drawn from the world of the interpreter, which are imposed anachronistically back onto the text. The second works with patterns of thought assumed to be operative at the time when the texts were written and then seeks to apply these, without modification or historical sensitivity, to contemporary questions. Stendahl is right to warn against these tendencies. Of course, to an extent, they are two sides of the same coin. This is amply illustrated by certain contemporary fundamentalist interpretations of Revelation, which *both* impose categories drawn from the interpreter's world (such

---

[3] Stendahl asserts: 'the tension between "what it meant" and "what it means" is of a competitive nature, and when the biblical theologian becomes primarily concerned with the present meaning, he implicitly (Barth) or explicitly (Bultmann) loses his enthusiasm for the descriptive task' (1962, p. 421). Whether the distinction between 'meant' and 'means' is quite as straightforward as Stendahl thinks is discussed below, on pp. 28–31.

[4] Stendahl (1962), p. 422.

[5] See the helpful discussion of this question in Ollenburger (1986), pp. 63ff.

[6] See, for example, the criticism of Stendahl in this respect in Lash (1986), pp. 77–8.

as superpower conflict) onto the text *and* then reapply the text in a literalistic way to contemporary events.[7] For Stendahl, there are only two credible ways for the interpreter to bridge the historical distance between the text and the present. The first is to conclude, with Tillich and Bultmann, that 'history is mute as far as theological meaning is concerned'.[8] Historical evidence is simply not an appropriate form of knowledge upon which to base faith commitment, and grounds for faith must be sought elsewhere, in Bultmann's case in the kerygma which challenges humans to decision in the present. The alternative, which Stendahl himself favours, is to work within an expressly historical framework, which acknowledges that both text and interpreter are products of their time, and which therefore eschews the ahistoricizing tendency in Bultmann and others. Stendahl argues that this approach helps to stress the vital need for continual comparison of contemporary theological formulations with scripture: 'all theological renewal and creativity has as one of its components a strong exposure to the "original" beyond the presuppositions and the inherited frame of thought of our immediate predecessors in the theological task'.[9]

Stendahl's position therefore rests on the idea that biblical interpretation consists of two separate stages, the descriptive and the hermeneutical, corresponding to the disciplines of biblical theology and systematic theology. It is a critical feature of his argument that the two stages should not be allowed to intermingle. Otherwise, there is a danger that existing theological commitments will dominate interpretation and prevent the Bible from being heard as a challenge to contemporary ideas.[10]

The issues raised by Stendahl's distinction between separate descriptive and hermeneutical disciplines have important implications for the ground covered in this study. In the debate which has occurred since 1962, some scholars have emphasized the separation between the descriptive and the hermeneutical, reinforcing Stendahl's view of biblical theology as a historical, descriptive discipline, and arguing against its straying into areas imagined to be the preserve of systematic theology.[11] Others have reacted against Stendahl's distinction between the descriptive and the

---

[7] For helpful surveys of modern fundamentalist interpretations of apocalyptic, see Boyer (1992) and O'Leary (1994).

[8] Stendahl (1962), p. 427.

[9] Stendahl (1962), p. 430. Stendahl's awareness of a broader historical perspective within which biblical interpretation takes place is helpful. His argument here has parallels in that put forward by Pannenberg (1970), pp. 96–136.

[10] Stendahl (1962), p. 422.

[11] Examples of this approach include J. Barr (1988), Collins (1990) and Räisänen (1990).

hermeneutical, arguing that this separation is misleading, undesirable, or both.[12]

In the following section, I look at some of the issues arising from Stendahl's position, offer some responses to them and draw out principles relevant to the approach of this study.

Lessons from the two-stage model of biblical interpretation

My conclusion below (pp. 28–31) is that the two-stage model proposed by Stendahl and others is ultimately unsatisfactory. However, Stendahl's model was formulated to guard against particular problems which can arise in the theological interpretation of scripture. These problems remain pertinent to this study. This section therefore seeks to draw out some of the important lessons which may be learned from the two-stage model, and which need to be borne in mind even when the model as a whole is not followed.

The limitations of biblical theology

One argument advanced in favour of the separation of tasks envisaged by Stendahl is that biblical theology cannot claim to be more than a historical discipline, and that straying into territory which is more properly the preserve of systematic theology leads it to make unwarranted and ill-informed assertions. James Barr suggests that the main reason for the decline, since the middle of the twentieth century, in the credibility of work labelled 'biblical theology' is that the discipline has claimed too much for itself. Since biblical theology takes the Bible as its horizon, he argues, it is unable to deal with wider theological questions raised by contemporary theology, a discipline which takes not the Bible, but God as its horizon. As a result, biblical theology 'did not necessarily oppose in principle, but was methodologically unable to handle, numerous kinds of questions that most theologians considered very important'.[13] Barr sees biblical theology as a point on a methodological continuum, between the two poles of biblical criticism and doctrinal theology. But although there is inevitably overlap between the different disciplines on this continuum, each needs to be aware of its limitations. Barr argues that in the case of biblical theology, this means recognizing that there must be more to

---

[12] Examples of this approach include Stuhlmacher (1979), and Ollenburger (1985; 1986; 1991). See also Hanson (1980; 1984a).
[13] J. Barr (1988), p. 7.

theology than merely organizing biblical materials. The Biblical theologians must acknowledge that systematic theologians may draw on resources other than scripture, and might not necessarily accept the conclusions of biblical theology. Biblical theologians should accept a limitation of their influence, and concentrate on the more focused task of historical study.[14]

John Collins adopts a similar line to that taken by Barr. He defines biblical theology as 'the critical evaluation of biblical speech about God'.[15] It is a historical discipline, and, as such, forms one resource among several upon which it is legitimate for systematic theology to draw. Like Barr, Collins stresses the limitations of biblical theology when drawing general theological conclusions. It is beyond the competence of biblical theology to assess the validity of ultimate truth-claims:

> The question is ... whether any of the biblical world views can be said to be true as well as useful ... It is not within the competence of biblical theologians as such to adjudicate the relative adequacy of metaphysical systems. Their task is to clarify what claims are being made, the basis on which they are made, and the various functions they serve.[16]

A more strongly worded version of this argument is provided by Gordon Kaufman. Kaufman not only limits the scope of biblical theology, but also asserts that it is the task of systematic theology to determine what the Bible is and how it is to be used. In other words, biblical theology is to be the servant of systematic theology, and is to be open to critical reassessment on the basis of contemporary theological reflection. The traditional view that biblical theology represents a critical check on doctrinal formulations is precisely reversed. Kaufman even argues that allowing the Bible to criticize theological formulations amounts to 'bibliolatry', since it places too much reliance on the ideas contained in 'this particular arbitrary collection of documents'.[17]

Thus it is possible to argue in favour of reinforcing Stendahl's division between the descriptive and the hermeneutical on the grounds that descriptive biblical theology cannot do justice to questions of contemporary theological judgement. Although, as I shall argue below, it

---

[14] J. Barr (1999), pp. 240–52, gives an expanded version of this argument. For a recent critique of Barr on this question, see Watson (1997), pp. 25–8.

[15] Collins (1990), p. 9.   [16] Collins (1990), p. 14.

[17] Kaufman (1991), pp. 62–3. Even if one goes along with Kaufman's claim that the canon is an 'arbitrary' creation, it remains the case that these documents have shaped the Christian tradition, and therefore the assumptions underlying the work of systematic theologians – including Kaufman himself.

is by no means straightforward to differentiate clearly between the descriptive and the hermeneutical, it remains of practical importance for scholars to be as clear as they can be about whether their focus at any particular point is primarily on the exposition of the text in its original setting or on the appropriation of the text for the purposes of contemporary theology.[18] Otherwise, there is a danger that conclusions drawn merely on the basis of interpreting the text may be imposed upon contemporary theology without proper account having been taken of the fact that the interpretation of scripture is just one of various resources upon which systematic theology may legitimately draw. For Ollenburger, who is otherwise critical of Stendahl's position, this is an important point which represents Stendahl's most significant lasting contribution to the debate.[19]

The arguments of Stendahl, Barr and Collins at this point have some force. For this reason, my reading of the text of Revelation alongside the proposals of contemporary theologians is not intended to represent a crude total assessment of the adequacy of such proposals. This study simply explores the extent to which a reading of the text might support these proposals, or question them. Where support is not evident, that does not necessarily call into question the validity of theological conclusions, which could well be supported by alternative interpretations of the same text or by interpretations of other texts. In any case, judgements in systematic theology will of course be shaped by interaction between scripture and other resources, such as church tradition, experience, and engagement with insights from other disciplines.

The limitations of systematic theology

In the previous section I dealt with the argument that exegetes have to be aware that the results of their work are only one of the resources on which systematic theology might draw, and that a 'biblical theology' may not therefore take the place of systematic theology. However, it is equally true that systematic theologians must be aware of the limitations of *their* discipline when appropriating scripture. If concerns of systematic theology are permitted to predominate, then the interests of contemporary theological agendas may operate to the detriment of open scholarly discussion of the text.

---

[18] This point is made by, for example, Dunn and Mackey (1987), pp. 21–2.
[19] Ollenburger (1986), p. 62.

Both Barr and Collins are anxious to guard against this danger. Barr characterizes the biblical theology movement of the middle decades of the twentieth century as being dominated by neo-orthodoxy, and suggests that 'theologians thus felt that biblical theology was a partisan movement, lined up on one side of a series of disagreements that were really a matter for doctrinal theologians to discuss among themselves'.[20] Elsewhere, Barr attacks Pannenberg and Moltmann specifically, claiming that they have in effect imposed their own theological agendas onto apocalyptic literature.[21] A similar charge, but from a very different angle, could be levelled at Bultmann, who appropriates New Testament texts in a highly selective fashion, according to the extent to which they support his theological agenda. Rather than manipulating apocalyptic for his own purposes, he practically ignores it.[22]

Perhaps the most sustained defence of the historical study of the Bible against a perceived danger of manipulation by confessional interests is still that of Van Harvey, whom I discuss at greater length in chapter 6 (pp. 157–9). Harvey's book is an analysis of the ways in which biblical scholars and theologians have sought to come to terms with Ernst Troeltsch's critique of traditional Christian views of faith and history, in the light of a rigorous application of historical method. Harvey's preferred solution to the dilemma is the adoption of what he calls 'soft perspectivism'. By this he means that the Christian historian is entitled to a particular faith perspective, but that this should not be allowed to interfere with honest assessment of the evidence. The problem with Harvey's approach is that it ultimately depends on the invocation of a variant of fact–value dualism which is similar in some respects to that upon which Bultmann also depends.[23] The theoretical legitimacy and practical application of such a framework are both open to challenge. But the problem Harvey is addressing – the potential of theological concerns to dominate exegesis – is none the less real.

---

[20] J. Barr (1988), pp. 7–8. See also J. Barr (1999) pp. 70–3 for his criticism of Barth's practice of including large sections of theological exegesis in his work, marked by a tendency to dismiss the findings of contemporary biblical scholarship.

[21] 'When we hear from Pannenberg that apocalyptic was the first locus for the idea of a universal history, what can that mean in terms relatable with the texts? Is it right to suspect that the terms of such an idea were first developed within the circle of modern theological problems and then imposed upon apocalyptic?' (J. Barr, 1975, pp. 30–1).

[22] Bultmann's *New Testament Theology* (2 vols., Eng. trans., London: SCM Press, 1952) devotes 160 pages to Paul, 72 pages to the Gospel of John and the Johannine Epistles, and just two, rather dismissive pages to the Book of Revelation.

[23] See my discussion of Bultmann above, in section 1.3, and my further discussion of Harvey below, pp. 157–9.

Stendahl's distinction between the descriptive and the hermeneutical tasks is also an attempt to tackle this problem. His solution is rigidly to separate the two tasks, thereby hoping to insulate exegesis from domination by contemporary theological concerns. As I discuss in the next section, Stendahl's method is ultimately unsatisfactory for a variety of reasons. But his concern that the imposition of theological frameworks onto the texts can produce distortions is well-founded.

A critique of the two-stage model

In the previous section I identified two difficulties which Stendahl's two-stage model was designed to address: first, the danger of the results of biblical exegesis being imposed onto contemporary systematic theology without sufficient regard for the wider theological questions with which systematics must also engage; and second, the danger of the concerns of contemporary systematic theology being allowed to dominate exegesis. These are both real problems, but the two-stage approach advocated by Stendahl and others is ultimately an unsatisfactory method of addressing them.

One weakness in the two-stage model is its distinction between the descriptive and the hermeneutical. Stendahl's contention is that biblical theology is solely 'descriptive' and never 'hermeneutical'; systematic theology, on the other hand, while it may be concerned with the interpretation of scripture, is 'hermeneutical' and 'normative' but not 'descriptive'. The key difficulty with this simple distinction has been well described by Ollenburger. 'Descriptive' and 'normative' are not antitheses. It is quite possible for a particular text, for example, to be both descriptive and normative. This is true at a mundane level: a computer manual is simultaneously a description of the way a program works *and* a normative statement of what the user needs to do in order to achieve certain tasks. More specifically, Ollenburger cites examples from the fields of systematic theology and metaphysics – he uses Kant and Barth, but could have used many others – where texts are clearly intended to function both descriptively and normatively.[24]

> To use Stendahl's own language, any 'common discourse' (or discipline) will have its descriptive and normative components. Stendahl is right to distinguish between history and theology, and to urge us to practice the kind of civility that does not try to

---

[24] Ollenburger (1986), pp. 72ff.

mount historical arguments that depend on theological warrants. But to contrast descriptive and normative as he does is to confuse the issue by asking us to contrast the descriptive component of one discipline with the normative component of another.[25]

A second weakness in Stendahl's model is that the distinction he wishes to draw between what a text *meant* and what it now *means* is not as straightforward as he suggests. He is not particularly clear about what he has in mind when referring to what the text *meant*: he could be referring to authorial intention, or its reception by its original readership, or something else, but it is not clear. Ollenburger concludes that Stendahl is probably working with a rather questionable assumption that the meaning of a text is a property inherent in the text at any particular point in its history. Such an assumption would appear to short-circuit the dynamic hermeneutical process involved in the appropriation of a text by its interpreters. Moreover, as Ollenburger points out, it is simply misleading to assume that biblical interpreters are interested solely in what a text 'meant', whereas systematicians are interested solely in what it 'means': 'It is true, of course, that we understand a biblical text differently today from when it was written ... But the point is that *all* of us understand such a text differently from when it was written, whether we are philologists, literary critics, or systematic theologians.'[26]

Another problem concerns the way in which the two separate disciplines envisaged by Stendahl actually relate to each other. In Stendahl's model there is no overarching methodological structure which includes both disciplines.[27] The result is a model which serves to reinforce the tendency of biblical studies and systematic theology to diverge from each other, resisting interrelation. Stendahl is clearly aware of the danger of biblical scholarship descending into what he calls 'historicism or antiquarianism, with its lack of interest in relevance'.[28] Indeed, his model, with its two phases, including the appropriation of scripture by contemporary interpreters, is partly an attempt to avoid just this danger. But the way he constructs his model in fact serves to reinforce division between the

---

[25] Ollenburger (1986), p. 78. J. Barr (1999, pp. 203–5) argues that 'descriptive' is not wholly adequate as a label for Stendahl's definition of biblical theology, since the discipline inevitably involves not merely description but also imaginative construction.

[26] Ollenburger (1986), p. 90.

[27] See Ollenburger (1986), p. 71. Part of the problem is that Stendahl is working with a cramped definition of hermeneutics, which in effect he wants to limit to being an aspect of systematic theology. However, the notion that exegesis can be isolated from hermeneutics is highly questionable.

[28] Stendahl (1962), p. 419.

descriptive and hermeneutical/normative tasks. As a result, the paradigm of biblical studies which emerges is one which avoids wider concerns of relevance, but rather ploughs its own isolated furrow.

Since Stendahl's proposals were first published, this division has of course come under increasing attack from inside and outside the guild of biblical scholarship.[29] Nicholas Lash has memorably described the two-stage approach as a 'relay-race' model: New Testament scholars produce packages of 'original meanings', which they then hand on, like the baton in a relay race, to the systematicians. Lash goes on to observe:

> Systematic theologians who subscribe to this model are some-times irritated by the fact that, because the work of New Testament interpretation is never finished, the baton never reaches them. The New Testament scholar appears to be 'running on the spot'; he never arrives at the point at which the baton could be handed over. The New Testament scholar, for his part, either ignores what the systematic theologian is doing (it is not his business: he is only running the *first* leg of the race) or disapproves of the fact that the baton is continually being wrenched prematurely from his hands.[30]

In Lash's view, a more convincing alternative to the 'two-stage' approach is to see the two tasks of exegesis and contemporary application as dialectically related. This is to acknowledge that the relationship between exegesis and systematics is not best seen as a one-way relationship in which the findings of biblical scholarship are reached totally independently and then passed on wholesale to a different set of scholars who seek to apply them to contemporary questions. As Lash comments:

> If it is true for us, as creatures of history, that some understanding of our past is a necessary condition of an accurate grasp of our present predicament and of our responsibilities for the future, it is also true that a measure of critical self-understanding of our present predicament is a necessary condition of an accurate 'reading' of our past. We do not *first* understand the past

---

[29] Levenson makes the point admirably: 'Much biblical scholarship is not practising any hermeneutic of retrieval. Instead, its operative technique is too often a trivializing antiquarianism, in which the bathwater has become more important than the baby and the enormous historical and philological labours are not justified by reference to any larger structure of meaning' (1990, p. 134). See also Watson (1997), pp. 1–29.

[30] Lash (1986), p. 79.

and *then* proceed to understand the present. The relationship between these two dimensions of our quest for meaning and truth is
dialectical: they mutually inform, enable, correct and enlighten
each other.[31]

It is not to say that biblical scholarship and systematic theology are the
same thing; and a dialectical approach does not prevent scholars from
engaging in only one of these disciplines. However, it does open the way
to examining exegetical and theological questions together, as in this
study.[32] I return to the idea of a dialectical relationship between scripture
and theology at the end of section 2.3.

From the arguments in this chapter so far, it will be clear that I am
seeking in this study to strike a difficult balance. On the one hand, I see
the text and the concerns of systematic theology in dialectical relationship. Equally, we need safeguards against the kinds of danger outlined
by Stendahl. Although the aim of the study as a whole is to examine certain contemporary questions about the nature of faith and history in the
light of the Book of Revelation, I have sought to prevent such questions
shaping from the start my exegesis of the text. Thus in chapters 3–5 I examine particular aspects of the theology of the text, through engagement
with the text itself and with recent New Testament scholarship. Within an
overall structure which treats scripture and contemporary theology dialectically, I aim therefore to give due weight to the text itself. Equally,
I am concerned to avoid the danger of imposing exegetical conclusions
onto systematic theology without taking account of the fact that systematic theology may legitimately draw on other resources. Thus my aim
is to ascertain the extent to which the interpretation of the text might
offer grounds to support or question certain conclusions in systematic
theology. Where support cannot be found, this is not necessarily an indication that the conclusions are unjustified. Throughout chapters 3–6
I shall be seeking to observe Morgan and Barton's guidance to the effect
that 'theological interpretation of the Bible seeks to relate the ancient text
to the religious questions of the modern reader, without doing violence to
either'.[33]

---

[31] Lash (1986), pp. 79–80.

[32] Some important attempts to define the discipline of biblical theology have also adopted
a dialectical approach, over against Stendahl, seeing biblical theology as a two-way bridge
between exegesis and systematics. The most prominent example is Brevard Childs, who
argues strongly that the relationship between exegesis and systematic theology is a two-way
process, and that 'there is a legitimate place for a move from a fully developed Christian
theological reflection back to the biblical texts of both testaments' (1992, p. 87).

[33] Morgan and Barton (1988), p. 37.

2.3   Scripture and theology: the nature and appropriation of scripture

In section 2.2 I examined debates about the nature and purpose of biblical theology, drawing from that debate issues of relevance to the approach adopted in this study. I now turn to consider the relationship between scripture and theology from a slightly different angle, this time with reference to debates about the nature of scripture and how it is used in systematic theology. Again, this is a very large subject, and it is not my primary purpose in this study to reach a view on it. But, just as with the debate about biblical theology, important questions arise from this debate which are relevant to the approach taken in chapters 3–6. In a way, this question is more fundamental than the previous one, since whatever one's view of the nature and purpose (or even legitimacy) of a discipline called biblical theology, the wider question of how scripture is to be used in theology remains.

David Kelsey and the functional view of scripture

A particularly influential treatment of this subject has been that of David Kelsey, whose *The Uses of Scripture in Recent Theology* was published in 1975.[34] Kelsey begins his account with a survey of different ways in which twentieth-century theologians have construed the role of scripture.[35] These different approaches include B. B. Warfield's idea of the plenary verbal inspiration of scripture; G. E. Wright's concept of scripture as the recital of the acts of God;[36] and finally a group of examples which argue that scriptural authority resides not in its presentation of doctrinal concepts, nor even in the content of its narrative, but rather in its non-informative force as expression. One example of this last approach is Bultmann's argument that God addresses humanity through the kerygma, which operates as an existential demand on the individual. For Bultmann, the narrative content of the New Testament is of secondary importance as a record of events. Unlike Pannenberg or Wright, for example, he does

---

[34] Kelsey's book has been very influential in shaping more recent treatments of the subject. See for example, Farley and Hodgson (1983) and Young (1990, pp. 167–75). Both make extended use of Kelsey's analysis.

[35] For Kelsey, the construal of scripture by theologians is an imaginative act (a *discrimen*) which is prior to the actual use of scripture in any particular context. It involves decisions about such matters as what kind of authority scripture is to be given (1975, p. 15).

[36] As Kelsey observes (1975, pp. 53–4), Pannenberg's idea of revelation as history has features in common with Wright's approach, especially in his stress on the revelation of God in events. There are also differences, however: Pannenberg's stress on the importance of the eschaton as the moment of complete revelation and his rejection of fact–value distinctions in the examination of history mark his approach out from that of Wright.

not see divine activity in the events of human history as an appropriate ground for faith. It is rather the kerygmatic address to the individuals in their own historical context which should evoke the response of faith.

Kelsey then proceeds to explore the ways in which theologians actually *use* scripture in the formulation of theological proposals. Kelsey is attracted to the sort of approach exemplified by Bultmann, seeing the authority of scripture as residing in the way it *functions* in the life of the reader. This leads him to argue that the use of scripture in theology is best seen as the appropriation of patterns for living rather than as the appropriation of concepts. 'So scripture is authority for theological proposals, not by being the perfect source of the content that they fully preserve, but by providing a pattern by which the proposal's adequacy as elaboration can be addressed.'[37] Thus, for Kelsey the metaphor of 'translation', often used to describe the process by which scripture is appropriated by theology, is inadequate. He argues that in detecting and elaborating patterns in scripture theology is not simply isolating concepts and 'translating' them into forms more readily accessible to contemporary understanding. Rather, theology may elaborate upon scripture in ways which imply *discontinuity* with the conceptual framework of the biblical writers, insofar as that may be reconstructed. He gives as an example Bultmann's elaboration of Paul's statement that Christ's death was 'for us'. Bultmann interprets the statement as opening up new possibilities of authentic existence, using categories drawn from existentialism. This is going beyond mere 'translation', since it is using concepts radically different from anything Paul might have envisaged.[38]

Kelsey's arguments about the construal of scripture and the use of scripture both point in the same direction. The authority of scripture derives not from its propositional content, but from its function in the life of the Christian community. And the use of scripture in theology is to be seen not as the translation of concepts from the world of the text to the contemporary world, but rather as elaboration upon patterns detected in the text. In both cases, it is more useful to consider not 'what does the Bible say?', but 'what is God using the Bible for?'[39]

---

[37] Kelsey (1975), p. 196.

[38] Kelsey (1975), p. 189. Farley and Hodgson (1983, p. 53) come to a similar conclusion: 'The actual authority of scripture derives not from its content but from its power to occasion new occurrences of revelation and new experiences of redemptive transformation when used in situations of proclamation, theological reflection, and personal self-understanding.'

[39] Kelsey (1975), p. 213. It is interesting to note the similarity between this debate on the relative importance of the function of scripture compared to its content and a parallel debate in social anthropology about the function and content of myth (see chapter 3, pp. 65–8). In both cases, I argue that due emphasis needs to be placed on *content*.

Two distinct but closely related issues emerge from the discussion. The first concerns the question of the way in which theologians construe the nature and authority of scripture. The shift by Kelsey and others to a functional view of the authority of scripture is partly a reaction to the breakdown of what Kelsey sees as the traditional view of the authority of scripture, which relies on the idea of scripture as an inerrant repository of doctrinal concepts. This classic position has been christened the 'scripture principle'. In Kelsey's opinion, the findings of the last two centuries of biblical scholarship have made such a view progressively more difficult to sustain.[40]

It is not clear, however, that Kelsey's response to the problem is justified. It is certainly true that the 'scripture principle' in its classic form is untenable if it means that scripture is to be seen merely as a repository of inerrant, timeless doctrinal concepts. And, as Young rightly argues, an extreme version of the scripture principle will find it impossible to do justice to the various genres of scripture and the different ways in which they need to be read: it is no good reading poetry or apocalyptic literature primarily as a resource for constructing a set of abstract propositions.[41] Sensitivity to the different genres contained in scripture is essential, and this is nowhere more important than in the interpretation of apocalyptic literature. The Book of Revelation is ill served by interpretations which seek to systematize it into a set of doctrinal abstractions, or which fail to give due regard to the multivalent and allusive nature of apocalyptic symbolism.

Insofar as it moves interpretation away from trying to read doctrinal statements off the face of the text, acknowledgement of the way a text functions is to be welcomed. The problem is that a functionalist approach often tends to go much further: its logical conclusion is that so much emphasis is placed on the *function* of the text that the importance of its *content* is inevitably downgraded. As Childs comments,

> Just as it was a serious mistake for scholastic Protestantism to attempt to defend rationally an infallible biblical text apart from the working of the Holy Spirit, it is equally erroneous for a modern theology to separate the function of the Spirit from the content of the written Word which continues to voice the one will of God for the church.[42]

[40] Farley and Hodgson state the position starkly, framing their essay as a response to the breakdown of the scripture principle. They adopt a functionalist view of scripture on the lines proposed by Kelsey (Farley and Hodgson, 1983, pp. 51–60). The problem with their analysis, however, is that the version of the scripture principle they present is an extremely conservative one, which is all too easy to reject.

[41] Young (1990), pp. 168–9.   [42] Childs (1992), p. 663.

An additional feature of functionalist approaches is that the the relationship of scripture to historical events may be seen as less important. This is ironic, since part of the motivation for adopting a functionalist approach in the first place is to avoid the ahistoricizing tendency of the position which sees scripture merely as a source-book of timeless doctrine. Moving to a thoroughgoing functionalist approach to the nature of scripture can be an overreaction caused by an unnecessarily crude perception of what a cognitive element in the understanding of scripture might actually involve. But in fact, even if one takes a relatively pessimistic view of the prospects for the scripture principle, this need not lead one in a Bultmannian direction – quite the reverse. Pannenberg is equally persuaded of the demise of the scripture principle, but far from abandoning history, he emphasizes all the more strongly the reality of divine revelation as history, albeit located in the events themselves, rather than in the text.[43] In chapter 6 (pp. 145–54) I make use of Pannenberg's work in this area as applied particularly to apocalyptic, with the idea that the authority of the text depends upon future vindication in history.

The contention in chapters 3–5 will be that the impact of the Book of Revelation comes from the way it reveals dimensions of reality underlying the world of human events, and as a result seeks to bring about a change in the way its readers live in the present. Of course, this implies a rhetorical element in the operation of the text. But the power of the rhetoric comes from the combination of the content and function of the text. A *merely* functionalist explanation will not suffice, hence the criticisms below of interpretations such as those offered by Gager and Yarbro Collins, which appear to emphasize the psychological operation of the text at the expense of its content.[44] Attaching importance to the content of the text and the truth claims it makes does *not*, however, mean a return to seeing the text primarily as a quarry for timeless, abstract principles. Sensitivity to the apocalyptic genre will mean dealing with the text *as a whole*, and not seeking to strip away its symbolism as somehow constituting a secondary husk surrounding a set of central concepts.[45]

The second important issue to emerge from my discussion of Kelsey is the question of how far the use of scripture in systematic theology should be seen as the translation of concepts from the world of the text

---

[43] Pannenberg (1970), pp. 1–14.   [44] Gager (1983), Yarbro Collins (1984).

[45] Of course, there remains the issue of how to bridge the gap between the two very different genres of apocalypse and systematic theology. However, I believe that the method adopted in this study does enable the gap to be bridged. Young and Ford offer a brief but helpful discussion of the similar difficulties involved in moving from a New Testament Epistle to systematics, in their discussion of 2 Corinthians (1987, pp. 236–7).

to the contemporary world, and how far it should be seen as elaborations on patterns in scripture – elaborations which may result in conceptual discontinuity rather than continuity. Dissatisfaction with the more traditional idea of 'translation' as an overarching metaphor and attraction instead to ideas such as the metaphor of 'performance' have become popular recently.[46] The idea of performance has much to commend it, not least in respect of the interpretation of apocalyptic literature. One of the problems in interpreting the Book of Revelation is what to make of the symbolism in which it is couched, and the first-century world-view upon which its narrative structure so obviously depends. The metaphor of performance, with its connotation of conveying the sense and spirit of the original in a creative way which 'connects' with the contemporary audience, is potentially a most helpful way of seeing the interpretation of apocalyptic literature. However, it should not be assumed that the idea of performance is necessarily at odds with taking seriously the ontological truth-claims made in scripture. 'Performing' the Book of Revelation adequately today will involve doing justice not only to the pattern of Christian living it advocates, but also to its fundamental assertions about the nature of reality.[47] This would seem to entail more emphasis on *continuity* between text and theology than Kelsey thinks necessary.

So a balance needs to be struck. A theological interpretation of the text needs to offer an elaboration, or 'performance', of the original which is meaningful in the context of the interpreter's own culture, and which *also* retains continuity with the truth-claims made in the text. The danger of the approach taken by Kelsey is that too much attention is devoted to the first half of this balance and not enough to the second.

George Lindbeck and the cultural-linguistic view of doctrine

Another attempt to address the issue, in a way which consciously seeks to balance continuity and discontinuity, is that of George Lindbeck. Lindbeck's seminal work *The Nature of Doctrine* seeks to chart a new way forward in the understanding of how doctrine is formed and developed, but it is also highly relevant to the use of scripture in theology. He begins with an analysis of two established paradigms for the understanding of

---

[46] See, for example, 'Performing the Scriptures' in Lash (1986), pp. 37–46; Young (1990), *passim*.

[47] See the criticisms levelled against Kelsey, Farley and Hodgson, and others in this regard in Childs (1992), p. 723. N. T. Wright has adapted the metaphor of performance to describe the activity of biblical interpretation, in a way which certainly allows for the retention of a propositional element (1992, pp. 139–43).

doctrine. The first, which he terms the 'cognitive-propositional' approach, is for Lindbeck characteristic of historic Christian orthodoxy: doctrines 'function as informative propositions or truth claims about objective realities'.[48] The second, which he terms the 'experiential-expressivist' approach, is characteristic of Protestant liberalism, and interprets doctrines as 'noninformative and nondiscursive symbols of inner feelings, attitudes, or existential orientations'.[49] Lindbeck is dissatisfied with both of these approaches: with the cognitive-propositional approach, because it lacks the resources to allow reconciliation between different traditions, and with the experiential-expressivist approach, because it destroys any notion of the objective meaningfulness of doctrine.

Lindbeck's response is to propose a third approach, which he terms 'cultural-linguistic', in which doctrines are seen 'not as expressive symbols or as truth claims, but as communally authoritative rules of discourse, attitude, and action'.[50] This third approach relies on the assumption that religions resemble languages, and that just as a language depends on the application of grammatical rules, so also doctrine may be seen to function as a set of rules. These basic rules do not specify exactly how doctrinal statements are to be framed in any particular cultural setting. Nor should any one doctrinal articulation of the rules – no matter how venerable – be simply slavishly repeated: it requires reformulating in varying cultural circumstances. Thus, for example, in the area of Christology, Lindbeck detects three rules, or 'regulative principles', which he regards as foundational to mainstream Christian identity. These are: monotheism; 'historical specificity' (Jesus was a particular person who lived and died in a particular place); and 'Christological maximalism' (every possible importance is to be ascribed to Jesus consistent with the first two rules). Lindbeck argues that particular formulations of these rules, such as the Nicene and Chalcedonian definitions, may function as authoritative paradigms, but they do not themselves have doctrinal authority: such authority belongs rather to the rules which the formulations instantiate.[51]

Lindbeck argues that this framework offers a mechanism which can accommodate both continuity and change in doctrinal formulation. It also offers a potential way forward in ecumenical dialogue, since different confessional formulations may be understood as legitimately varying expressions of the same underlying regulative principles. And importantly, it seeks to shift the emphasis away from doctrine as a set of abstract

---

[48] Lindbeck (1984), p. 16.   [49] Lindbeck (1984), p. 16.
[50] Lindbeck (1984), p. 18.   [51] Lindbeck (1984), pp. 92–6.

propositions and towards the way in which fundamental truth is actually embodied by the community in a particular situation:

> What is important is that Christians allow their cultural con-
> ditions and highly diverse affections to be molded by the set
> of biblical stories that stretches from creation to eschaton and
> culminates in Jesus' passion and resurrection. The experiential
> products of this shaping process, however, will be endlessly var-
> ied because of the differences of the affective materials on which
> it works.[52]

Underlying this point is a basic distinction which Lindbeck draws between the cultural-linguistic approach and the classic cognitive-propositional approach. He argues that the cognitive approach lays greatest emphasis on a correspondence theory of truth, in which theological assertions are held to reflect ontological reality. A cultural-linguistic approach, by contrast, lays emphasis on a coherence or intrasystematic theory of truth: what matters is whether the action of an individual or a community in a particular situation is consistent with the overall system of Christian belief set out in its basic rules. According to a cultural-linguistic approach, therefore, 'for a Christian, "God is Three and One", or "Christ is Lord" are true only as parts of a total pattern of speaking, thinking, feeling, and acting'.[53] Lindbeck is at pains to argue that this does not mean that a cultural-linguistic approach is inimical to epistemological realism. Rather, he argues, intrasystematic truth is in fact a necessary – though not sufficient – precondition for ontological correspondence between asser-tion and reality. A cultural-linguistic understanding of doctrine is fully capable of accommodating ontological truth-claims. However, whereas a cognitivist-propositional approach would locate propositional truth at the level of doctrinal assertion, a cultural-linguistic approach would see propositional truth as characterizing 'ordinary religious language when it is used to mold lives through prayer, praise, preaching, and exhortation'.[54]

Lindbeck's treatment of the use of scripture in theology reflects his more general concerns about the nature and transmission of doctrine. He refers again to the importance of coherence or intrasystematic truth. His difficulty with the cognitive-propositionalist approach to scripture is what he sees as its resort to translating scripture into extratextual propositions which form the basis of doctrine. Instead, he argues, the focus should

---

[52] Lindbeck (1984), p. 84.   [53] Lindbeck (1984), p. 64.
[54] Lindbeck (1984), p. 69.

be on the 'system' of scripture itself, rather than outside it (whether on abstract doctrines, as in cognitive-propositionalism, or on the individual's religious experience, as with experiential-expressivism):

> For those who are steeped in [authoritative, canonical texts], no world is more real than the ones they create. A scriptural world is thus able to absorb the universe. It supplies the interpretative framework within which believers seek to live their lives and understand reality ... intratextual theology redescribes reality within the scriptural framework rather than translating scripture into extrascriptural categories. It is the text, so to speak, which absorbs the world, rather than the world the text.[55]

This formulation is in fact a problematic one.[56] As I argue later in this section, the rhetorical power of a text like Revelation comes from the interplay of the text and the reality to which it relates: to postulate either the absorption of the world by the text or the text by the world is therefore to assume a false antithesis.

A more promising way forward is that suggested by Anthony Thiselton. He critiques approaches such as those of Jacques Derrida and Roland Barthes, in which language is no longer assumed to have any external referent. He makes use of Wittgenstein, to argue that communication depends on a life-context for it to have any meaning, and that to speak of language divorced from an external referent is meaningless.[57] Thiselton also develops this conclusion in the context of his discussion of speech-act theory, in engagement with writers such as John Searle.[58] He makes two points here of particular relevance to this study. First, a hermeneutic such as that of Bultmann, which emphasizes the self-involving nature of the text at the expense of its propositional content, is unbalanced, and fails to take account of the fact that statements such as 'Jesus is Lord' (1 Cor. 12:3) rely upon a dual function of propositional assertion *and* self-involvement for their impact. Second, extralinguistic reference is critical in respect of two contrasting but characteristic forms of biblical utterance: promise and assertion. The logic of promise (or command) is that the utterance 'gets the world to match the words'; the logic of assertion involves getting 'the word to match the world'. In both cases, the utterance derives force only from the interaction between language

---

[55] Lindbeck (1984), pp. 117–18.

[56] Childs is also uneasy with Lindbeck's argument, partly on the grounds that it seems to assume that the world of the text is somehow distinct from the world of human reality (Childs, 1992, pp. 21–2).

[57] Thiselton (1992), pp. 80–141.   [58] Thiselton (1992), pp. 272–312.

and reality. If a promise can have no effect in reality, it has no meaning. If the assertion does not match reality, *it* has no meaning. Thiselton brings out the interrelation of these two opposite 'directions of fit', world to word and word to world, with reference to the Fourth Gospel:

> whenever promises, pledges, or other world-to-word utterances are effective and fully operative, a context and a background is presupposed concerning which word-to-world assertions can be made. In the enfleshment of the divine word of promise in the world in the incarnation of Jesus Christ (John 1:14) these two 'directions of fit' come together as one single transforming personal reality. Jesus comes and addresses the reader in the Johannine writings as the word who, on the one hand, articulates a pre-existing ultimate reality (John 1:1–18), but who, on the other hand, promises world-to-word transformation (John 20:31).[59]

This intertwining of 'directions of fit' is abundantly clear in the Book of Revelation. The seer makes assertions about the ultimate nature of reality (word-to-world fit), on the basis of which it is possible to articulate promises of transformation (world-to-word fit) (see chapters 3–5 below).

Lindbeck's proposals, particularly as they relate to the interpretation of scripture, raise important questions which are relevant to my argument. Some features of his model provide helpful insights for interpreting apocalyptic literature in the context of contemporary theology: his reminder that the interpretation of scripture should not primarily be a matter of extracting abstract doctrinal statements, but rather should do justice to the shape of the text itself; his emphasis on the living-out of the text by the community of faith; and his stress on the need consciously to interpret the text in the context of the interpreter's own culture. However, the way in which Lindbeck's model concentrates on intrasystematic consistency at the expense of extratextual reference is open to question. As I noted earlier, Lindbeck certainly does not see his proposal as ruling out ontological truth-claims. The problem is that his proposal divorces the question of the intrasystematic consistency of religious belief from the question of its ontological truth or falsity. In the context of the interpretation of Revelation this is ultimately an unsatisfactory approach, because the text derives its impact precisely from the truth-claims implied by its rhetoric and symbolism.

[59] Thiselton (1992), p. 307.

Alister McGrath and the importance of content

In his 1990 Bampton Lectures, Alister McGrath offers a helpful critique of Lindbeck's position. He begins by arguing that the cognitive-propositional model has historically been much more flexible than Lindbeck is prepared to allow. It has classically seen doctrine as perception of the divine, rather than an attempt at total description: it is capable of accommodating metaphor and symbol, and is not restricted to some crude correspondence theory of truth. So Lindbeck's dissatisfaction with the cognitive-propositionalist approach may not be wholly justified. McGrath's criticism is that Lindbeck has in fact erected a 'straw man' of an extreme version of the cognitive-propositional model ('the view that an exhaustive and unambiguous account of God is transmitted conceptually by propositions'), with which he then takes issue, whereas a more measured view (merely 'that there is a genuinely cognitive dimension, component or element to doctrinal statements') would have suggested a more restrained conclusion.[60]

McGrath goes on to suggest that Lindbeck's alternative cultural-linguistic model, with its concentration on a coherence theory of truth, fails to account for the origin of the 'grammar', or regulative principles, on which it is based, and sets aside the question of whether Christian assertions have any external referent: 'This grand retreat from history reduces doctrine to little more than a grammar of an ahistorical language which – like Melchizedek – has no origins. It is just there.'[61] Lindbeck's view of doctrine, and of scripture from which it draws, is therefore 'strongly reductionist'.[62]

McGrath makes his point forcefully and clearly, although it is perhaps a overreaction to call Lindbeck strongly reductionist. Lindbeck is careful not to rule out the possibility of correspondence between doctrine and reality. He is rather saying that his approach does not *depend* on making the assumption that such correspondence exists. Nonetheless, part of my contention in chapters 3–5 is that John of Patmos is seeking to reveal hidden layers of reality which encompass the visible world of human events. I shall take issue with interpretations which see as secondary this connection between the assertions in the text and ultimate reality, and which stress rather the psychological impact of the text upon its audience.

McGrath's own view of the relationship between scripture and systematic theology begins with the observation that there is 'a perceived

---

[60] McGrath (1990), p. 20.
[61] McGrath (1990), p. 34. See also Reimer (1991), pp. 51–2.
[62] McGrath (1990), p. 34.

need to transfer theological reflection from commitment to the limits and defining conditions and vocabulary of the New Testament itself, in order to preserve its commitment to the New Testament proclamation. The genesis of doctrine lies in the exodus from uncritical repetition of the narrative heritage of the past.'[63] The key problem is how to manage this transition from foundational narrative to systematic doctrine and how to test the adequacy of doctrinal formulations as interpretative frameworks for scriptural narratives.

Like Lindbeck, McGrath resists the idea that scripture is primarily a set of propositions, from which deductions may be made. Rather, scripture is 'a specific mode of discourse and pattern of thinking, which requires transposition into an interpretative framework. This involves a shift in modes of discourse and patterns of thinking, in that two quite different genres – narrative and metaphysics – require correlation.'[64] In an important passage, he offers a framework within which this correlation might be sought:

> There is...a dynamic relationship between doctrine and the scriptural narrative. That narrative possesses an interpretative substructure, hinting at doctrinal affirmations. It is evident that there are conceptual frameworks, linked to narrative structures, within scripture: these function as starting points for the process of generation of more sophisticated conceptual frameworks in the process of doctrinal formulation. On the basis of these scriptural hints, markers and signposts, doctrinal affirmations may be made, which are then employed as a conceptual framework for the interpretation of the narrative. The narrative is then re-read and re-visioned in the light of this conceptual framework, in the course of which modifications to the framework are suggested. There is thus a process of dynamic interaction, of *feedback*, between doctrine and scripture, between the interpretative framework and the narrative itself.[65]

This seems to me an admirable summary of the way in which scripture and doctrine should interact. The idea of dynamic interaction between

[63] McGrath (1990), p. 7.

[64] McGrath, (1990), p. 62. He echoes Lindbeck's concern that extratextual factors should not be allowed to dominate scriptural interpretation: 'Doctrine provides the conceptual framework by which the scriptural narrative is interpreted. It is not an arbitrary framework, however, but one which is suggested by that narrative, and intimated (however provisionally) by scripture itself. It is to be discerned within, rather than imposed upon, that narrative' (McGrath, 1990, pp. 58–9).

[65] McGrath (1990), pp. 60–1.

text and theology brings us back to the arguments of Lash and others, to which I referred above (pp. 28–31). Thus the two discussions in this chapter, of the relationship between the disciplines of biblical exegesis and systematic theology, and of the use of scripture in systematic theology, have both arrived at the same point.

2.4 Conclusions

This section sets out some conclusions, in the light of the discussion in this chapter, which will provide a foundation for the more detailed study in chapters 3–6.

The first conclusion is that scripture and theology should be seen in dynamic interrelationship. This arose in the discussion of the interdisciplinary relationship between biblical studies and systematics in section 2.2, in the critiques by Lash, Ollenburger and others of the two-stage model of biblical interpretation proposed by Stendahl. It also arose in the discussion of the use of scripture in systematic theology in section 2.3, in particular in relation to McGrath's proposals for a framework for testing the adequacy of doctrine as far as it represents elaboration of scripture. McGrath's proposals provide a good working basis for the overall task of chapters 3–6. Hence, although Revelation is a work of apocalyptic prophecy, not a set of propositions, it does indeed contain 'hints, markers and signposts', on the basis of which theological assertions may be made. This will enable judgements to be made about the extent to which the text might offer grounds to support or question the positions reached by the theologians whom I consider in chapter 6.

Second, however, we must heed the warnings of Stendahl, J. Barr and others that neither side of the balance in this dynamic interaction should be permitted to dominate the other. The way in which the study is structured is designed to strike this balance. I began in chapter 1 with a set of contemporary theological questions; chapters 3–5 will concentrate on detailed engagement with the text and its interpretation; chapter 6 will return to questions of systematic theology. The intention is to provide space to do justice to both the text and contemporary theology, within an overall framework which will bring them together.

The third conclusion relates to the discussion about the relationship between the function and content of scripture. This arose both in my discussion of Kelsey's approach to the construal and use of scripture in theology, and also in connection with Lindbeck's rejection of cognitive-propositionalist explanations of doctrine in favour of cultural-linguistic ones. Kelsey, Lindbeck and others argue that scripture is not primarily a set of doctrinal propositions; this does not, however, rule out the idea that scripture has a propositional element to it. Both Kelsey and Lindbeck appear to erect 'straw men' in the form of extreme versions of a cognitive-propositionalist approach, which they (not surprisingly) then reject. McGrath has argued convincingly for a more flexible understanding of what a cognitive-propositionalist approach might involve. He concludes that 'Christian doctrine is...concerned with the unfolding and uncovering of the significance of the history of Jesus of Nazareth, in the belief that this gives insights into the nature of reality.'[66]

Fourth, however, according a central place to ontological truth-claims in the text does *not* entail a process of stripping away the rich and varied imagery of the text, as if this were some secondary husk within which might be found timeless abstract principles. This would quite simply not do justice to the apocalyptic genre. Hence, the approach in chapters 3–5 is not to try to boil the text down to abstract points. Rather, the study will try to do justice to the total shape of the text, including the whole of its narrative sweep, the imagery the seer uses, and to what is known of the historically conditioned circumstances in which the text originated.

It is with these four conclusions in mind that I now turn to the text.

[66] McGrath (1990), pp. 74–5.

3

WAYS OF APPROACHING THE BOOK OF REVELATION

3.1   Introduction

In the next three chapters, I turn to the Book of Revelation. My particular concern will be to analyse the way in which the dimensions of space and time are used in the text to develop the theological argument. I shall consider this in detail in chapters 4 and 5, but first I examine in this chapter three important ways in which interpreters have approached Revelation. In section 3.2 I consider different ways in which the text has been treated as a resource for reflection on the development of human history. The seer is profoundly concerned with human history. However, his concern for history stems not from an attempt to provide a speculative chronology of the future or to discern abstract principles at work in the course of history. Rather, he provides a spatial and temporal framework within which to address the present situation of his readers. In section 3.3 I consider various interpretations of the rhetorical situation and impact of the text. My conclusion is that the seer aims to evoke a practical response from his readers to the threats which he perceives from the enemies of Christ. He achieves this by revealing hidden dimensions of reality, both spatial and temporal, to demonstrate the true nature of the readers' situation, and therefore to exhort and encourage them. In section 3.4 I turn to the recent debates about the genre of the text. My main conclusion is that Revelation should be seen not only as an apocalypse, or as a prophecy, or as a letter, but as all three. This combination of different generic backgrounds strengthens an interpretation of the text as *both* reaching out to ultimate spatial and temporal realities *and* focusing sharply on the earthly present. Taken together, my conclusions from each of the sections in this chapter form the framework for the detailed analysis in chapters 4 and 5.

3.2   Revelation as the key to history?

The interpretation of the Book of Revelation has traditionally been dominated by the question of how it might be seen to relate to human history.[1] Speculation about this relationship has sometimes taken the form of 'futurist' interpretations. These regard the text as an inspired, detailed prediction of the course of end-time events, which the interpreter usually expects to begin imminently. At a popular level, such interpretations are still widespread, especially among churches influenced by dispensationalism.[2] Other interpreters, sometimes labelled 'historicist', have seen the text as a prediction of the whole of human history. A difficulty with this kind of approach is that each interpreter following it tends to impose on the book a pattern leading up to his or her own particular time. Neither the 'futurist' nor the 'historicist' method shows convincingly what the message of the book might have been for its original audience. It is not my purpose to provide a detailed account of interpretations of this kind, popular though they remain in some quarters. Rather, in this section, I shall concentrate on an analysis of the ways in which mainstream twentieth-century theologians and biblical scholars have considered the text as a resource for reflection on the nature of history.

Preterist interpretations

This method seeks to ground the meaning of the visions of the text firmly in the historical events of the time of the seer. Fiorenza describes it as trying to establish that 'John points to the immediate past or present history of the Christian community to show that the final time has already been inaugurated and is realising itself in the present.'[3] Giet provides a good illustration of this method at work. His central argument is that the seer detects in the recent past certain historical patterns or rhythms which it is believed will somehow replicate themselves in the future. Thus, Giet argues, certain episodes in the vision sequences in Revelation relate to phases in the Jewish War of 66–70.[4] For example, the third phase of the war (actually four separate campaigns) from 67–70 lasted for around three and a half years, and therefore relates to the three visions in chs. 11–13, each of which mentions that length of time.[5] Giet argues that the seer

---

[1] For brief surveys of the history of the interpretation of Revelation, see, for example, Swete (1906), pp. cciiiff.; Mounce (1977), pp. 39–45; Court (1979), ch. 1; Beale (1999), pp. 44–9.

[2] For surveys of this kind of approach, see Boyer (1992) and O'Leary (1994).

[3] Fiorenza (1985), p. 37. Fiorenza's essay 'History and Eschatology in Revelation' (pp. 35–67 of her 1985 volume) offers a helpful critique of different attempts to relate Revelation to history.

[4] Giet (1957), ch. 1.   [5] See 11:2; 11:3; 12:6; 12:14; 13:5.

scrutinizes history to discern 'un certain rythme qui lui permet d'augurer "ce qui doit arriver bientôt"'.[6]

In her critique of writers such as Giet, Fiorenza concludes that temporal-developmental interpretations of this kind are invalid.[7] She argues that they could be justified only if it could be demonstrated that the seer is consciously borrowing the presuppositions of historical development typical of Jewish apocalyptic thought, in which the past is used to predict the future. However, since the two hallmarks of the Jewish apocalyptic view of history – pseudonymity, and the dating of the work to a period earlier than that of the author – are absent from Revelation, such justification is not available. This specific critique is only partly convincing: Collins, for example, has argued that the lack of pseudonymity and predating should not be taken as necessarily excluding Revelation from the genre of apocalypse.[8] Fiorenza is on firmer ground when she concludes more generally that preterist interpretations are misconceived, given the overall purpose of the text: 'The author does not aim to present a historical sequence; nor does he seek to justify and deduce the future from history. Rather he understands his book as a prophecy for the present which receives its justification from the future, that is, from the coming of Christ (22:20).'[9]

'Theology of history' interpretations

Philosophy of history

Unlike the preterist approach, these interpretations do not seek to link the text to individually identifiable historical events from the seer's own time, but rather conclude that the seer is using the text to convey principles underlying the development of human history in general.[10] Schlier provides an example of this approach, beginning his account with the declaration 'Die Offenbarung Johannis ist das einzige Buch des Neuen Testaments, das die Geschichte zum Thema hat.'[11] Schlier's premise is that although there is an underlying meaning to human history, this cannot be read from actual historical events in themselves. It can be discerned only through

---

[6] Giet (1957), p. 199.   [7] Fiorenza (1985), pp. 37–42.
[8] Collins (1977).   [9] Fiorenza (1985), p. 42.
[10] As Fiorenza (1985) puts it, these interpretations assume that Revelation is 'the prophetic charter of the dialogue which God carries on with humanity in world history. The visions and images of Rev. are types of what lies "behind" the history of the world and what constitutes the meaning of all history' (p. 43).
[11] Schlier (1956), p. 265.

faith. Moreover, one cannot understand history 'from a distance', but only from within it, in the context of historical encounter. Christ's ability to unseal the scroll (5:5) should be taken to mean that he is the one worthy to enable history to be resolved; in other words, God will use the events of history in order to bring the world into accord with the future of the resurrected Christ.[12] This process will be resisted by the world, which sets itself against the future to which Christ's death and resurrection point. The seals, trumpets and bowls of Revelation are symbols of the divine response to this earthly resistance. The aim of the text is to help Christians as they seek to live in 'the present future of God in Christ', conscious of the importance of the present moment of decision.[13]

The approach of Ernst Lohmeyer has much in common with that of Schlier, in its quest to detect fundamental principles to do with the nature of history. However, Lohmeyer begins from the premise that the underlying concern of the text is not so much the nature of historical development as such, but rather the eschatological judgement of God and the powers which seek to stand in the way of that consummation. For Lohmeyer, this is the lens through which the whole text should be seen. The result is a reduced sense of historical progression; in its place there is a timeless sense of the struggle between good and evil. A central feature of Lohmeyer's analysis is that every eschatological event described in the text is *both* future *and* timeless (or unlimited to any one particular temporal location). It is future because it relates to the liberation of the church from the eschatological tension of its present existence, and timeless because this liberation is in a sense already present, prefigured both in Christ's earthly existence and in the faith of the church.[14] Thus past and future become interchangeable as both are caught up in the eternal reality of God and Christ. Lohmeyer illustrates this by drawing attention to some of the ambiguous temporal references in the text. Thus in 5:9 the Lamb is found to be worthy to initiate the future events heralded by the opening of the seals, but in 3:21 Christ is already said to have sat on God's throne. In 7:4ff. the faithful are sealed, yet their names were written in the book of life from the foundation of the world (17:8).

Fiorenza finds Lohmeyer's approach more satisfactory than that of Schlier because of his acknowledgement that the text's fundamental concerns relate to eschatology rather than history, although she nonetheless

---

[12] 'Geschichte ist das Welt-Geschehen, in dem und durch das Gott seine von dem gekreuzigten und auferstanden Jesus Christus übernommene zukünftige Herrschaft vorläufig zur Geltung bringt' (Schlier, 1956, p. 268).
[13] Schlier (1956), pp. 272–3.   [14] Lohmeyer (1926), p. 188.

criticizes him for not placing sufficient emphasis on the actual historical location of the text.[15] I believe that Fiorenza is right to criticize approaches which assume that John was seeking to convey a kind of philosophy of history to his readers. His text is rather concerned with present realities in the light of an imminent future; to assign a sense either of gradual historical development or of timeless abstraction to the text is to impose alien categories upon it. But Fiorenza is wrong to suggest that the text therefore has nothing to contribute towards an understanding of the nature of history. Her contention that 'the main concern of the author is not the interpretation of history but the issue of power' is oddly phrased.[16] John may not have been setting out a projected calendar of history – but how can a concern for the way in which divine power operates in the world be divorced from the question of history?

Salvation history

As with the interpretations in the previous section, those based on the concept of salvation history seek to discern from the text overall principles at work in history. However, they stress much more strongly the notion of a continuous line of salvation history running through scripture and beyond, centred on the Christ event. The most notable attempt at this method of exegesis is that of Rissi (1966), which takes as its starting point the work of Oscar Cullmann.

In his influential books *Christ and Time* and *Salvation in History* Cullmann sets out a series of important theses about the treatment of history in scripture. First, he argues that the Christ event stands at the centre of history, inaugurating the turn of the ages.[17] Second, Cullmann postulates a division between 'biblical' and 'general' history, similar to the traditional distinction between sacred and secular history. 'Biblical' history consists of the interventions of God within history to bring about salvation, centring on the Christ event, and it is this form of history with which the New Testament writers are concerned. Third, Cullmann maintains that in assessing the nature of biblical myth, the interpreter should resist the temptation to regard it as somehow the opposite of history. Myth, far from being separated from history, serves to interpret it, disclosing the hidden connections between different events in the thread of salvation history. For Cullmann, there is certainly a distinction to be made between the purely prophetic, such as Revelation, and prophetically

---

[15] Fiorenza (1985), p. 44.   [16] Fiorenza (1985), p. 24.
[17] Cullmann (1951), pp. 17ff.

interpreted history, such as Acts, but this does not undermine the point that both should be viewed as lying on the same time line.[18]

Rissi's exposition of the text is an attempt to apply Cullmann's ideas to a particular New Testament book. He accepts the basic premise of a line of salvation history, stretching from the beginning through the story of Israel to the Christ event and on into the future. The Christ event is for Rissi, as it is for Cullmann, the central feature of the line of salvation history, towards which the past points, and from which the future flows. He therefore argues that the understanding of the relationship between eschatology and history in Revelation is fundamentally different from that of Jewish apocalyptic: 'while in the Jewish apocalyptic all history is directed toward the End and moves on according to plan, John recognizes in the historical Christ event an eschatological event already occurred, he sees in Jesus the revelation of the meaning and goal of all history, and in the risen Lord, the lord of final history'.[19]

Rissi discerns a repeated pattern in the text, in which the time between the first and second comings of Christ is symbolically represented from different viewpoints. Thus, for example, the block of material in chs. 12–14 begins with the historical Christ event (the birth of the Messiah in 12:5) and finishes with the parousia (the twin images of the harvest and vintage of 14:14–20). Just as for Cullmann myth is not separate from history but rather interprets it, so for Rissi the repeated symbolic portrayals of this age serve to invest it with meaning: 'God's plan in John's Revelation is ... a goal-directed sequence of intrusions by God into human history ... But individual events of world history to come are not predicted – John rather portrays the characteristic features of all coming history which are disclosed by the victory of Jesus Christ.'[20] Nonetheless, like Cullmann, Rissi wants to preserve an element of contingency in the seer's picture of history, and in this context contrasts Revelation with Jewish apocalyptic:

> All the visions of judgement, which stand under the divine 'must', have finally a very evident 'if not' before them. So long as the world despises the gospel, the gracious word will turn into a word of judgement. In this, John distinguishes himself basically from the historical images of Jewish apocalyptic, for which history constitutes a determinate, inclusive unity.[21]

---

[18] Cullmann (1951), p. 97.   [19] Rissi (1966), pp. 49–50.
[20] Rissi (1966), pp. 113, 115.   [21] Rissi (1966), p. 104.

Although the salvation-history approach is a serious attempt to deal with the temporal dimension of the text, it has some flaws. First, it is questionable whether this approach is right to lay such an emphasis on a supposed conscious attempt by New Testament writers to set out an account of the progression of salvation history, as for example in Rissi's detection of patterns in the text of Revelation portraying the history of the world between the first and second comings of Christ. There is certainly an irreducible element of temporality in the text, and a strong sense of eschatological tension. But the stress in the text is heavily upon the *imminence* of the end-time events (cf. 1:1, 3; 22:7, 12, 20), rather than upon a sense of historical *development*. To this extent, Fiorenza's comments which I noted above, to the effect that the text is concerned with issues of power and eschatology rather than with history, are justified. However, as I argued there, this does not necessarily lessen the importance of the text in contributing to a Christian understanding of history.

Second, much of the rhetorical power of the text comes from the dissonance it creates between 'what is', in the perspective of God's ultimate sovereignty, and 'what appears to be', in the earthly present. The magnificent climax of the passages relating to the New Jerusalem are in a sense as much of a starting point as a conclusion, since it is from that symbol that the reader/hearer is led back into the world of 'what appears to be', to wrestle with the realities of this world, albeit equipped with a new perspective. The inexorable time line of salvation history is perhaps too linear to deal adequately with this effect, since it tends to move the reader's focus to the future and away from the present, rather than holding the two in tension.

Moltmann and Pannenberg both attack Cullmann's position for different reasons. Moltmann argues that the salvation-history approach leads to the transposition of eschatology into time, which is inevitably transient. Thus, even the 'not yet' of the 'already–not yet' polarity of salvation becomes transient: the fundamental transformative power of eschatology is lost.[22] For Pannenberg, Cullmann's philosophical conclusions about the relationship between salvation history and general or secular history are open to serious question:

> The conception of a redemptive history severed from ordinary history ... is hardly acceptable on theological grounds, and is judged not to be so in the first instance because of historical presuppositions. It belongs to the full meaning of the Incarnation

[22] Moltmann (1996), pp. 6–13.

that God's redemptive deed took place within the universal correlative connections of human history and not in a ghetto of redemptive history.[23]

Orientation to the present

A significant number of commentators have concluded that it is wrong to seek to detect a chronological framework in the visions of Revelation. Fiorenza argues: 'Since Revelation does not progress in historical-successive fashion but reveals in ever-new images and visions the present time of the community as the eschatological end time, it is impossible to reconstruct a historical-chronological development of events.'[24] From another perspective, Boring's view is that since there is constant interaction in the text between different narrative levels, it cannot be analysed in a purely diachronic fashion.[25] Prigent rightly argues that the language of temporal succession in the text should not be taken literally; rather, it is an attempt by John to convey the point that present reality will include persecution, but that God has the ultimate triumph.[26]

In this context, insights from sociology about the perception of time are illuminating. In *Temporal Man: The Meaning and Uses of Social Time*, published in 1981, Robert Lauer argues that a highly influential tradition in western philosophy has sought to deny ultimate significance to temporal perception. Lauer relates this to a Platonic tendency to seek escape from the finitude of human existence, and hence to escape from time. He therefore sets out to provide an alternative approach, which would take seriously the reality of time. His method is to concentrate on what he calls 'social time' as opposed to 'clock time'. He defines social time as 'the patterns and orientations that relate to social processes and to the conceptualization of the ordering of life'.[27] In this context he concludes that if a future orientation is too short (i.e. its horizon is too imminent), 'life becomes insignificant, meaningless and dreary, since the present leads to nothing of enduring value'. If on the other hand, a future orientation is too long, focusing on the remote future, 'the present is rendered equally valueless and dreary because nothing humanly desirable or satisfying is permissible'.[28]

---

[23] Pannenberg (1970), p. 41.   [24] Fiorenza (1985), p. 138.
[25] Boring (1992), p. 721. Boring postulates three distinct, though interrelated, narrative levels, consisting of John's story, God's/Christ's story and the world's story.
[26] Prigent (1980), pp. 243–4.   [27] Lauer (1981), p. 21.
[28] Lauer (1981), pp. 355, 356. These conclusions are in fact quotations by Lauer from Lawrence Frank, *Society as the Patient: Essays on Culture and Personality*, New Brunswick, N.J.: Rutgers University Press, 1949.

Lauer's point about future orientation is relevant to my main contention about the way in which Revelation deals with time. The text assumes an irreducible element of temporality, which is wrongly excluded by interpretations which would seek either to reduce the text to an expression of timeless abstractions about the nature of history, or to read it as an attempt to escape out of history completely. One might say that one problem with such interpretations is that the future orientation they assume is too short. It is interesting to notice the similarity between Lauer's description of the problems of truncated future orientation ('the present leads to nothing of enduring value...') and the interpretation by Russell or Hanson of apocalyptic, with its stress on pessimism regarding this world and this age.[29] On the other hand, interpretations of Revelation which appear to overemphasize chronology may have the effect of focusing future orientation at a point too distant in time. Certainly, interpretations which see the text as relating chronologically either to the sweep of history or to a small set of eschatological events yet to come in the twentieth or twenty-first century are often criticized for rendering the text meaningless to its original audience. Could an alternative way of expressing this meaninglessness be precisely that used by Lauer to describe the problems associated with a too-remote future orientation?

From within the New Testament guild, Bruce Malina has taken up the question of temporal orientation and applies it to the perception of time among New Testament writers, including John of Patmos. Malina is reacting against the deeply entrenched tradition of assuming that the temporal orientation of New Testament writers was essentially future. Drawing on work on the attitude towards time among the peasants of Algeria, he argues that Mediterranean culture is predominantly present-orientated, and that descriptions of the New Testament as future-orientated represent the imposition of an alien, north European/North American temporal orientation onto the text.[30] The title of Malina's essay, 'Christ and Time: Swiss or Mediterranean?', heralds a critical approach towards the salvation-history method of Oscar Cullmann. Malina draws on the anthropologist Pierre Bourdieu's study of the Kybale of Algeria. Bourdieu summarizes the present-orientated culture of the Kybale thus:

> The lapse of time which constitutes the present is the whole of an action seen in the unity of a perception including both the retained past and the anticipated future. The 'present' of the action embraces, over and above the perceived present, an

[29] See my discussion below, pp. 73–5.   [30] Malina (1989), p. 9.

horizon of the past and of the future tied to the present because they both belong to the same context of meaning.[31]

Malina stresses that he is *not* saying that New Testament writers ignored the past or the future, but simply that their primary orientation was to the present. In other words, events from the recent past which are still relevant to the present and events in the near future which will grow out of the present are all included in the horizon of the present.[32] That which is forthcoming is organically linked to the present, and precise chronology is not important. Malina adds that the nature of social time typical of peasant cultures is polychronic: time is not conceived of as a linear sequence with events following one after the other, but rather as non-directional, accommodating more than one event simultaneously. Developments such as the onset of old age, or child-bearing, are not associated with particular time periods, but simply occur when the appropriate time arrives. Malina sees apocalyptic as reflecting this perspective, and thus retaining a present orientation. His overall conclusion is that there is in fact no 'now–not yet' tension in the New Testament, that the New Testament writers were instead orientated to the present, and that the accepted assumption that apocalyptic thought is future-orientated therefore needs reappraisal.[33]

Malina's article is both suggestive and challenging. In the context of Revelation it is a healthy corrective against interpretations which place too much emphasis on the future without relating the message of the text sufficiently to the present. At the same time, his overall conclusion about the lack of eschatological tension seems to go too far. It is precisely *because* Revelation has a central concern for the present situation, and describes dissonance between 'what appears to be' in human history and 'what is' in the perspective of God's ultimate sovereignty, that tension between the

---

[31] Bourdieu (1963), pp. 59–60. For the Kybale, times are not specified chronometrically, but rather in accordance with vague conventions. For example, the timing of an exact appointment might be unknown; the parties might simply agree to meet 'at the next market' (p. 59).

[32] Malina refers to 'operational time', as defined by Rayner (1982) in his study of the perceptions of time and space in egalitarian sects. Rayner suggests that in small, tightly knit groups, operational time is emphasized within the group. Since the group defines itself sharply over against the rest of society, one effect of this is to collapse wider temporal perspectives (i.e. past and future historical dimensions) into the present. The result is a telescoping of the perception of historical distance between the original founder of the movement and the current group, and a tendency to claim certain knowledge of the future.

[33] Malina (1989), p. 29. See also Malina (1995), in which he makes the extraordinary statement that 'there is nothing in the book of Revelation that refers to the future' (p. 266).

'now' and the 'not yet' is surely implied. My conclusion is therefore that Malina is right in his criticism of over-chronological interpretations, but less persuasive in his dissolution of temporal tension.[34] His case for interpreting apocalyptic as present-orientated rather than future-orientated is unproven.

In their recent analysis of the relationship between time and space in Revelation, Howard-Brook and Gwyther draw on Malina's work.[35] They are concerned to guard against an unhelpful temporal dualism which would divorce the outworking of divine justice from the present, and against an unhelpful spatial dualism which would divorce heavenly realities from each other. They therefore emphasize (rightly) the interchange between heaven and earth as two coexistent realities.[36] However, their dependence on Malina leads them to a less persuasive conclusion in respect of the temporal dimension of the text. They argue that 'Once we put aside our future-oriented lens on time and perceive time from the present orientation of John's world, we can see how Revelation bifurcates time into two simultaneously present realities.' Thus, the grammatically future verb tenses in Revelation are 'literal references not to a sequential future but to the always co-present other reality in which God and the Lamb have already conquered empire'.[37] This is to underestimate the sense of temporal tension in the text between the 'now' and the 'not yet'. It also raises more theological difficulties than it solves in respect of the current reality of political, social and religious pressures faced by John's readers. If the coming of divine justice is a completely present reality, how can the apparent dominance of the empire and the imperial cult be accounted for? The most convincing way of guarding against the dualism which Howard-Brook and Gwyther want (rightly) to avoid is not to dissolve the temporal tension of the text into an extended present, but rather to hold the spatial and temporal dimensions of the text together, as I argue at the end of chapter 5.

---

[34] The conclusions of Bourdieu about Mediterranean peasant culture have in any case been disputed within the field of social anthropology. Gell argues convincingly that Bourdieu's claim that peasant societies such as the Kybale of Algeria can do without the 'laws of succession' is misplaced. It is true that their descriptions of time periods are apparently very inconsistent. Their calendar is essentially structured by agrarian rather than celestial factors, so that lengths of time can differ markedly. But this does not mean that it does not function, logically, as a calendar, in which Y follows X but comes before Z (Gell, 1992, pp. 297–9).

[35] Howard-Brook and Gwyther (1999), pp. 120–35.

[36] Howard-Brook and Gwyther (1999), pp. 126–31.

[37] Howard-Brook and Gwyther (1999), p. 126.

Conclusion

The aim of the seer is indeed to enable a true understanding of the present. Bauckham expresses this well, discussing the overall purpose of the book:

> [the seer] is given a glimpse behind the scenes of history so that he can see what is really going on in the events of his time and place. He is also transported in vision into the final future of the world, so that he can see the present from the perspective of what its final outcome must be, in God's ultimate purpose for human history.[38]

But the text is not focused purely on the present. It reveals hidden dimensions of the past, present and future, within which the present must be seen. The text achieves this result through the adoption of a framework which is temporal yet not chronological. It is the presence of this paradoxical combination in the text's treatment of time which makes the different kinds of approach set out above unsatisfactory. Preterist approaches do not do justice to the future dimension of the text. Interpretations which seek to discern some kind of philosophy of history in the text are importing modern concerns which would have been alien to John. Salvation-history approaches run the risk of not dealing adequately with the sense of imminent divine intervention which runs through the text.[39] Malina's argument for emphasizing the present orientation of the New Testament writers appears not to take seriously the strong element of unrealized eschatology in Revelation.[40]

My conclusion is that an analysis of the temporal dimension of the text needs to give due weight to the sense of temporal progression in the narrative, without seeking to discern specific future chronologies. It also needs to do justice to the fact that John's primary purpose is not to provide a view of the nature of history (although what he says should certainly inform a Christian understanding of history). Rather, his concerns are the

---

[38] Bauckham (1993b), p. 7. In a valuable study of the Christology of Revelation, Boring has noted the emphasis given to the present. He analyses all the references to Christ in the text and concludes that forty-nine relate to the present (i.e. the period between the resurrection of Christ and the onset of the end-time events), nineteen to the past and forty-one to the future (Boring, 1992, p. 716).

[39] The same difficulty applies to Caird's argument that although the New Testament writers believed that the world would literally end, they habitually used end-of-the-world language to relate to what they knew was not the end of the world (1980, pp. 243–71). This argument only really works if it can be shown that these writers believed the eschaton not to be imminent; see the critique in Allison (1987), pp. 84–90.

[40] See Fiorenza (1985), pp. 114–32, in which she argues that John, like Paul, was concerned to counter over-realized eschatology.

tough questions facing his communities in the earthly present. How can God's sovereignty be affirmed in a world of ambiguities? Will justice be restored? Will God's people be vindicated?[41]

3.3 The rhetorical impact of the text

In the previous section I argued that the primary purpose of the Book of Revelation was to deal with questions arising out of the present experience of the communities to whom the text was written. The weakness of many of the different approaches to Revelation and history is precisely their failure adequately to explain what the purpose of the book might have been in its first-century context. In this section, I shall examine various attempts which have been made to place the argument of the text in a rhetorical context.

The text in context

The majority view among commentators is that the text of Revelation originated towards the end of the reign of Domitian (81–96).[42] Domitian has traditionally been regarded as the instigator of sustained and fierce persecution of the church, so that Revelation could be seen as responding to such a grave crisis by offering consolation to its readers.[43] However, more recently, it has been generally accepted by interpreters that the available evidence does not support the view that Christians in the last years of the first century were undergoing systematic persecution.[44] Alternative explanations for the book's purpose have therefore been sought.

Perhaps the most influential recent attempt to articulate a plausible rhetorical context for Revelation is that of Adela Yarbro Collins. She

[41] My approach therefore has something in common with that of Beale (1999), to which he gives the rather complex label 'Eclecticism, or a Redemptive-Historical Form of Modified Idealism' (p. 48)! Beale resists the identification of particular symbols in the text with specific historical referents on a one-to-one basis. His is not a 'futurist' or 'historicist' approach. At the same time, he avoids dissolving the message of the text into timeless abstraction, by maintaining that the text certainly does envisage future transformation through 'the final coming of Christ to deliver and judge and to establish the final form of the kingdom in a consummated new creation' (p. 48).

[42] I accept this dating as the most likely, on grounds of both internal and external evidence. For a good general survey of the arguments, see Yarbro Collins (1984), pp. 54–83. Some scholars argue for an earlier date, in the late 60s; see, for example, Rowland (1982), ch. 14.

[43] For an account of this view of Domitian, see Swete (1906), pp. lxxxiff. Some interpreters (e.g. Boesak, 1987) continue to assume that the book emerged against a background of severe oppression.

[44] See, for example, Yarbro Collins (1984), pp. 69–73, or, in more detail, L. L. Thompson (1990), chs. 6–9.

dates the text to Domitian's reign, and regards the traditional claims for widespread persecution as overstated. Any persecution suffered by Christians at this point would have been sporadic, not systematic.[45] Her conclusion is that 'rather than simply consoling his fellow Christians in a situation of grave crisis, [John] wrote his book to point out a crisis that many of them did not perceive'.[46] Yarbro Collins seeks to identify various components which, taken together, would have been perceived by John as a crisis. First, she identifies underlying factors in the social situation of Christians in Asia Minor, such as hostility on the part of Jewish communities and pagan society, and economic hardship.[47] She couples these underlying factors with more specific 'experiences of trauma', such as memories of the Neronic persecution, the growth of the imperial cult, the martyrdom of Antipas (2:13) and John's own exile to Patmos (1:9). Yarbro Collins argues that the combination of these factors would have appeared to contradict Christian confidence in the rule of God and Christ in the world, producing a sense of 'cognitive dissonance'.[48] Although John may not have been suffering extreme persecution, it is possible that he was suffering from 'relative deprivation' as a result of this contradiction: 'It was the tension between John's vision of the kingdom of God and his environment that moved him to write his Apocalypse.'[49] John's message is a call to an exclusivist social radicalism which will resist compromise with Roman authority. Yarbro Collins detects several elements within this stance, including a boycott of Roman coinage, sexual abstinence, and a readiness to embrace martyrdom.[50]

In his detailed examination of the situation within which the text may have arisen, Leonard Thompson takes a rather different line. He also rejects the idea of a systematic persecution under Domitian.[51] Like Yarbro

---

[45] Yarbro Collins (1984), pp. 69–73.   [46] Yarbro Collins (1984), p. 77.

[47] Yarbro Collins (1984), pp. 84–99.

[48] Yarbro Collins (1984), p. 141. Yarbro Collins describes this dissonance as being caused by 'disparity between expectations and reality', or 'between what is and what ought to be'. Although I agree that addressing cognitive dissonance is at the heart of the text, I have expressed the disparity rather differently, as being between 'what appears to be' (in the earthly present) and 'what is' (from the perspective of God's ultimate sovereignty). The point is that for John the sovereignty of God, now manifest in heaven only, but in due time to become manifest also on earth, is not merely something which ought to apply, but something which, at a fundamental level, *does* apply. The ambiguities and difficulties of the earthly present are not the ultimate reality. However, I should emphasize that by describing the earthly present as that which 'appears to be', I am not in any sense denying its reality, merely stressing that for John, its apparent status as *ultimate* reality is illusory.

[49] Yarbro Collins (1984), p. 106.   [50] Yarbro Collins (1984), pp. 124–34.

[51] Thompson produces helpful and detailed evidence to the effect that the sources for the traditional view of Domitian (particularly Pliny, Suetonius and Tacitus) had a vested interest in undermining his reputation (1990, ch. 6).

Collins, he therefore sees John as attempting to provoke a response from his community to a perceived threat, rather than responding to actual oppression. However, whereas Yarbro Collins argues that a combination of social factors and experienced trauma led John to perceive a crisis, Thompson presents a more hopeful picture of life for Christians under Domitian. He argues that far from being socially isolated or harassed, Christians at this period were probably playing a full role in the life of Asian cities, enjoying, for the most part, peaceful coexistence with their pagan fellow-citizens.[52] There is an element of crisis in Revelation, but this originates from John's perception that compromise with the religious and political demands of urban society is dangerous, rather than from any actual or perceived hardship. 'John reports surprisingly few hostilities towards Christians by the non-Christian social world. He anticipates conflict, but conflicts stemming from his fundamental position that church and world belong to antithetical forces. In other words John *encourages* his audience to see themselves in conflict with society; such conflict is a part of his vision of the world.'[53] Thompson sees the crisis perceived by John as the result not of social pressures, but of conflict between two opposing views of reality.[54]

In another important study Fiorenza uses a critical-rhetorical approach to seek to establish the purpose of the text. She argues that while there was no widespread persecution under Domitian, Christians in Asia Minor were nonetheless suffering 'everyday experiences of harassment, persecution and hostility from pagan as well as Jewish neighbors and from the provincial authorities'.[55] This experience would have run counter to Christians' expectations, given their conviction that Christ was the ruler of this world, and the text is an attempt to deal with this contradiction. Fiorenza associates official harassment particularly with the increased promotion of the imperial cult, which appears to have taken place under Domitian.[56] John's message is a call to resist the temptation

[52] L. L. Thompson (1990), ch. 7. For a general discussion of the social and economic conditions in the Asian cities of this period, see Macro (1980).

[53] L. L. Thompson (1990), p. 174.

[54] See also Kraybill (1996), whose detailed assessment of the role of the imperial cult and commerce in the Apocalypse uses the work of L. L. Thompson and Yarbro Collins as a starting point. For Kraybill, the purpose of the text was to urge Christians to avoid being seduced into compromise with Roman ideology and the imperial cult. 'Christian communities of Asia Minor probably experienced more internal *desire* to conform to pagan society than external *pressure* in the way of persecution' (p. 196).

[55] Fiorenza (1991), p. 55.

[56] For a full account of the imperial cult in Asia Minor, see S. R. F. Price (1984), who concludes that there may well have been increasingly intense pressure on Christians to conform to the cult during this period (p. 198).

to compromise with the authorities and the idolatry of the surrounding culture, especially the imperial cult. John and his followers 'view the de-humanizing powers of Rome and its allies as theologically so destructive and oppressive that a compromise with them would mean a denial of God's life-giving and saving power'.[57] The text is a prophetic interpretation of events, designed to help Christians discern the eschatological forces lying behind the political oppression they face, and to enable them to resist that oppression on the basis that God's objective is to end all oppression and bring in universal salvation. John 'seeks to persuade and compel readers to a certain Christian praxis, one of resistance and hope'.[58]

These three different approaches to the text, all of which seek to re-construct a possible *Sitz im Leben* within which it might have arisen, are highly stimulating. They reinforce the importance of considering the message the text might have had for its original readers, a dimension often neglected in attempts to relate Revelation to an understanding of history. Given the lack of evidence for a systematic persecution under Domitian, all three are justified in seeing John as seeking to *provoke* a decisive shift (or crisis) in his readers' understanding of their situation, rather than as responding to an existing crisis.

The three approaches differ in their assessment of the factors motivating John: Yarbro Collins stresses the phenomenon of relative deprivation and perceived crisis; Thompson argues rather for a conflict between two different views of reality; Fiorenza is more ready to assume an element of actual persecution in the background. Ultimately, however, it may be misleading to seek to tie the genesis of the text down to one particular social setting. The text itself suggests strongly that the book was addressed to a variety of different settings. The messages to Smyrna, Pergamum and perhaps Philadelphia suggest an atmosphere of oppression, while those to Thyatira, Sardis and Laodicea do not appear to refer to any existing persecution. The book's message of judgement against Babylon (and hence the need to avoid compromise), the expectation that Christian witness will provoke hostility, and the assurance of ultimate vindication are relevant to a variety of different situations.

There are dangers in taking an over-restricted view of the setting of the text. For example, Fiorenza's concern to focus on the text's context leads ultimately to an impoverished view of the text's meaning. She argues that the world of vision opened up by Revelation is valid as a 'theo-ethical response' only in a rhetorical situation similar to that originally

[57] Fiorenza (1991), p. 57.   [58] Fiorenza (1991), p. 36.

addressed by the text. Since she assumes that this original situation was one of persecution, she argues, 'Revelation will elicit a fitting theo-ethical response only in those sociopolitical situations that cry out for justice.' Reading the text from other situations, for example in a position of stable authority, risks allowing it to function oppressively.[59] This seems to me a misleading conclusion. If the text itself was originally addressed to a variety of situations, there would seem to be no reason in principle why its relevance today should be limited to any one group. For example, the account of the destruction of Babylon in 18:1–24 could function as an effective critique of, and challenge to, the modern West.[60] Seeing the text in its context should not lead the interpreter to conclude (as Fiorenza appears to conclude) that the text is only relevant to a closely defined set of socio-political circumstances. Although interpreters should always be sensitive to the original circumstances in which Revelation may have arisen, the text can surely 'speak' to a variety of situations in different ways. Indeed, the argument of the present study, that Revelation is of relevance to contemporary systematic theology, depends fundamentally on that premise.

The symbolic world of the text

In the previous section I considered some approaches to identifying the purpose of the text in its first-century context. I turn now to a closely related issue, which has also been the subject of critical debate. This is the question of how the symbolic world of the text functions. From seeking to identify what the *aims* of the text were in its context, I am now switching the focus to the debate about how John seeks to achieve those aims. Important recent work in this area has been influenced by the work of Claude Lévi-Strauss on the use of symbol in myth.[61]

Lévi-Strauss argues that humans apprehend their environment by imposing a structure upon it, by dividing it into mental categories, and especially into binary oppositions. In analysing the way in which humans use symbols, Lévi-Strauss distinguishes between what he calls 'metaphor', which represents sets of possibilities from which the individual elements of symbolic narrative can be constructed, and 'metonym',

---

[59] Fiorenza (1991), p. 139.

[60] Rowland (1993) remarks, 'If Revelation seems to highlight divine judgment rather than mercy, that is a message which an idolatrous generation needs to hear' (p. 83).

[61] The classic account of Lévi-Strauss's position is in *Structural Anthropology* (1972), ch. 10, 'The Effectiveness of Symbols'.

the actual sequence of symbols used in a particular context. Lévi-Strauss uses these two sets of relationships to form a grid which he overlays onto mythical narrative in order to analyse it. He argues that a characteristic of 'metaphor' is that it has a timeless quality to it: it is a store-house of ideas waiting to be used. 'Metonym' on the other hand consists, in myth, of narrative in a chronological sequence, projected into a supposed temporal (often primordial) context. He argues that myth consists of a potentially infinite series of diachronic patterns overlaid on a set of synchronic oppositions. In a mythical narrative, a series of slightly varying sequences of events is overlaid in a repetitive pattern over the same structure. For example, he analyses the Oedipus myth by plotting the various episodes in the myth as diachronic sequences. These interact with constant underlying themes in the synchronic structure to produce the message that if society is to continue, daughters must be disloyal to their parents and sons must destroy their fathers.

Lévi-Strauss sees the purpose of myth as being 'to provide a logical model capable of overcoming a contradiction'.[62] Humans are faced with contradictions in their environment between the way things are and the way they would like them to be. Myth provides a pattern of thought which provides a way through the dilemmas. An illustration of this is Lévi-Strauss's essay, 'The Effectiveness of Symbols', a study of a shamanistic ritual for the alleviation of difficult childbirth, recorded among the Cuna Indians of Panama.[63] Lévi-Strauss argues that the technique represents a form of 'abreaction', a process also used in psychotherapy, in which deep-lying conflicts within the patient are brought to the surface to be resolved. For Lévi-Strauss, whether or not the content of the myth bears any relation to reality is irrelevant. The point is that it becomes 'real', a 'living myth', as the patient's mind appropriates and orders it.

---

[62] Lévi-Strauss (1972), p. 229.

[63] The purpose of the ritual is to help a woman through a difficult childbirth. At no stage does the shaman touch the woman or administer any remedies. Rather, he recounts a mythical story of a battle within the woman's internal organs between the spirits summoned by the shaman and the hostile spirit, Muu. Lévi-Strauss analyses the process as follows: 'The cure would consist . . . in making explicit a situation originally existing on the emotional level and in rendering acceptable to the mind pains which the body refuses to tolerate. That the mythology of the shaman does not correspond to an objective reality does not matter. The sick woman believes in the myth and belongs to a society which believes in it. The tutelary spirits and malevolent spirits, the supernatural monsters and magical animals, are all part of a coherent system on which the native conception of the universe is founded. The sick woman accepts these mythical beings or, more accurately, she has never questioned their existence. What she does not accept are the incoherent and arbitrary pains, which are an alien element in her system but which the shaman, calling upon myth, will re-integrate within a whole where everything is meaningful' (1972, p. 197).

Revelation as the enactment of myth: John Gager

In his analysis of Revelation Gager acknowledges explicitly his debt to Lévi-Strauss. He argues that the book was produced in the context of persecution and martyrdom, and that its purpose was to provide consolation for the believer, 'not simply as the promise of a happy fate for the martyr in the near future but through the mythological enactment of that future in the present'.[64] This analysis has clear affinities with Lévi-Strauss's arguments about the purpose of myth outlined above. For Gager the point of the text, like the shamanistic childbirth ritual, is to overcome a contradiction (in this case the contradiction between faith in God's protection on the one hand and the experience of persecution on the other).

Gager produces an analysis of the central section of the book (4:1–22:5) which sees the narrative overlaid onto the binary oppositions of 'victory/hope' and 'oppression/despair'.[65] For example, the vision of heaven (victory/hope) in 4:1–5:14 is followed by the opening of the first six seals (oppression/despair) in 6:1–17, and the vision of the multitude of the faithful and the opening of the seventh seal (victory/hope) in 7:1–8:4 by the first six trumpets (oppression/despair) in 8:5–9:21. The pattern continues throughout the book, culminating in the ultimate victory and hope represented by the new heaven, new earth and the New Jerusalem in 21:1–22:5. Gager has therefore produced an analysis of the text on classic Lévi-Straussian lines: a series of sequences superimposed onto binary oppositions. He points out that the interrelationship between the two contradictory poles is complex, such that, for example, the patterns of seven disasters represented by the seals and trumpets sequences are in each case broken by visions of final glory.

> By thus substituting a dynamic for a static relationship between oppression and hope, these broken series serve to undermine any tendency among the audience to treat them as permanent, unbearable contradictions. The glimpse of final victory in each case shatters the anticipation of perfect despair and points to an experience of exultation not just in the future but in the immediacy of the myth itself.[66]

Gager argues that the net effect is that the reader experiences the future as present: for a fleeting moment, the visions of glory within the text become real. For Gager, this transient effect would have enabled the

---

[64] Gager (1983), p. 147.
[65] It is a weakness of Gager's analysis that he omits 1:1–3:22 and 22:6–21.
[66] Gager (1983), p. 151.

community to withstand persecution, since they clearly believed that the time of God's final judgement, and hence their deliverance, was imminent.

Revelation as catharsis: Adela Yarbro Collins

In her reading of the text Yarbro Collins is also indebted to Lévi-Strauss. In the previous section, on the rhetorical function of the text, I explained that Yarbro Collins assumes that John was experiencing a sense of 'cognitive dissonance' between 'what was and what ought to have been'.[67] Yarbro Collins therefore argues that Lévi-Strauss's theory of myth as providing 'a logical model capable of overcoming a contradiction' is an appropriate one to use in analysing the text.[68]

Yarbro Collins has accordingly analysed the text on structuralist lines, in terms of three contradictory poles: persecution, punishment and salvation. For example, persecution (chs. 12–13) is followed by punishment (14:14–20), and salvation (15:2–4), and in the bowls sequence, persecution (16:4–7) is followed by punishment (16:17–18:24) and a vision of salvation (19:1–10).[69] The repetition of these three themes of persecution, punishment and salvation produces a therapeutic effect which Yarbro Collins terms 'catharsis': feelings of fear and resentment within the reader are brought to the surface and purged.[70] As in Gager's analysis, the complex juxtaposition of hope and despair enables the readers to resolve the manifest contradictions in their existence: 'The solution of the Apocalypse is an act of creative imagination which, like that of the schizophrenic, withdraws from empirical reality, from real experience in the everyday world... Through the use of effective symbols and artful plots, the Apocalypse made feelings which were probably latent, vague, complex, and ambiguous explicit, conscious and simple.'[71]

---

[67] Yarbro Collins (1984), p. 141.   [68] Yarbro Collins (1984), p. 142.

[69] Yarbro Collins (1980), p. 189.

[70] Yarbro Collins understands the term 'catharsis' to have a medical origin, relating to the removal of alien and painful matter from the body. She argues that Aristotle uses the term in the context of dramatic tragedy to mean that 'the emotions of the audience are purged in the sense that their feelings of fear and pity are intensified and given objective expression' (1984, p. 153). However, David Barr (1984) has argued that while Yarbro Collins's idea of Revelation as catharsis may provide a partial explanation of how the text 'works', it does not get to the heart of the matter because her definition of catharsis is inadequate. Barr argues that the text does not operate simply as a psychological safety valve, but that it aims to have a concrete effect on the reader's *understanding* of how the world really is (p. 49). Barr acknowledges a debt to Golden (1976), who argues that Aristotle's idea of catharsis is much better understood as 'intellectual clarification'.

[71] Yarbro Collins (1984), pp. 155, 160.

Yarbro Collins offers a subtle and powerful account of how Revelation might 'work' in the lives of its readers. Her case for a situation of relative deprivation, rather than outright persecution, is well argued. The themes of persecution, punishment and salvation are indeed clearly central to the text. Yet some questions about the application of Lévi-Strauss's ideas to the text remain. Does this kind of approach emphasize too much the function of the text in providing a psychological mechanism, rather than the content of the text? Does it overemphasize the role of the text in *responding* to a real or perceived crisis as opposed to its role in *shaping* circumstances?

Critiques of Lévi-Strauss and functionalism

One potential difficulty with using Lévi-Strauss's approach in the analysis of a text like Revelation is that the resulting conclusions may be too heavily functionalist, stressing the importance of the psychological and/or sociological mechanisms at work, rather than the content of the material. In Lévi-Strauss's analysis of shamanism, he makes the point explicitly that the extent to which the myth bears any relation to reality is irrelevant. What matters is that the narrative takes on a life within the mind of the subject and therefore produces the desired psychological effects. When applied to apocalyptic, this results in an emphasis on the psychological mechanisms which are operating, at the expense of the theological content. It is almost as though the *content* of the text is irrelevant: it is the operation of its *structure* which counts.

This stress on function rather than content has been attacked from within the discipline of social anthropology. In a recent study of the social history of marginalized groups, the American scholar James C. Scott has also stressed the importance of the *content* of traditions held by such groups. For Scott, it is inadequate to see such traditions as mere safety valves enabling the group to cope with oppressive reality.[72] Scott attempts to penetrate beneath the surface of the apparent terms on which the socially dominant and the socially subordinate relate, to try to discover what the subordinate might really be thinking. He distinguishes between the 'public transcript', which he defines as 'the open interaction between

---

[72] Whether or not one regards the *Sitz im Leben* of Revelation as a situation of actual persecution, it certainly represents a view from those who do not have access to political or economic power. As I noted earlier, Gager (1983) and others assume a background of actual persecution. Several recent interpreters, such as Yarbro Collins and L. L. Thompson, argue that there may not have been systematic persecution under Domitian (see above, pp. 57–61).

subordinates and those who dominate', and which often serves to form the documented history of such interaction, and the 'hidden transcript', or discourse that takes place 'offstage', beyond direct observation by power holders.[73] In chapter 6 of his book Scott discusses the phenomenon of symbolic inversion of the world, exemplified by the 'world-upside-down' genre of old broadsheets, and the carnival tradition. Scott attacks functionalist interpretations which see such traditions as psychological safety valves, draining away otherwise harmful social tensions. The *content* of the traditions is vital. He asks pointedly why, if carnivals, for example, were serving the purpose of allowing harmful tensions to dissipate, the authorities were often so keen to suppress them.

Scott concludes that the 'safety-valve' theory, popular as it has been among sociologists, is flawed, for two key reasons. First, history suggests that phenomena such as carnivals, where hidden transcripts break the surface, are more plausibly seen as ritualized expressions of genuine resentment rather than diversions away from the experience of oppression. Second, interpretations of hidden transcripts which rely on explanations based on functionalism or catharsis assume too readily that what is at stake is a merely idealist, abstract debate, rather than a struggle with a material dimension. His conclusion is that the hidden transcript is a condition for practical resistance, rather than a substitute for it. That is *not* to say that every hidden transcript is necessarily a prescription for revolt (Revelation certainly is not); but it *is* to challenge any assumption that hidden transcripts are always purely psychological devices which seek to escape from reality rather than to face it and change it.

In this context, the contribution of Dan Sperber to the understanding of symbolism is helpful. Sperber argues that approaches such as the structuralist analysis of Lévi-Strauss, which concentrate on the way that symbols 'work', rather than on what they mean, are misguided.[74] The danger is that apparent indifference to the content of a text leaves a vacuum, into which the interpreter's own preconceived ideas on the meaning of the myth or the text can too easily be imported. As Sperber asks pertinently: 'what guarantees that the structure outlined accounts for the properties of the object and does not derive simply from the systematizing

---

[73] Scott (1990), pp. 2, 4.

[74] Sperber is highly critical of structuralism. He argues that it is notoriously difficult to test the validity of its underlying assumptions. Lévi-Strauss's basic suppositions about the underlying homogeneity of human thought processes and their affinity with the structure of myth are, it can be argued, no more than suppositions (1975, p. 64).

gaze of the analyst?'[75] This problem appears most strikingly when the interpretation of what the text is *really* about appears to bear little relationship to any natural reading of the text. As Mary Douglas comments in relation to Lévi-Strauss's interpretation of the Oedipus myth: 'All the majestic themes which we had previously thought the Oedipus myth was about – destiny, duty, and self-knowledge, have been strained off, and we are left with a story about how the species began.'[76] Instead of seeing symbols as signs which can be paired with particular interpretations in a code structure, Sperber argues that symbolism is in fact a form of *knowledge* in its own right. In this respect, symbolism is different from semantic knowledge, which is concerned with classification, and encyclopaedic knowledge, concerned with empirical fact. Symbolism can quite happily exist alongside encyclopaedic knowledge in apparent contradiction, as a kind of 'knowledge about knowledge, a meta-encyclopaedia in the encyclopaedia'.[77]

Sperber's account is relatively brief and represents only a first step to a comprehensive theory of symbolism, but it is highly suggestive. His contention that symbolism represents a meta-knowledge which may exist in apparent contradiction with encyclopaedic knowledge may be another way of expressing one of the basic arguments in this study – that Revelation uses symbolism to convey deep truth which appears to be at odds with the reader's experience. Sperber is also helpful in seeking to understand the way in which the symbolism of Revelation evokes memories from previous symbolic accounts in scripture and elsewhere,

---

[75] Sperber (1975), p. 57. As Sperber recognizes, this would not be a problem for Lévi-Strauss, since a fundamental connection between the thought processes of the observer and the ritual (or text) being observed is in any case presupposed by structuralist analysis.

[76] Douglas (1967), p. 63.

[77] Sperber (1975), pp. 108–9. Sperber gives as an example the fact that the Dorze of Ethiopia believe on the symbolic level that leopards are Christians and therefore observe fast days, but their encyclopaedic knowledge of leopards means that they still guard their cattle every day against attack. Sperber's proposals for understanding *how* symbolism operates are stimulating when considering the use to which John puts his store of symbols. Sperber suggests that the 'symbolic mechanism' (i.e. how the mind deals with symbol) takes over when the mind meets information which cannot be successfully assimilated through conceptualization associated with encyclopaedic knowledge. The mind adopts an alternative strategy, accessing the memory by a more evocative, tangential route, to try to make sense of the information. Sperber calls this switch 'focalization'. There then follows a second stage, which Sperber terms 'evocation', attempting to understand the information at a symbolic level so that the result can then be fed back into the conceptual mechanism. Sperber suggests that often this is simply the beginning of a dialectical process of interaction between the mind's symbolic and conceptual mechanisms which can continue indefinitely as more inputs of information appear. Thus the activity of the symbolic mechanism has the effect of repeatedly reordering the encyclopaedic memory (1975, ch. 5).

in a way which both reworks them imaginatively and calls for imaginative effort on the part of the reader.

This brings us to the helpful distinctions made by Philip Wheelwright between stenosymbolism and tensive symbolism. Wheelwright characterizes stenosymbolism as one-for-one relationships between signifier and signified, which tend to have 'meanings that can be shared in exactly the same way by a very large number of persons'.[78] Tensive symbolism presses beyond such one-for-one relationships, and serves to trigger complex and shifting patterns of association in the mind of the reader. Many symbols in Revelation, such as the 'Lamb', the 'whore of Babylon', the 'great city' and the 'New Jerusalem', do not relate straightforwardly to a delimited set of referents, but rather are used by John in a way which matches Wheelwright's description of tensive symbolism.[79]

Wheelwright also notes that the use of tensive language is especially characteristic of liminal, or threshold, situations, in which human beings are trying to come to terms with that which cannot be fully grasped or explained in stenosymbols. He describes three such thresholds: that of time, where tensive language is used to express the tension between the present moment and continuity; that of otherness, where tensive language expresses the complex interrelationships between the self and its environment; and that of upwardness, or the sense of the transcendent.[80] All three thresholds are operating in Revelation. The threshold of otherness is present in the whole question of the reader's understanding of the nature and destiny of the people of God and their place in the world. The threshold of upwardness is of course present in the way in which the text sets the reader's experience in divine perspective, culminating in the new creation and the descent of the New Jerusalem. The threshold of time is present in the relationship between the present time of John and the communities he addresses, and the wider canvas of God's sovereign action in history as a whole. This relationship is not fully graspable in the sense that the precise place of the present community in some overarching chronology is not known – indeed, cannot be known. And yet *something* is known of this relationship in the sense that certain events (for example, the creation, or the earthly life, death and resurrection of Christ) are past, and certain are future, some of which will have transient significance, and others of which will have permanent significance. John is wrestling with

---

[78] Wheelwright (1962), p. 33.

[79] See Beale's helpful critique of approaches to Revelation which focus (wrongly) on supposed one-to-one references between symbols in the text and particular historical events, either past or future (1999, pp. 50–5).

[80] Wheelwright (1968), ch. 2.

these half-grasped realities, and uses the language of tensive symbol in order to express his understanding.

Revelation and reality: a further debate

Discussion of how the symbolic world of the text operates leads on to consideration of the relationship which the world that is opened up by the text might be understood to bear to empirical reality. This question has sparked an important debate in the interpretation of the text.

L. L. Thompson has produced a full and stimulating account of Revelation based on the premise that 'an apocalypse does not reveal another world, it reveals hidden dimensions of the world in which humans live and die; that is, an apocalypse is not world-negating but, rather, world-expanding: it extends or expands the universe to include transcendent realities, and it does this both spatially and temporally'.[81] Thompson gives detailed examples of the ways in which different narrative and descriptive techniques in the text set the understanding of the reader in this ultimate perspective, while maintaining a strong sense of unity in both spatial and temporal planes. For example, in the spatial dimension, Thompson describes what he terms the 'blurred boundaries' among godly forces in the text. Characteristics associated with the forces of heaven stray across the spatial boundary into the earthly level: the glorious effulgence surrounding God (4:3) is also a feature of the description of the strong angel who crosses the boundary onto earth (10:1), while the sacrificial and priestly characteristics of the Lamb as seen in heaven (5:10) are imitated by his earthly followers (14:4). The temporal dimension is united by various narrative techniques: features which appear at different points in the narrative are related to one another by contrast (the protected 144,000 of 7:4 are contrasted with the judgement delivered upon earth; the beasts are contrasted with the Lamb). Another example is the use of equivalent measures of time for the duration of different events (e.g. the trampling of the holy city in 11:2, the prophetic activity of the two witnesses in 11:3, the nourishment of the woman in the wilderness in 12:6, and the beast's exercise of its authority in 13:5 – all last 1260 days). Thompson also argues that the language of worship is important in establishing the unity of the universe in Revelation. Thus, heavenly worship is performed by those who have been through tribulation on earth (7:14–15; 15:2). And the fact that the glory of God which is manifest in heaven is seen as both a present (4:11; 5:12–13; 11:13) and a future phenomenon (21:11, 23) is

---

[81] L. L. Thompson (1990), p. 31.

an example of how a feature of the spatial dimension of the text can hold together the temporal dimension.

The interplay of spatial and temporal dimensions also occurs at the level of the reality to which the seer believes his symbols point. Thompson argues that lying beneath the surface of the language one can detect a vision of 'unbroken reality': 'the vision transmitted by the seer is not merely a "literary world" or a "symbolic universe" – a vision separate from the everyday life of John and his audience. The seer is constructing an *encompassing* vision that includes everyday, social realities in Asia Minor.'[82]

For Thompson, Revelation does not present a symbolic universe separate from social and political realities. Nor is it merely an attempt to address conflicts or crises in the mind of the audience. Rather, it offers a particular understanding of what the *whole* world is like. In contrast, he argues, the suppression of time, the enactment of the future in the present envisaged in Gager's scheme is an illusion. It represents a fleeting glimpse of millennial bliss, which does not alter empirical reality: 'Nothing fundamental is changed by the myth. The world of social, political realities is too real for the alternative symbolic world of the myth.'[83] Thompson characterizes the approaches of Gager and Yarbro Collins as ultimately escapist: 'both resolve the religious crisis of faith in a temporary imaginative experience that does not affect the hard social and political realities of Asian life'.[84]

While Thompson's arguments about the unitive nature of the vision of the text are generally convincing, he presses his point too far in places, especially when he claims to detect an underlying unity between the descriptions of good and evil in the text. Thompson argues that while there are important contrasts between good and evil in the text, the seer's vision

---

[82] L. L. Thompson (1990), p. 74.

[83] L. L. Thompson (1990), p. 207. Fiorenza makes a similar point in criticism of Gager's argument that Revelation offers an escape by collapsing the future into the present for a fleeting moment: for Fiorenza, this fails to do justice to the strong sense of eschatological tension in the text – John is all too aware of the reality of present experience (1985, pp. 167–8).

[84] L. L. Thompson (1990), p. 210. While Thompson's criticism of Gager's interpretation for being escapist seems justified, his criticism of Yarbro Collins at this point needs careful qualification. While it is certainly arguable that her view of the operation of the symbolism of the text is 'escapist' in the sense that she sees it as projecting an alternative world rather than an encompassing world (in Thompson's terms), it is not fair to criticize her approach as denuding the text of its political impact. She certainly argues that John sought to evoke a clear socio-political response by his readers. It *is* true, however, that she views the response which John was seeking as rather more sectarian and exclusivist than Thompson's 'cosmopolitan sectarianism'.

of an unbroken reality means that there is also considerable blurring across the boundaries between good and evil: 'Evil contrasts with the godly, but evil is not of a fundamentally different order from good. Humans belong to the earthly plane, the divine belong to heaven above, and the demonic belong to the plane below; but those three tiers of the seer's universe are not separated absolutely.'[85] Thompson supports this argument by pointing to the apparent structural similarities between good and evil forces in the text. Thus, for example, the Lamb's relationship to God may be seen as a parallel of the beast's to Satan; the seal of the Lamb is parallel to the mark of the beast; several symbols, such as the city, the woman and the wilderness, are ambiguous, sometimes representing good, sometimes evil. Thompson concludes: 'The logic of the vision does not progress from oppositions to their resolution. Rather, in all its aspects the language speaks from unbroken wholeness to unbroken wholeness.'[86] He is therefore doubtful about the use of sets of oppositions (as, for example, by Gager and Yarbro Collins) to analyse the text.

Thompson's argument goes too far at this point. He is certainly right to affirm that the cosmic view of the seer is unitive, not dualistic. But in asserting a unitive vision of reality, the seer is stressing the sovereignty of God and his assured victory in the cosmic conflict, rather than some underlying structural unity between good and evil. There are undoubtedly striking parallels between the two opposing camps, as Thompson points out, but these often perform an ironical purpose: the fact that the beast from the sea, like the Lamb, has been wounded is more to do with parody and deception than with underlying unity. Laws has effectively demonstrated how certain features of the portrayal of the beast parody the image of the Lamb. The beast has been wounded (13:3), as has the Lamb (5:6); the beast has two horns like a lamb (13:11); the beast has a mysterious name (13:18), as does the Lamb (2:17; 3:12).[87] Thompson's analysis of the temporal dimension of the text suffers similarly from a tendency to blur distinctions between present and future to an unhelpful extent, dissipating eschatological tension. He sees, for instance, no sharp distinction between this age and the age to come, and stresses the nature of Christ's crucifixion as a motif lying in the 'deep structure' of reality rather than as a historical event.[88] Stuckenbruck comments that Thompson's analysis 'tends to collapse time into one interrelated, spatially-conceived continuum that blurs past, present, and future into an interchangeable reality'.[89]

[85] L. L. Thompson (1990), p. 81.   [86] L. L. Thompson (1990), p. 91.
[87] Laws (1989), ch. 3.   [88] L. L. Thompson (1990), p. 85.
[89] Stuckenbruck (1995), p. 41.

Conclusion

In section 3.2 I examined ways in which commentators have sought to relate Revelation to an understanding of human history. I suggested that John *is* profoundly concerned with human history, but not as a set of abstract principles, nor as a speculative chronology. Rather, he is concerned to reveal hidden dimensions of reality in order to influence how his readers live in the present.

In this section I have gone on to consider recent assessments of the possible rhetorical situation within which the text arose, and of the ways in which the symbolism of the text operates in the mind of the reader. I have concluded, in line with several important recent interpretations of the text, that in writing Revelation John was not simply responding to an existing crisis in the Christian communities of Asia Minor, but rather that he was seeking to reveal to his readers the true nature of the situation in which they found themselves. Essentially, his message was fourfold: divine judgement on the political, economic and religious structures of the empire; consequently, a call to his readers to live distinctively, avoiding compromises which would conflict with their loyalty to Christ; assurance that in the expected tribulation which would accompany such a stance, God would provide ultimate protection; and finally, the promise of eschatological bliss for those who stood firm.

I have also argued that readings which concentrate on how the symbolism of the text might function as a psychological mechanism, to enable the reader to cope with present earthly difficulties, are inadequate unless they also give due weight to the *content* of the text and the truth-claims it makes. Hence, interpreters such as Thompson are correct to argue that the vision of the text is of a single reality which *encompasses* the earthly present of the reader, placing it within ultimate spatial and temporal horizons. This is a more convincing reading of the text than interpretations which see it as postulating a symbolic universe *separate* from that of the earthly present, into which the reader is invited to escape in the imagination. At the same time, it is important to recognize the extent to which the text contains conflicts and oppositions which need to be resolved, and that blurring these into a over-homogeneous view of the cosmos is misleading.

3.4   The genre of the Book of Revelation

Much recent research on Revelation has been motivated by a concern to discover the most appropriate generic framework within which to read the book. Judgements made about the genre of a text can be of great importance for reflection on its message. In the case of Revelation, much discussion has centred on whether the text should be regarded as an apocalypse or a prophecy. Although the first verse of Revelation ('Ἀποκάλυψις 'Ιησοῦ Χριστοῦ...) has given the name to the genre of apocalypse, this is not necessarily the end of the story.[90] John himself referred to the text as προφητεία (1:3). To complicate matters further, at least part of the text (chs. 2–3) is in epistolary form.[91]

Is the Apocalypse an apocalypse?

Jewish apocalyptic

Scholars have often argued that one of the main features distinguishing Jewish apocalyptic from Old Testament prophecy is the way in which it views the relationship between history and faith. In a standard textbook on Jewish apocalyptic, D. S. Russell states that apocalyptic grew out of Old Testament prophecy as 'essentially a literature of the oppressed who saw no hope for the nation simply in terms of politics or on the plane of human history'.[92] An influential strand of twentieth-century interpretation, including such writers as H. H. Rowley, P. D. Hanson and Russell himself, has maintained that Jewish apocalyptic is a development stemming from prophecy. It is certainly possible to trace the antecedents of apocalyptic in certain passages of Old Testament prophecy, such as Isaiah 24–7 and Ezekiel 38–9.[93] Hanson argues that the fall of the Israelite monarchies produced a crisis of confidence in the Deuteronomic view of history, which had been based on a schema of promise and fulfilment. At first, argues Hanson, this situation was met by developments in late prophecy, in which a cosmic vision was added to the earthly plane, with the two held in dialectical tension. He sees Isaiah 51:9–11 as a good example of this development.[94] However, Hanson suggests that this sense of optimism faded subsequently. Despairing of the possibility of divine intervention on behalf of Israel on the earthly plane, the apocalyptic writers began to

[90] The designation ἀποκάλυψις is of course of itself no guide to genre, since Revelation is the earliest known example of a document describing itself thus.
[91] Beasley-Murray (1978), pp. 12–29, gives a good general introduction to the threefold form of the text. In what follows I concentrate on the genres of apocalypse and prophecy, which have dominated discussion among commentators. For an unusual attempt to explore the *epistolary* character of the text as a whole (not just 1:1–8 and 2:1–3:22), see Karrer (1986).
[92] Russell (1964), p. 17.   [93] See Russell (1964), pp. 88ff.
[94] Hanson (1979), p. 25.

express a hope for vindication beyond history, illustrating what Hanson describes as 'growing indifference to and independence from the contingencies of the politico-historical realm'.[95]

While there is considerable truth in the analysis of Hanson, Russell and others, it needs careful qualification. For example, not all would agree that apocalyptic is descended only from prophecy. Von Rad argues that the origins of apocalyptic should be sought not in prophecy, but in wisdom literature.[96] Although von Rad's account has received relatively little support, it may be that the links between apocalyptic and wisdom literature deserve further exploration.[97] Attempts to modify the hypothesis that apocalyptic developed purely from prophecy are important, because they help to explain why apocalyptic is not merely concerned with eschatological issues, but also seeks to relate knowledge of heavenly secrets to the present.

Moreover, common descriptions of Jewish apocalyptic as holding an unremittingly pessimistic view of this world and a naïvely deterministic view of history do not always do justice to the complexities of this literature. It is true that apocalyptic often looks to vindication of the elect beyond earthly history (see *1 En.* 58; *2 Bar.* 74), and therefore appears pessimistic about this world. But that does not necessarily mean a lack of interest in this world and, by extension, the history of the present. Rowland stresses the meaning of apocalyptic for the present, arguing that 'the attitude towards the present age, such as we have it in the apocalypses, arises not so much from the conviction that the present world was too corrupt for the establishment of God's kingdom, but from the frank admission that without God's help the dominance of Israel and the coming of the new age could never be achieved'.[98] The key issue was therefore reliance on divine intervention, rather than, necessarily, a pessimistic view of this world.

On the subject of determinism von Rad accuses apocalyptic of 'dispensing with the phenomenon of the contingent'.[99] This is a rather sweeping statement. It is true that one of the standard devices of apocalyptic is the portrayal of history as a preordained process (see *1 En.* 41:3ff.; 93:1ff.; *Jub.* 1:4–6). However, this does not exclude the possibility of individuals making decisions which will affect their destiny (see *Jub.* 5:13; 41:24ff.; *Pss. Sol.* 9:7). And in some cases, for example the story of Taxo and his

---

[95] Hanson (1979), pp. 11–12.   [96] See the account in Koch (1972), pp. 45ff.

[97] VanderKam (1986) suggests that there are in fact considerable affinities between mantic wisdom and late prophecy, to the extent that it is wrong to push a distinction between prophetic and sapiential origins of apocalyptic too far.

[98] Rowland (1982), p. 38.   [99] See the discussion in Koch (1972), pp. 43–4.

seven sons in the *Testament of Moses* 9–10, the actions of the faithful are seen to result in divine intervention and hence change the course of earthly history.[100]

Defining the genre of 'apocalypse'

Much scholarly interest in the last twenty-five years has centred on the question of defining the genre of apocalypse, and reaching judgements on the extent to which the Apocalypse of John, which gave its name to the genre, might actually be classified within it.[101] While this concern may sometimes be overplayed, it has nonetheless proved very useful in clarifying the framework within which the interpretation of apocalyptic texts might take place. In an extremely important article in *Semeia* 14, reflecting the work of the SBL Apocalypse Group, Collins proposes a definition of the genre of apocalypse, as follows: '"Apocalypse" is a genre of revelatory literature with a narrative framework, in which a revelation is mediated by an otherworldly being to a human recipient, disclosing a transcendent reality which is both temporal, insofar as it envisages eschatological salvation, and spatial insofar as it involves another, supernatural world.'[102] Collins argues that while apocalypses might vary considerably, all can be seen to contain these core elements. The definition put forward by Collins covers questions both of form (narrative framework, mediation by a heavenly being) and of content (disclosure of transcendent reality).

Others have since argued that some reference to the *function* of the text is necessary. In *Semeia* 36 (1986), Hellholm proposes the following addition to Collins's definition: 'intended for a group in crisis with the purpose of exhortation and/or consolation by means of divine authority'. Hellholm is correct to resist what he sees as the separation of text from its context. However, it is often difficult to come to clear judgements about the *Sitz im Leben* of apocalyptic texts. Our knowledge of the communities to whom Revelation was addressed is very flimsy. Moreover, it appears from the text itself that the seven churches found themselves

---

[100] See Collins (1984), pp. 104–5. See also Allison's discussion of the tradition that the timing of the eschaton was dependent on the repentance of Israel (1987, pp. 155–6).

[101] Here I am using the term 'apocalypse' to mean a literary genre, following the distinctions set out in Hanson (1979), pp. 427ff. As well as using 'apocalypse' to describe a literary genre, he advocates the use of 'apocalyptic eschatology' to describe the theological perspective characteristic of apocalyptic, and 'apocalypticism' to describe religious movements associated with apocalyptic.

[102] Collins (1979), p. 9. Note that this definition enables Revelation to be classified as an apocalypse even though it lacks two features – pseudonymity, and (with the arguable exception of 17:9–10) *vaticinia ex eventu* – often taken to be typical of apocalypses.

in varying situations; at the very least, 'crisis' in Hellholm's definition needs modification, since it is not clear that all the communities perceived themselves to be in crisis (Laodicea springs immediately to mind). In her editorial introduction to *Semeia* 36 Yarbro Collins expresses reservations along these lines, and proposes a much more convincing addition to the 1979 definition, to cover the question of function: 'intended to interpret present, earthly circumstances in light of the supernatural world and of the future, and to influence both the understanding and the behavior of the audience by means of divine authority'.[103]

Of course, the fact that Revelation is a Christian work sets it apart to some extent from Jewish apocalyptic, and this is recognized by scholars who, like John Collins, nonetheless want to include it within the genre of apocalypse. Collins uses Revelation's Christian character to explain the absence of *vaticinia ex eventu* from the work. Since the critical moment of history, the Christ event, had already occurred, there was no need for John to engage in elaborate historical reviews after the event in order to demonstrate that the end was near: the imminence of the end could be taken for granted.[104] Collins concludes: 'The Christian adaptation of apocalyptic did not involve a rejection of either the forms or the values of Jewish apocalypses, but rather an intensification.'[105]

In assigning Revelation to the genre of apocalypse, Collins and others are prepared to acknowledge that its Christian nature gives it a unique place in the genre, and the SBL definition is sufficiently widely drawn to accommodate it. Nevertheless, some have felt that the uniqueness of Revelation, when seen alongside Jewish apocalypses, makes trying to fit it into the same genre a misleading exercise. Is there, then, an alternative solution to the quest for a generic framework within which to read Revelation?

Is the Apocalypse a prophecy?

Although John refers to his account as an ἀποκάλυψις (1:1), he also uses the term προφητεία (1:3; 22:7, 10, 18, 19), and refers at several points to groups of prophets, of which he may have been a member.[106] A number of writers have therefore argued that Revelation should be seen as falling under the genre of prophecy rather than apocalyptic. I mentioned above (pp. 73–6) some of the ways in which scholars have sought

---

[103] Yarbro Collins (1986), p. 7. I have used the SBL 1979 definition, as amended by Yarbro Collins, as a working description of the genre of apocalypse.
[104] See Collins (1977).   [105] Collins (1977), p. 342.
[106] See 10:7; 11:18; 22:6, 9.

to distinguish between the view of history typically expressed in Old Testament prophecy and in Jewish apocalyptic. Those who argue that Revelation should be considered primarily as a prophecy therefore seek to demonstrate that in its view of the relationship between history and faith it manifests characteristics of Old Testament prophecy, such as a concern for the present, and a measure of hope for divine intervention in this world. Hill suggests that although Revelation displays some features typical of apocalyptic, the dominant feature of the seer's attitude to history is a sense of salvation history:

> For the apocalypticists the events of their own time were not a locus of divine action and revelation: the present age was meaningless and evil, and would be swallowed up and destroyed in the End-time. The prophetic *Heilsgeschichte*, on the other hand, speaks, not of the termination of history, but of its fulfilment through God's disclosure of himself in history ... John's starting point is the saving action of God in Christ: this event is the pivot of his confidence in the power and victory of God in the present and throughout the short space of time till the establishment of God's sovereignty.[107]

For Hill, therefore, Revelation should be regarded as an example of prophecy (albeit one using apocalyptic imagery) rather than as an apocalypse.

Hill has been followed more recently by Mazzaferri. Mazzaferri is uneasy with the attempts by Collins and others to define the genre of apocalyptic, arguing that a definition on these lines is far too broad, and would encompass not only works widely regarded as apocalyptic, but also gnostic apocalypses (which he would prefer to classify differently) and even some works, such as *2 Enoch* and *3 Baruch*, which Mazzaferri does not regard as apocalypses at all.[108] He offers a much tighter definition of apocalypse, according to which a work should display a dominating sense of imminent eschatology, marked by ethical, spatial and temporal dualism, profound pessimism about the current order, and a determinist view of history. This has important consequences for the way in which he reads Revelation, since he concludes that the text will not fit his tighter criteria, and cannot be classified as an apocalypse.[109]

---

[107] Hill (1972), pp. 404–5.   [108] Mazzaferri (1989), pp. 164ff.

[109] He argues that only seven known works meet this tighter definition of apocalypse: *Life of Adam and Eve, 1 Enoch, Apocalypse of Abraham, Testament of Moses, Jubilees, 2 Baruch* and *4 Ezra*.

Mazzaferri argues: 'The simple fact of the matter is that when John speaks so assuredly in his own name and authority, he stands utterly apart from the genre of normative apocalyptic.'[110] He gives various reasons for this position. First, the central role of the Christ event *within* history suggests that Revelation represents a return to the salvation-history tradition of the prophets. Second, unlike Collins, Mazzaferri sees pseudonymity as an essential feature of apocalyptic. Third, while he assumes that a radical pessimism about this world is central to apocalyptic, such pessimism is not present in Revelation. Fourth, Mazzaferri argues that the determinism which commentators often detect in Revelation is only surface-deep, and that in fact the view of history in the text is strongly marked by conditionality, which again sets it apart from apocalyptic. He points out that the text includes threats and promises of a conditional nature. As examples, he suggests the sword of 19:15, poised over the Pergamenes in 2:16, indicating that the gift of salvation depends upon human response, and the time given to Jezebel to repent (2:21). He also draws attention to the point, noticed by many commentators, that the plague sequences are accompanied by opportunities for repentance (cf. 9:20–1; 16:9, 11). Mazzaferri's conclusion is that Revelation should be regarded as 'proximate classical prophecy' (i.e. very like, although not identical to, classical prophecy), rather than as apocalyptic.

Mazzaferri is certainly correct to stress the prophetic features of Revelation, which tend to be missed by many commentators content simply to see the text as an apocalypse.[111] However, his conclusions about genre are misguided. Revelation has important features which set it apart from Jewish apocalyptic, as I have discussed. At the same time, it seems perverse to argue that the clear similarities with works such as *4 Ezra* and *2 Baruch* should not weigh heavily in decisions about genre. By drawing the criteria for classifying works as apocalypses very tightly, Mazzaferri makes it impossible for Revelation to be considered an apocalypse. But it is questionable whether the end result is very helpful, since it tends to underestimate the undoubted apocalyptic characteristics of the text.

A much more convincing approach is to acknowledge that genre is a complex issue and that to seek to press texts into only one genre, to the exclusion of others, can be unnecessary and misleading. The peculiar form of Revelation requires that it be read as an apocalypse *and* as a prophecy. Elisabeth Schüssler Fiorenza argues exactly this, classifying Revelation as 'apocalyptic-prophetic'.[112] She finds that certain features of the text,

---

[110] Mazzaferri (1989), p. 228.   [111] See Fiorenza (1985), pp. 133–4.
[112] Fiorenza (1985), p. 138.

such as the way in which history is taken up into eschatology, have clear affinities with apocalyptic. Yet for Fiorenza the text is also prophetic, not because it operates within a *Heilsgeschichte* framework, but because of the centrality of the proclamation of redemption through the death and resurrection of Christ.[113] She turns on their head the arguments of Collins (1984) that the lack of *vaticinia ex eventu* and pseudonymity in Revelation are merely superficial differences flowing from the inauguration of the end-time in the Christ event. For Fiorenza, it is precisely this kind of difference which demonstrates that Revelation is *not* simply apocalyptic, but should be considered in its own right.

Conclusion

Revelation is clearly an apocalypse. Yet the sense of conditionality running through parts of the work (typified by opportunities for repentance), the lack of certain traditional features such as pseudonymity and *vaticinia ex eventu*, and above all the centrality of the Christ event make it a particular kind of apocalypse. The unique combination of apocalyptic and prophetic form in Revelation leads to a transformation of the apocalyptic view of history. The apocalyptic nature of the text brings with it a sense of the universal scope of history and ultimate temporal and spatial perspectives, while the prophetic and epistolary nature of the text serves to focus attention on the present situation of the communities to which it is addressed. There is therefore a twofold dynamic at work, in which temporal and spatial horizons are expanded *outward*, while at the same time there is heavy *inward* concentration on the meaning of the text for the present.

3.5   Conclusions

In this chapter I have examined three different kinds of approach to the Book of Revelation: interpretations which explore its possible relationship to historical development; interpretations which explore the way in which its symbolism functions; and interpretations which seek to clarify the genre of the text.

The findings in each section point to one overall conclusion: the seer seeks to influence his readers' present lives by locating the earthly present in the context of ultimate spatial and temporal horizons. In the case of attempts to relate the text to an understanding of history, I concluded that

---

[113] Fiorenza (1985), p. 138.

John seeks to illuminate the present by placing it within the framework of the past and the future. As far as the rhetorical purpose of the text and the operation of its symbolism are concerned, I concluded that John seeks to influence his readers in the earthly present by revealing the true nature of ultimate reality, spatially and temporally. With regard to the genre of the text, I concluded that as an apocalypse the text makes claims about ultimate spatial and temporal realities, while as a prophecy and as a letter it focuses intensely on the earthly present.

The conclusions from this chapter will serve as a basis for my analysis of the text in the next two chapters. Essentially, my argument will be that the seer seeks to set the reader's present experience within an ultimate spatial and temporal framework; and that, having accomplished this, the seer then seeks to focus the reader's attention back to present experience, now seen in the light of the ultimate realities which the text has revealed. My conclusions in respect of both the spatial and the temporal dimensions of the text will therefore be mutually reinforcing. Over the course of the following two chapters, I hope to demonstrate a strong *correlation* between the expansion and intensification of spatial and temporal horizons in the text.

Briefly, my analysis of the text will seek to demonstrate the following pattern: In 1:1–3:22 John begins to set the present position of the Christian community within ultimate spatial and temporal perspectives. The vision of heaven in 4:1–5:14 serves as a marked contrast to the situation of the faithful: within the vision, 4:1–11 poses the question of how the dissonance between the manifest rule of God in heaven and the apparent power of evil on earth is to be overcome, and the appearance of the Lamb in 5:1–14 points to the solution to the problem. 6:1–20:15 describes the outworking of divine judgement on the earth, and the salvation of the faithful amid persecution, preparing the way for the consummation. In 21:1–22:21 the descent of the New Jerusalem from heaven acts both to *resolve* spatial and temporal dissonances and paradoxically to *intensify* them, focusing back on the earthly present of the reader.

4

THE SPATIAL DIMENSION OF THE BOOK OF REVELATION

4.1   The spatial setting of the text

The importance of the temporal dimension of apocalyptic thought has long been recognized, given the central role which eschatology often plays in apocalypses. However, recent analyses of apocalypses have sought to underline the importance of the spatial dimension of the genre alongside the temporal dimension. This is reflected in the important definition of the genre of apocalypse, put forward in 1979 as a result of work in the SBL Apocalypse Group: '"Apocalypse" is a genre of revelatory literature with a narrative framework, in which a revelation is mediated by an otherworldly being to a human recipient, disclosing a transcendent reality which is both temporal, insofar as it envisages eschatological salvation, and spatial insofar as it involves another, supernatural world.'[1] It is the idea that the Book of Revelation seeks to disclose a transcendent spatial reality which underlies my treatment of the spatial dimension of the text in this chapter.

In an influential reassessment of apocalyptic thought Rowland has laid particular emphasis on the importance of the spatial dimension of this literature, in the sense of the revelation of heavenly secrets. It is this feature of apocalyptic which is for Rowland its most distinctive characteristic – more distinctive even than the eschatological interest which is usually held to be central to the genre.[2] Rowland's suggestion that eschatology should not be regarded as the central feature of the apocalyptic genre has been criticized.[3] And certainly, whatever might be the case in terms of the genre as a whole, the Book of Revelation itself has a critically

---

[1] Collins (1979), p. 9. See my discussion of this definition and the various proposals to modify it (chapter 3, pp. 75–6).

[2] See Rowland (1982), ch. 2.

[3] Collins sees it as an overreaction to the tendency, identified by Rowland, to equate apocalyptic thought and eschatology. He accepts that the eschatological component of apocalypses may have been overstressed by scholars, but wants to retain it as part of a core definition of the genre; see Collins (1984), p. 8.

important eschatological dimension. However, Rowland's insistence that the prime focus of the apocalypticists was on the needs of communities in the present, rather than on speculation about the future for its own sake, is well-founded. My argument in due course will be that, as far as Revelation is concerned, both the expansion of spatial horizons to include transcendent spatial reality and the expansion of temporal horizons to include transcendent temporal reality have the effect of concentrating attention upon the earthly present of the reader. The result is that the reader is encouraged to resist compromise and face possible oppression, in the knowledge of the ultimate perspective within which the earthly present is to be seen.

The stage upon which the action of the Book of Revelation takes place consists of heaven, earth, the region under the earth, and the sea.[4] I shall be concerned primarily with the relationship between the spatial planes of heaven and earth, although I shall refer to the other two divisions of creation at particular points. The text is punctuated by expressions which bring together the whole of creation. Thus, in 5:13 a doxology is offered by 'every creature in heaven and on earth and under the earth and in the sea', while at 14:7 an angel calls for worship to be given to 'him who made heaven and earth, the sea and the springs of water'.[5] At one level, therefore, the seer sees the various spatial planes of creation as related together, not least because of the duty they owe to God as their common creator. At the same time, there are of course clear distinctions between the different spatial planes, not least in the extent to which their inhabitants choose to acknowledge God. The juxtaposition of 4:1–11 with 1:1–3:22 establishes a dissonance between heaven, where God's just sovereignty is eternally and completely acknowledged, and earth, where evil appears to mask the working of God's power. The remainder of the text deals with the resolution and (paradoxically) the intensification of that dissonance.

---

[4] Since John's primary interests are theological rather than cosmological, the radical differences between modern and ancient conceptions of the cosmos do not in themselves prevent the use of the text in contemporary theological reflection. As Caird puts it: 'No doubt the ancients really believed in a three-storey universe, but this is not quite the same thing as saying that they took it literally. They believed in it for theological rather than geographical reasons' (1984, pp. 118–19). John's relative lack of interest in cosmological detail when compared with other apocalypticists has often been noted. One widely quoted example is that he uses the relatively simple concept of a single heaven rather than the multiple pattern found in, for example, *2 Enoch* or *3 Baruch* (see Gruenwald, 1980, p. 48).

[5] Commentators have often noted that within the complex numerical patterns of the text, the figure four is used to signify the world, and references to the whole of creation tend to be fourfold in nature, as in all the examples I have cited here. See also the references to the four corners of the earth in 7:1 and 20:8. For a helpful recent discussion of the use of number in Revelation, see Bauckham (1993a), pp. 29–37.

4.2 The spatial dynamic of the text

The spatial dimension of the text is not a fixed, static framework within which events take place. Rather, the theological message of the text is developed by the interaction of different spatial locations in the text (principally heaven and earth) with each other, and by movement in the narrative between different spatial planes.[6]

Movement from earth to heaven: the revelation
of heavenly secrets

In the definition which I noted above from the SBL Apocalypse Group, mention is made of the mediation of a revelation to a human recipient. A common device to enable this mediation to take place is the ascent of the human recipient into heaven in order to receive heavenly secrets. The information thus gained sets earthly events in a wider context. For example, from the perspective of heaven the ultimate sovereignty of God can be asserted, providing assurance and the promise of vindication to his people on earth. Yet the fact that the human recipient needs to penetrate beyond the spatial plane of earthly reality in order to discern this ultimate truth offers a mechanism which reflects the apparent limitation of that divine sovereignty from the earthly perspective. This pattern is present in Revelation. John is invited into heaven at the beginning of Revelation 4. This enables him to see from a heavenly perspective both the true nature of ultimate reality, in which God rules justly and his sovereignty is acknowledged by his creatures (4:1–11), and the starting point of the whole process of judgement and salvation by which God's sovereignty is explicitly restored on earth (the appearance of the Lamb in Rev. 5).[7] John

---

[6] John sometimes uses particular terms indicating intermediate positions between heaven and earth to locate activity which involves interaction between heaven and earth. Two such terms are νεφέλη (cloud) and μεσουράνημα (midheaven). These two terms suggest spatial location in the firmament between heaven and earth, but they also play an intermediate role at a symbolic level within the seer's scheme. Νεφέλη occurs at 1:7 (the coming of Christ), 10:1 (the descent of the strong angel), 11:12 (the ascent of the two witnesses), and 14:14–16 (the visions relating to the harvest and vintage of the earth). For a brief survey of the use of clouds as transport in Jewish tradition, see Aune (1998a), p. 625. Μεσουράνημα occurs in 8:13; 14:6, 8, 9; and 19:17; in each case an important announcement is made to foretell or to initiate activity relating to the earth.

[7] Enoch's journeys in the *Book of the Watchers* (*1 En.* 1–36) also serve to demonstrate divine sovereignty in the midst of earthly suffering. *1 En.* 14:8ff. recounts his ascent to heaven and his throne vision, in which the sovereignty of God is depicted. His tour of earth and sheol in chs. 17–19, and particularly his second journey in chs. 21–36, with its geographical and cosmological detail, emphasize that destiny is not left to chance, but is rather under the command of God, and built into the structure of the cosmos. See the helpful discussion in Collins (1984), ch. 2.

appears to remain in heaven to see the effects of the opening of the seven seals and the sounding of the first six trumpets (6:1–9:21). From 10:1 onwards he is once again on earth, yet he continues to see and hear events which take place in heaven as well as those on earth. This heavenly perspective enables him to discern the true nature of earthly events. As Bauckham comments in relation to martyrdom, which appears on the surface to represent defeat, 'the perspective of heaven must break into the earth-bound delusion of the beast's propaganda to enable a different assessment of the same empirical fact: the beast's apparent victory is the martyrs' – and therefore God's – real victory'.[8] The expansion of spatial horizons has the effect of unmasking reality, of revealing the divine hand at work and exposing the nature of evil in its many forms.

Movement from heaven to earth: the execution of divine action

In addition to the ascent pattern noted in the previous section, Revelation is marked by a series of downward movements from the heavenly plane to the earthly plane, as actions which are initiated in heaven are executed on earth.[9] This dynamic marks the whole of the process of salvation and judgement in chs. 6–20. Mauser argues that in Revelation 'Everything that happens on earth is first decided, recorded, and often acted out, in heaven . . . The initiative for all history on earth, including human history, goes out from the vitality of heaven.'[10] Downward movement is an important feature of the three judgement sequences of seals, trumpets and bowls, which are initiated in heaven with earthly effects. The defeat of God's enemies is described in terms of being thrown (βάλλω) downwards (Satan in 12:9–10, 13; 20:3, 10; Babylon in 18:21; the beast in 19:20; death and Hades in 20:14).[11]

---

[8] Bauckham (1993b), p. 91.

[9] This idea can also be found widely in other apocalyptic literature. An interesting example is the Son of Man figure in *1 En.* 46ff. Collins (1984, pp. 147–50) suggests that there is a 'structural homologue' between this figure and the righteous on earth: when the Son of Man is hidden, the righteous suffer, and when he is exalted, so are they.

[10] Mauser (1987), p. 41. There is therefore a strong pattern of events being determined in heaven and worked out on earth. This need not, however, lead to a deterministic interpretation of the relationship between God and humanity in the text. Mazzaferri (1989) and Bauckham (1993a) have both recently stressed the element of contingency in the text, given the need for a human response to divine initiative.

[11] Kvanvig describes Revelation as a 'cosmic exorcism'. The realm of creation has been invaded by hostile powers, whom God attacks. The devil is first expelled from heaven (Rev. 12), subsequently builds his kingdom on earth (Rev. 13) and is in turn exorcised from there (Rev. 20). The aim of the exorcism is the creation of a new universe freed from demonic corruption (1989, pp. 50ff.).

Salvation is seen as descending from heaven, most obviously in the form of the New Jerusalem which comes down from heaven (3:12; 21:2, 10). In the interim, before the establishment of the New Jerusalem on earth, the ultimate protection of the servants of God is also expressed in spatial terms (the martyrs in heaven, 6:9–11; the two witnesses ascending to heaven, 11:12; the child caught up to heaven, 12:5). This process of judgement and salvation is triggered by the appearance of the Lamb in 5:6ff., whose worthiness to open the scroll and begin the process is ascribed to his having 'conquered' (5:5), a reference to his death and resurrection. In a stimulating essay on heavenly ascent in apocalyptic literature Segal argues – rightly, I think – that references to Christ in Revelation, especially 1:18 (descent into Hades) and 1:5 (his implied ascent from the world of the dead to be ruler of the kings of the earth), assume a descent–ascent pattern, in common with Philippians 2:6–11 and the Fourth Gospel.[12]

4.3   Analysis of the text

Introduction

My purpose in analysing the spatial dimension of the text is to explore the way in which John uses it to make theological points. As a starting point, I have therefore made use, in a greatly modified form, of the approach used by Elizabeth Struthers Malbon in her structural analysis of narrative space in the Gospel of Mark. Malbon is 'searching for a homology (similarity in structure) between the geopolitical system and a cognitive (philosophical or theological) system'.[13] She deals with three different categories of space: geopolitical, topographical and architectural. In each category her technique is to examine all the spatial references which occur in the text, in the order in which they occur, in an attempt to discern diachronic sequences in the narrative, and then to produce a diagrammatic analysis based on the detection of binary oppositions underlying the text. For example, in the case of topographical space, Malbon sees a fundamental opposition in the narrative between heaven and earth, within earth

---

[12] Segal (1980), p. 1375. Segal distinguishes between two kinds of journey between heaven and earth, an *anabasis* type (ascent–descent), which he finds in *1 Enoch*, *2 Baruch*, *Ascension of Isaiah* and elsewhere, and a *katabasis* type, which he finds in the Book of Revelation. As I have noted, however, Revelation in fact includes examples of both patterns: there are similarities between the ascent of John to heaven in 4:1ff. and Segal's *anabasis* pattern.

[13] Malbon (1986), p. 15.

between land and sea, within land between isolated areas and inhabited areas, with a convergence between these last two in the idea of the 'way' of discipleship.

However, in chapter 3 I set out some underlying problems with structuralist analysis. In particular, I noted the danger that the operation of the *structure* of the text (as discerned by the interpreter) can be overstressed at the expense of the *content* of the text. This has given rise to the criticisms by Douglas and others that the apparent meaning of texts is evaporated by an over-rigid application of alien categories.[14] The structuralist technique – applied fairly rigorously by Malbon – which seeks to detect diachronic sequences overlaid on sets of synchronic oppositions runs this risk, since the diachronic sequences need bear no relation to the obvious divisions within the text. In an attempt to counteract this problem, I have adopted an approach which is much more flexible than that followed by Malbon. Revelation consists largely of a series of interconnected visions, each of which takes its place within a cosmic framework of heaven, earth and the demonic realm. The ways in which these different visions and auditions interrelate are the subject of many different theories.[15] But the boundaries between individual visions in the text are usually reasonably clear, and indeed are often signalled by textual devices such as movement from earth to heaven or vice versa. To ignore such divisions would be perverse. I have therefore divided the text into fairly large units, each of which contains passages which are widely recognized as belonging together (for example, the seven messages of 2:1–3:22). Using these units as a framework, I have examined all apparent spatial locations referred to in the text. This facilitates an analysis of the spatial dimension of the text which does justice to the obvious divisions within the text, and which deals in distinctions, conflicts and resolutions which are clearly present in the text, not imported into it. This method is a long way removed from Lévi-Strauss, though it still owes something to ideas from structuralist analysis. I should stress that I am *not* seeking to produce a comprehensive analysis of the structure of the text, with detailed arguments about how the various parts of the text might best be seen in conjunction with one another. This would involve a more detailed examination of smaller units of text. My aim is simply to produce a framework within which the spatial development of the text can be considered.

---

[14] See above, pp. 65–9.

[15] Yarbro Collins has commented that there are almost as many outlines of the book as there are interpreters. Proposals which I have found helpful include those by Lambrecht (1980), Fiorenza (1985), Hellholm (1986), Giblin (1991) and Bauckham (1993a,b).

Patmos and divine epiphany (1:1–20)

The introduction to the book is given from an earthly perspective on Patmos, yet already the seer is beginning to intertwine the everyday context of Asia Minor with an encompassing wider reality. This is clear from the structure of this opening section. The seer has received an ἀποκάλυψις from God, through Christ and an angelic intermediary (1:1), relating to ἃ δεῖ γενέσθαι – the things to come – which the book will describe in graphic symbolism embracing the entire cosmos. Yet this grand cosmic context is juxtaposed with the particular earthly context in the macarism and injunction about right reception of the message of the book in 1:3, and John's address to the seven churches (1:4ff.). The interweaving of address of this kind with a strong and imminent expectation of direct divine intervention in earthly space through the coming of Christ is characteristic of 1:1–8 and 22:8–21. Although both passages are clearly linked to adjacent text, they are distinct from the rest of the book and form an *inclusio* to the text as a whole.[16]

John's use of spatial references is already beginning to stretch the limits of his vision. References to heaven (the seven spirits in 1:4 are before the throne) and Hades (to which Christ holds the key in 1:18) help to establish the universal context in which the action of the book is to take place. The divine statement in 1:8 is particularly important in this regard. I shall deal with the self-description of God as ὁ ὢν καὶ ὁ ἦν καὶ ὁ ἐρχόμενος in chapter 5 (pp. 115–19). For the purposes of the present chapter the use of the term παντοκράτωρ is significant. Apart from 2 Corinthians 6:18, where it forms part of a citation from the Old Testament, the term is unique to Revelation in the New Testament. It carries the force of God's supremacy over all things, rather than omnipotence.[17] As Beasley-Murray notes, the term underlines that 'Revelation is a book concerned with the purpose of God not solely for believers, nor even for the Church alone, but for the nations and for history in its broadest sweep, indeed for the universe as a whole.'[18]

This passage illustrates two important narrative techniques which the seer adopts in relation to movement *between* spatial locations. First,

---

[16] Significantly, the phrase ἐγώ [εἰμι] τὸ Ἄλφα καὶ τὸ Ὦ occurs only in these two passages (1:8; 22:13) and in the crucial divine statement related to the descent of the New Jerusalem at 21:6.

[17] Thus Michaelis (1965), p. 915. Giblin points to the use of παντοκράτωρ in the LXX to translate צְבָאוֹת, rendered often in English as 'Lord God of hosts' (see 2 Sam. 5:10; 7:8–11; Amos 4:13; Mic. 4:1–4), and argues that 1:8 therefore 'states the cohesive thematic of the entire apocalypse as God's coming in the Holy War' (1991, p. 43).

[18] Beasley-Murray (1974), p. 60.

important movements of the seer from plane to plane and from place to place, especially when connected with the granting of prophetic discernment, are said elsewhere in the book to be in the Spirit (ἐν πνεύματι).[19] Movement between spatial planes and the discernment this brings are thus linked clearly with divine initiative. The term appears at 1:10 ('I was in the Spirit on the Lord's day'). It does not seem that the seer is translated spatially at this point, in contrast to the other occasions when the term is used.[20] Prophetic discernment is certainly in view, however, as the following verse includes a commission to the seer to write what he sees and proclaim it to the churches.[21] And although the seer does not change location within his visionary experience at this point, his sense of space is surely changed (his spatial horizon is expanded) by the vision of the one like a son of man, who transcends earthly reality. The spatial location of the figure in 1:12–20 is ambiguous. Christ appears to John on Patmos, yet features of the description suggest a heavenly figure. Christ has passed through the realm of the dead, and holds the keys of death and Hades (1:18). As Ford notes, the figure possesses a combination of different attributes which transcends conventional boundaries between the human and the divine. The hair which is white as wool and the flaming eyes of 1:14 recall the Ancient of Days of Daniel 7:9–10, but the expression ὅμοιον υἱὸν ἀνθρώπου (1:13) recalls the one like a son of man of Daniel 7:13. Ford also draws attention to the combination of cosmic, inanimate and human elements in the description (stars, sun, wool, snow, fire, bronze, water, hair, eyes).[22] In this sense, John's being in the Spirit at 1:10 entails crossing a boundary.[23] The identity of the seven spirits before

---

[19] Bauckham (1993a, pp. 150ff.) gives a good analysis of the use of this term, and argues persuasively that it refers to the Holy Spirit, rather than John's own spirit.

[20] See, however, Aune (1997), pp. 71, 82–3, who argues that ἐν πνεύματι is associated in Revelation with a change of location. In its three other occurrences, it is associated with movement to heaven (4:2), to the wilderness (17:3) and to a high mountain (21:10). Aune therefore argues that use of the term in 1:10 implies that the vision of 1:10–20 is set in the heavenly throne-room.

[21] Jeske (1985) argues that ἐν πνεύματι should not be understood as referring to John's personal visionary experience, but rather as a relational symbol signifying John's identification with his community, and his reception of a prophetic message on behalf of the community. Phrases such as 'I saw', 'I was carried', etc., should be understood simply as literary conventions which mean that 'the mythology of the translation of the apocalyptic visionary is transformed into the codes of the community' (p. 459). Jeske may well be right that ἐν πνεύματι should be understood as having a corporate dimension, but this does not seem incompatible with its also signifying an aspect of the seer's private visionary experience, and Jeske does not offer sufficient evidence to rule out the latter.

[22] See Ford (1975), pp. 384–5. Aune (1997, pp. 90ff.) gives a comprehensive analysis of parallels with Jewish and Graeco-Roman descriptions of epiphanies.

[23] Wheelwright's conclusions about the importance of the upward threshold and a sense of the transcendent for the use of tensive symbol (see above, pp. 68–9) are relevant here.

the throne (1:4) has been much debated. The most likely explanation is that there is a reference here to Zechariah 4:1–14, in which seven lamps are seen as the seven eyes of the Lord, ranging actively throughout the earth. Within the text of Revelation, the seven spirits may be associated therefore with the seven eyes and horns of the Lamb (5:5–6), and with the two witnesses of 11:3–13, who are described as olive-trees, again recalling Zechariah 4:1–14. Thus there is a complex of ideas relating to the Spirit of God, in which God's activity and the church's witness are interconnected.[24]

Second, as I mentioned in note 6 of this chapter, John makes particular use of two terms, νεφέλη and μεσουράνημα, to signify interaction between heaven and earth. Νεφέλη occurs at 1:7, in connection with the coming of Christ. This is of course in line with New Testament adaptation of Daniel 7:13, applying it specifically to the figure of Christ, especially in Mark 14:62. Nonetheless, one must always analyse carefully the precise phrases used by the seer, and it can be argued that one of the reasons why John places this reference at this point is indeed to stress that Christ intervenes decisively to bring the spatial plane of earth into a right relationship with the spatial plane of heaven.

This first section of the text thus begins to place the earthly situation of John and the churches in a broader spatial context which embraces heaven, earth and Hades, setting the stage for all that follows.

The messages to the seven churches: earthly realities
in heavenly perspective (2:1–3:22)

As in 1:1–20, the setting here is earthly, yet the spatial horizon of the narrative is stretched to encompass a wider reality. Still in a sense a prologue to the forthcoming visions, the prophetic declarations of the seven messages anchor the message of the one like a son of man into more specific earthly situations, while at the same time consistently pointing beyond them. The messages demonstrate the solidarity of the one like a son of man (who transcends spatial boundaries) with the earthly communities of his followers, whatever their situation. Their life in the cities of Asia is to be lived in the light of the promised eschatological reality of the New

---

[24] Bauckham (1993a), pp. 162–6. The implication may well be that God's purpose in restoring justice to the earth will be accomplished 'not by might, nor by power, but by my spirit' (Zech. 4:6). The link with Zech. 4 is also accepted by Ladd (1972), pp. 24–5; Caird (1984), p. 15; and Beale (1999), pp. 189–90. An alternative interpretation, seeing the seven spirits as relating not to the spirit of God active in the world, but rather to the seven 'angels of the presence' of Tobit 12:15, is followed by Giblin (1991), p. 41; Roloff (1993), p. 24; and Aune (1997), pp. 34–5.

Jerusalem, which descends from the spatial plane of heaven in chs. 21–2, as the distinctions between heaven and earth are abolished.

Commentators have often noted the similarities in the structure of the seven messages. Each includes an instruction to write to the angel of the relevant church, a prophetic utterance of the risen Christ prefaced by the formula τάδε λέγει, an eschatological promise, sometimes linked with a warning, and an exhortation to hear what the Spirit says to the churches. To my knowledge, however, commentators have not noted the way in which this repeated rhetorical pattern reproduces in microcosm both the spatial and the temporal structures of the whole text.[25]

Firstly, each message begins with a self-reference to the risen Christ. These references relate back to the description of Christ in 1:12–20, which transcends the boundaries between heaven, earth and Hades.[26] In 2:1 (the message to Ephesus) Christ is described as holding seven stars (the angels of the churches) in his right hand, yet also walking among the seven lampstands (the seven churches): heavenly and earthly features are thus combined. In 2:8, at the head of the message to Smyrna, Christ is described as ὁ πρῶτος καὶ ὁ ἔσχατος, ὃς ἐγένετο νεκρὸς καὶ ἔζησεν.[27] Taken with 1:18, this also implies a transcendence of spatial boundaries, this time between Hades and the earth: Christ has passed through, and now controls access to, the realm of the dead. In 2:12 (the message to Pergamum) Christ is ὁ ἔχων τὴν ῥομφαίαν τὴν δίστομον τὴν ὀξεῖαν. This is a central feature of the description of Christ in 19:11–16, as a figure bursting through the opened boundary between heaven and earth to execute judgement. The description at the head of the message to Thyatira (2:18) refers back to 1:14–15 and the recollection of the description of the heavenly figure of Daniel 10:6. In 3:1 (the message to Sardis) the idea of the seven spirits of God, which, as I noted earlier, suggests active movement down from heaven to earth, is repeated.[28] The reference in 3:7 (the message to Philadelphia) to ὁ ἀνοίγων καὶ οὐδεὶς κλείσει καὶ κλείων καὶ οὐδεὶς ἀνοίγει suggests, when taken with the following verse, a means of access to the kingdom of God. Finally, the description of Christ in 3:14 (the message to Laodicea) as ἡ ἀρχὴ τῆς κτίσεως τοῦ θεοῦ refers to the whole of the cosmos. These descriptions of Christ therefore serve to set the messages in a wider framework which extends outwards to ultimate spatial horizons.

---

[25] Here, I am concerned with the spatial dimension of this pattern. For my comments on its temporal dimension, see chapter 5, pp. 119–22.

[26] See above, pp. 87–9.

[27] Beale (1999) suggests that 2:8 describes Christ as 'the divine sovereign over history who alone possesses the attribute of eternity' (p. 239).

[28] See above, pp. 87–9.

Secondly, each message includes a reference to the earthly situation of the church, introduced by οἶδα, I know. The ambiguity and trial of the church's earthly experience is thus set within the ultimate spatial horizons suggested by the descriptions of Christ. This earthly experience includes the threat of false teaching (2:2, 14–15, 20–3); persecution (2:9–10, 13); loss of commitment (3:1–3, 15–19) and powerlessness (3:8). But the deeper reality conveyed by the descriptions of Christ – and by the claims he makes – serves to place that experience in context.

Thirdly, each message contains a promise relating directly or indirectly to the New Jerusalem. The New Jerusalem which descends from God out of heaven is explicitly mentioned in 3:12 in the message to Philadelphia, but connections are present in all the other messages also. The church at Ephesus is promised that everyone who conquers will be allowed to eat from the tree of life which is in the paradise of God (2:7). The tree of life appears in 22:2 in the New Jerusalem, and twice again in the epilogue to the book, where the right to eat from the tree is explicitly linked to membership of the holy city (22:14, 19). The church at Smyrna is promised that the one who conquers will not be harmed by the second death (2:11): in 21:4, a voice from heaven declares that death will be no more in the New Jerusalem, whereas in 20:14–15 and 21:8 the enemies of God suffer the second death, in the lake that burns with fire and sulphur. In 2:17 the promise to the church at Pergamum includes a new name: God's (or the Lamb's?) name is on the foreheads of his servants in the city in 22:4.[29] The morning star is promised to the church at Thyatira in 2:28 – although the morning star is not mentioned in the vision of the New Jerusalem itself, it does appear as a title of Jesus in 22:16, and of course the Lamb is indeed present in the city, which is described as his bride. Similar correspondences are present in relation to Sardis (the book of life, 3:5; cf. 21:27), and Laodicea (the throne, 3:21; cf. 22:3). These references to the New Jerusalem point forward to the expected resolution of spatial dissonance between heaven and earth at the end of the book.

Fourthly, each message includes the exhortation ὁ ἔχων οὖς ἀκουσάτω τί τὸ πνεῦμα λέγει ταῖς ἐκκλησίαις. This brings the spatial focus back to the earthly situation of the churches. This formula, as used in Revelation, is related to the hearing formula in the synoptic tradition (Matt. 13:9–17, 43; Mark 4:9, 23; Luke 8:8; 14:35), which is a development of Isaiah

---

[29] In addition, the 'hidden manna' of 2:17 may carry overtones of descent from heaven to earth. Swete (1906, p. 38) and others have suggested a background in the traditions referred to in 2 Macc. 2:4–8, where Jeremiah hides the ark (according to Heb. 9:4, the ark held a golden urn of manna), and in *2 Bar.* 29:8 ('And it will happen at that time that the treasury of manna will come down again from on high, and they will eat of it in those years because these are they who will have arrived at the consummation of time').

6:9–10. Many commentators therefore argue that in Revelation 2–3 the force of the hearing formula is to underline to believers the need to understand God's message and remain faithful in the earthly present, while at the same time it somehow hardens the hearts of unbelievers.[30]

I have thus established a strong pattern in the spatial structure of the seven messages. Each is introduced by a reference to the figure of Christ, who transcends the spatial boundaries between heaven and earth. The earthly experience of the church is placed in the ultimate context of the expected descent of the New Jerusalem. Yet there is also a refocusing back to the earthly present with the exhortations to repent, stand firm and listen to the Spirit. This pattern reproduces in microcosm the structure of the whole text, with its expansion outwards to ultimate horizons and its refocusing back to the earthly present of the reader.

The first two sections of the book establish that its message is for the church in its earthly situation. At the same time, the seer has clearly set the church's situation in a wider spatial context, embracing heaven and Hades. Already the reader is being urged to look beyond visible reality to the divine promise. There is more to the world than appears on the surface.

Revelation of the heavenly perspective (4:1–11)

At 4:1 the scene changes abruptly, and many commentators regard this as marking the beginning of the central visionary content of the book. However, it is a mistake to stress this division too heavily, given that, as I shall argue, much of the point of the vision in 4:1–5:14 stems precisely from its relationship to what has preceded it.[31]

A door is opened in heaven, and a voice tells John to go up and enter. The opening of a door is a traditional apocalyptic motif, linked with ascent to heaven.[32] John is transported up to heaven ἐν πνεύματι, where he sees a glorious vision of heavenly worship.[33] The critical point for present

---

[30] See, for example, Beale (1999), pp. 236–9. In contrast, Enroth (1990) argues that this synoptic context of the hearing formula has been lost in Revelation.

[31] The connections between 2:1–3:22 and 4:1–11 are not limited to the level of the overall logic of the narrative. There are also interesting textual connections, most obviously the throne (4:2; cf. 3:21–2), white robes (4:4; cf. 3:4–5), crowns (4:4, 10; cf. 2:10; 3:11), and the seven spirits of God (4:5; cf. 3:1). These reinforce the point made on pp. 89–92 to the effect that the seven messages already contain within them references to the resolution of spatial dissonance.

[32] See also *1 En.* 14:15; *Asc. Isa.* 6:9. There is a full discussion of the motif of the open door in Aune (1997), pp. 279–82.

[33] See above, pp. 87–9 for a discussion of John's use of ἐν πνεύματι.

purposes is not simply that John sees a divine reality which transcends reality as it appears in the cities of Asia. It is also vital to grasp the relationship, represented by the use of spatial categories, between 4:1ff. and the text in which it is embedded.

The opening vision of Revelation 1 and the messages to the seven churches reflected the struggle of the earthly situation of the church (later to be expressed more graphically in 11:1–13:18), together with the deeper reality underlying that existence, represented by the promises relating to future intervention from a different spatial sphere – the descent of the New Jerusalem. The tension inherent in this juxtaposition is now intensified: John's vision in 4:1ff. reveals a present heavenly reality in which the good and omnipotent God is offered continual worship,[34] but there is a discrepancy between this picture and how things appear to be on earth. This is represented by the spatial distinction between heaven and earth. Sperber's analysis of symbolism is relevant: the symbolic vision of heaven represents a perspective which is at odds with the encyclopaedic, empirical knowledge of John's readers. The process of symbolic focalization (in Sperber's terms) therefore leads to intense contradictions, which need to be resolved.[35]

At the same time, it can be argued that although the spatial focus of 4:1–11 is very much in heaven, the imagery employed suggests transcendence of the boundary between heaven and earth. Davis lists a number of such features: the twenty-four elders (4:4), which he links with the twenty-four courses of priests of 1 Chronicles 24; the four living creatures (4:6), which he relates to the four chief tribes of Numbers 2; and the seven spirits of God (4:5), which he connects with the seven eyes of God ranging over the earth (Zech. 4:10).[36] Some of Davis's examples are more convincing than others. But his analysis does suggest that heaven and earth form an 'ontological cosmic unity', in line with my contention

---

[34] The presence of ὡς θάλασσα ὑαλίνη ὁμοία κρυστάλλῳ (4:6) in heaven has occasioned much debate. Caird (1984, pp. 65ff.) and Sweet (1979, p. 113) see it as referring to the waters of chaos in primeval creation myths and thus suggesting a discordant element in the picture of heaven. This is, I think, pressing the evidence too far. More likely is a reference either to the tradition of some kind of celestial sea which does not imply an evil presence (Ladd, 1972, pp. 76–7; Beasley-Murray, 1974, p.116; Ford, 1975, pp. 73–4), or even merely to decoration of the divine throne-room (since the text refers only to something *like* a sea of glass: cf. Mounce, 1977, pp. 136–7). Beale (1999, pp. 327–8) suggests a combination of these two approaches: that the sea represents chaotic power calmed by divine sovereignty. Generally, the *earthly* sea in Revelation is an ambiguous symbol. It is part of creation and, as such, offers praise (5:13) and suffers judgement (16:3). Yet it is of course absent from the new creation (21:1).

[35] See chapter 3, pp. 66–8.

[36] Davis (1992), pp. 148–57. See the discussion of links to Zech. 4 above, pp. 88–9.

that the text seeks to *expand* the spatial horizons of the reader, rather than to offer a picture of an *alternative* reality.[37]

The combination of imagery suggesting cosmological unity with the manifest distinction between the acknowledged sovereignty of God in heaven and the injustice and ambiguity of earth generates tensions in the spatial dimension of reality. First, as O'Donovan puts it, 'the prophet poses his problem: how can the created order which declares the beauty and splendour of its Creator be the subject of a world-history, the events of which are directionless and contradictory?'[38] How can there be such a discrepancy between what is in heaven and what appears to be on earth? Second, John is deliberately building a log-jam in the development of the text. How is this unsatisfactory state of affairs to be rectified? How is God's rule, manifest already on the spatial plane of heaven, to be made manifest on earth?[39]

The Lamb: the possibility of earthward manifestation of heavenly reality (5:1–14)

The precise relationship between 4:1–11 and 5:1–14 has been a source of important debate among interpreters. Rowland argues that Revelation 4 'shows no evidence at all of Christian influence, and, treated in isolation, it is evident that it is entirely Jewish in its inspiration. Indeed, the author obviously intends a deliberate contrast between the description of the divine court in Revelation 4 and the transformation which takes place as the result of the exaltation of the Lamb.'[40] This position has been attacked strongly by Hurtado, who argues that 4:1–11 and 5:1–14 are closely related and that 4:1–11 does indeed show Christian influences. Of the Christian influences which Hurtado claims to find in 4:1–11, the most convincing is probably the twenty-four elders. This symbol is not present in Jewish apocalyptic: it is a new, unparalleled group, given all the more prominence because of the relative restraint in describing

---

[37] Davis (1992), pp. 21–2.

[38] O'Donovan (1986), p. 71. Rowland also draws attention to the contrast between God's rule in heaven and disobedience on earth: 'The antithesis between theological affirmation and historical reality could not have been more starkly put' (1982, p. 425).

[39] In this context, Bauckham (1993a) refers back to the importance of John's use of Zech. 4:1–14, arguing that 'the question to which the message of Revelation is the answer was: Given the apparently irresistible might and worldwide power of the beast, how is God going to establish this rule of earth?' (p. 163). The implied answer – to be made explicit later – comes from Zech. 4:6, 'Not by might, nor by power, but by my Spirit, says the Lord of hosts.'

[40] Rowland (1982), p. 222.

heavenly beings in the scene. Hurtado suggests that they are heavenly representatives of the elect, demonstrating that 'the promises to the elect are based on heavenly realities'.[41] His conclusion is that the two chapters should in fact be understood as complementary scenes in the same vision.[42]

Hurtado is correct to link 4:1–11 and 5:1–14 closely together, and to place them both in a Christian framework. On the other hand, there are clearly distinctions between the two passages, and it is precisely in these distinctions that their interconnection within the overall structure of the text is best understood. I noted above (pp. 92–4) that 4:1–11 establishes that there are major problems in the relationship between heaven and earth; it is the action in 5:1–14 which begins to bring about a solution. Thus there are *both* close linkages *and* contrasts between the two passages.

The crucial development is the appearance of the Lamb. He is deemed to be worthy to open the scroll in 5:5, from which point flow the events associated with the seven seals, trumpets and bowls, and the visions of the church's struggle in 11:1–13:18.[43] This is, then, a critical moment in the narrative. As Hurtado argues, whereas 4:1–11 provides a picture of the 'idealized heavenly sovereignty of God', 5:1–14 'gives the means by which this heavenly reality... is to be made a historical reality upon the earth, the exaltation and triumph of the sacrificed Lamb, and shows that it is this exalted figure who is alone worthy to execute God's eschatological plan'.[44] Despite his different analysis of the nature of 4:1–11, Rowland's conclusion about the overall effect of the two passages taken together is similar: 'Theologically, one can say that a start has been made in the

---

[41] Hurtado (1985), p. 114. Aune (1997, pp. 287–92) sets out a comprehensive survey of the different possible identifications of the twenty-four elders (including that of Hurtado). Aune himself favours the theory that they are the heavenly counterparts of the leaders of the twenty-four priestly courses described in 1 Chr. 23:6; 24:7–18.

[42] Hurtado (1985), p. 117.

[43] The three series of seven seals, trumpets and bowls are certainly linked. Lambrecht (1980) argues that the structure of 4:1–22:5 is one in which the sequences of seals and trumpets are open-ended, each embracing all that follows. An additional point binding the beginning of Rev. 5 to the whole sequence is that the term ἄγγελος ἰσχυρός (strong angel) occurs only three times in the book: at 5:2, when the sealed scroll is first introduced; at 10:1, when the open scroll is brought down from heaven; and at 18:21, at the culmination of the bowls sequence, when Babylon is thrown into the sea. If one sees the process unleashed by the Lamb's unsealing of the scroll as a process of judgement and redemption moving earthward from heaven, then it is surely appropriate that the same term is used at the outset, as the move out from heaven begins; at 10:1, as the scroll itself is brought down to earth; and at 18:21, when the final act of judgement on Babylon (a highly graphic downward movement) is accomplished.

[44] Hurtado (1985), pp. 117–18. See also Beasley-Murray (1974), pp. 108–11.

attempt to bridge the gap between the divine intention for the world and the bleak reality of the situation.'[45]

This is shown in the way that the spatial coverage of this passage begins to reach downwards from heaven to embrace earth. At 5:3 there is a search of heaven, earth and under the earth to find someone worthy to open the scroll in the right hand of the one seated on the throne. Christ is introduced in 5:4 with reference to two titles (Lion of Judah, Root of David) which express messianic expectation in terms drawn from the earthly history of Israel. The descriptions of the Lamb as having conquered (5:5) and standing as if it had been slaughtered (5:6) are clearly references to the earthly death and resurrection of Christ. Following the Lamb's taking the scroll from the right hand of the one seated on the throne (5:7), there is a striking sequence of successively widening concentric circles of praise. At 5:8–10 the inner circle of heavenly beings, the four living creatures and the twenty-four elders offer a song of praise; they are joined by multitudes of angels in 5:11–12; in turn, every creature in heaven and on earth and under the earth and in the sea takes up the theme (5:13). Highly significant also is the reference in 5:6 to the seven eyes of the Lamb as the seven spirits of God sent out into all the earth.[46] It is through the Lamb that divine intervention on the spatial plane of earth is possible.

The outworking of divine initiative on earth (1) (6:1–9:21)

This section describes the interlocking patterns of judgement on the earth and preservation of the faithful, between the beginning of the opening of the seals in 6:1 and the appearance of the opened scroll in 10:1.

The action relating to the first six seals (6:1–17) and the first six trumpets (8:6–9:21) takes place virtually entirely on earth, although it is of course initiated in heaven.[47] The first four seals have, for example,

---

[45] Rowland (1982), p. 426.   [46] See above, pp. 88–9.

[47] There are in fact three references to heaven in ch. 6. However, of these, the scene associated with the opening of the fifth seal (the cry of the martyrs under the heavenly altar) is a reference to the preservation and service of the saints embedded in a narrative about judgement; οὐρανός in 6:14 is best translated as 'sky' (as in the NRSV) rather than 'heaven'; the reference to the heavenly throne in 6:16 is really a cry of anguish by those on earth relating to the earthly outworking of divine decrees. In the case of the six trumpets (8:6–9:21), οὐρανός is mentioned as the place from which stars fall in 8:10 and 9:1; again, these references might legitimately be regarded as referring to the natural sky (Caird (1984) translates the first in this way), although the fact that the star in 9:1 appears to be a living supernatural being leads translators to give οὐρανός as 'heaven' in that verse. The remaining spatial locator indicating action in heaven, at 9:13, describes the source of a voice whose command relates nonetheless to earthly consequences.

certainly been interpreted by many as indicating tribulation which arises on earth, and which, though permitted by God, originates directly in human sin, war and exploitation.[48] O'Donovan suggests that this is part of a development in which the hand of God behind events is gradually revealed: the seal judgements occur within nature; the trumpet judgements take place more directly at divine initiative; the bowl judgements are clearly shown as direct judgement from God.[49] With the sixth seal comes a vision of cosmic catastrophe, marked by the spatial displacement of the natural order (there is a great earthquake; the stars fall; the sky vanishes; mountains and islands are removed from their places). Humanity is also displaced, to caves in the mountains, and ironically cries to the mountains and rocks to be removed from their places to provide shelter from the wrath of God and the Lamb.

The trumpets sequence brings the first mention of the spatial category of the abyss, from which smoke and the locusts arise at the blast of the fifth trumpet (9:1ff.). Caird interprets the role of the abyss as that of 'a reservoir of evil from which human wickedness received constant reinforcing supplies'.[50] It is the place from which the beast ascends (11:7), and it serves as a temporary prison for Satan (20:3). It is thus a source of chaos and sinful rebellion.[51]

The aim of these judgements on the earthly plane is not purely retributive, as is clear from the final verse of this section (9:21), which records humankind's failure to repent as a result of the judgements. Rather, the sequence represents a revelation, initiated by divine fiat, of the consequences

---

[48] Fiorenza (1991, p. 63) argues that the first four seals should be seen not as a series of events, but rather as a series of images which 'reveal and highlight the true nature of Roman power and rule'.

[49] O'Donovan (1986), pp. 73ff. A parallel intensification is often remarked upon by commentators: in the seals sequence Death is given authority over one quarter of the earth (6:8); in the trumpets sequence one third of various categories of creation is affected (8:7–12; 9:18); in the bowls sequence no such limits are expressed.

[50] Caird (1984), pp. 118–19. For the background to the symbol of the abyss, see Aune (1998a), pp. 525–6; Beale (1999), p. 493.

[51] The abyss is not mentioned after 20:3. Certainly the implication of the text as a whole is that with the establishment of the New Jerusalem, the forces which were associated with the abyss have been finally overcome. In a study of the symbol of the abyss Pippin (1994) takes a radically different view. She argues that 'the abyss represents what in postmodernism is the unrepresentable, the indeterminate, the fragmented, the self-less and the depth-less' (p. 252). She attacks the traditional reading of Revelation as the re-establishment of the rule of God, arguing instead that 'the presence of the abyss in the text makes all boundaries useless' (p. 262), thus preventing the establishment of ordered space in the New Jerusalem. This view runs counter to a natural reading of the narrative shape of the text as a whole, in which forces of chaos are conquered.

of human sin and refusal to worship God, with at least a partial aim of encouraging repentance. It represents one side of the divine initiative to rectify the fundamental problem apparent by the end of Revelation 4: how is God's rule to be manifested?

Interlocked with these stark judgements is material dealing with the redemption and the preservation of the saints, recorded in 7:1–17, and with synergistic activity by the faithful (6:9–11; 8:1–5). It is important to notice the way in which the spatial coverage of the text in these sections contrasts with that around them. In contrast to the earthly situation of the surrounding text, the material in 6:9–11, 7:1–17 and 8:1–5 spreads its spatial coverage across both heaven and earth. In 6:9–11 the martyrs under the heavenly altar are linked with their brothers still on earth who have yet to join them. In 7:1–17 the implication is that the 144,000 are sealed on earth, since the sealing is to protect them from the outworking of judgement in the natural world which is referred to in 7:1–3. Yet the great multitude which the seer subsequently sees is described in terms which transcend spatial boundaries, including references to heaven (the throne in 7:9), an earthly tribulation/martyrdom (7:14) and the eschatological New Jerusalem (cf. the similarities between 7:15 17 and 21:3ff.).[52] 8:1–5 represents an important example of synergistic activity on the part of the faithful.[53] The prayers of the saints (presumably those on earth and those in heaven) are offered in heaven (8:4), returning to the earth in wrath (8:5).

Thus, spatial references are being used by the seer to distinguish between the fate of the faithful and that of the enemies of God. The faithful suffer on earth, but divine protection, originating in heaven but with earthly effect, catches them up into the ultimate positive purposes of God, to be consummated at the descent from heaven to earth of the New Jerusalem (6:9–11; 7:1–17). By contrast, the enemies of God will be subject to divine judgement which originates in heaven with earthly effect (6:1–8, 12–17; 8:6–9:21).

---

[52] On the relationship between the two groups in Rev. 7, and between 7:15–17 and 21:3ff., see chapter 5, pp. 125–7.

[53] The relationship between the actions of God and the accompanying actions of his saints is subtle. Bauckham (1993a, ch. 8) argues that the Old Testament contains two broad traditions of holy war. The first, typified by Exod. 14, has God fighting with his people against the enemy. The second (e.g. Isa. 59:16), which is common in later apocalyptic, has God fighting alone. Bauckham argues that Revelation is exceptional. It belongs largely in the second tradition, since no military involvement of the faithful is expected, yet it does envisage a role for them which is not entirely passive, given the importance of witness and martyrdom. See also Yarbro Collins (1977) and Kraybill (1996, pp. 200–5), who reach similar conclusions.

The scroll brought down from heaven (10:1–11)

The divine initiative to restore just rule to the cosmos begins with the Lamb's enabling the process to start by unsealing the scroll, and continues with the contrasting accounts of judgement and eschatological preservation in 6:1–9:21. With the appearance of the open scroll brought down from heaven, 10:1–11 introduces a new phase of the book. Just as the first appearance of the scroll was associated with the extension of the spatial coverage of the text from heaven to earth with the appearance of the Lamb in 5:6ff., so now an actual descent by the strong angel from the heavenly to the earthly plane signals the bringing of the scroll to earth.[54]

The judgements of 8:7–9:21 were announced in heaven and executed on earth, with the action focusing primarily on the earthly effects of the judgements. 10:1–11 sees a public announcement on earth itself, and the spatial coverage of the passage, in contrast to the primarily earthly focus of 8:7–9:21, spans heaven and earth. The angel descends from heaven, wrapped in a cloud (10:1),[55] a voice from heaven orders the sealing of the seven thunders (10:4) – yet the proclamation of the scroll (10:7, 11) is clearly to take effect on earth. Very significantly, the angel bearing the scroll of the prophecy stands on the sea and the land while at the same time raising his hand to heaven (10:2–6). The spatial symbolism could hardly be clearer: the angel's message is from heaven, and is addressed to the whole earth (land and sea). Yet the spatial development of the text has also moved on since Revelation 5. Whereas the scroll at that point was in heaven, the angel is here making a highly public proclamation on earth. The juxtaposition of this with the following vision of the church's earthly tribulation (where the power of the angel's disclosure is hidden to the world) is especially ironic. Or, to adapt Scott's language, that which is a very public transcript in the vision is in the present life of the church a hidden transcript.[56]

---

[54] I understand the βιβλίον of 5:1 and the βιβλαρίδιον of 10:2 to be the same scroll; see Mazzaferri (1989), pp. 265ff.; Bauckham (1993a), pp. 243–57; and Michaels (1997), pp. 133–4. This is a minority view among commentators. See Aune (1998a), p. 571 for a brief survey of the strengths and weaknesses of this position. Interestingly, Beale (1999, pp. 526ff.) sets out many arguments for the close identification of this scroll with that of ch. 5, and indeed concludes that the two scrolls are 'generally the same' (p. 545), but still prefers to understand the scroll in ch. 10 as 'a "little book" on a smaller theological scale than the bigger book of chapter 5' (p. 532). 'The little book is a new version of these same purposes symbolized by the book in chapter 5, insofar as these purposes are now to be accomplished by the people of God' (p. 545).

[55] See the discussion of νεφέλη above, in section 4.2, n. 6.

[56] See chapter 3, pp. 65–6.

In the narrative to follow, the witness of the church on earth becomes much more central (11:1–13:18). And the judgements upon those who reject that witness (the seven bowls in 16:1–21; the judgement of Babylon in 17:1–18:24; and the last judgement in 20:11–15) are no longer limited to a quarter of the earth (as with the fourth seal) or a third (as with the first, second, third, fourth and sixth trumpets): these judgements are final.

The witness of the church on earth (11:1–13:18)[57]

The expansion in spatial coverage from heaven to earth as a result of the Lamb's appearance in 5:6ff. was followed by the outworking on earth of the effects of the opening of the first six seals and the sounding of the first six trumpets, coupled with the account of the eschatological preservation of the saints in ch. 7. The descent of the strong angel from heaven to earth is followed by the second half of the book, in which the themes of judgement and preservation are repeated, now intertwined more specifically with the witness of the church.

Immediately, there is a group of three visions, which relate the witness of the church on earth, the opposition from the enemies of God, and, again, the ultimate protection of the faithful. This is a critical section of the book, since it seeks to reveal the hidden spatial dimensions behind the actual experience of the church in the present from three different perspectives.[58] It is characterized by intense interaction between the heavenly and earthly planes, especially in the first two visions. In each vision the themes of persecution and preservation/vindication are present, but gradually through this part of the book, different spatial dimensions of the universe are revealed, to unmask the true nature of events.

In the first vision (the two witnesses) the focus is clearly on action on the earthly plane, following the strong angel's descent. The action has definitely shifted dramatically to the church's mission on earth, and, despite the measure of protection afforded to the two witnesses in 11:5–6, the mission ends in apparent defeat in 11:10. Shrinkage of the spatial horizon of the text (the momentary apparent powerlessness of heaven)

---

[57] In this section I take the three visions of the two witnesses, the woman and the dragon, and the two beasts together. All relate to the tribulation of the church, and are united by a common duration of time (1260 days/42 months); see chapter 5, pp. 129–31. A detailed attempt to offer an overall structure of the text would, however, need to take full account of the apparent break between chs. 11 and 12, which leads many commentators to argue that 12:1 marks the beginning of a major new section in the text.

[58] See the further discussion in chapter 5, pp. 129–31.

therefore coincides with tribulation and martyrdom.[59] The positive side of that theme – the vindication of the faithful – is graphically combined with the renewed expansion of spatial horizons in 11:11ff., as God intervenes on earth and the witnesses are vindicated in their ascent to heaven (in a νεφέλη) see section 4.2). The interlude in 11:15–19 following the sounding of the seventh trumpet also intertwines these two themes: the expansion of the spatial horizon to encompass heaven affirms the reality of God's authority despite the apparent initial victory of the enemies of the two witnesses (11:15–16), while the vindication of God's servants is also reaffirmed (11:18).

In the second of the three visions, that of the woman and the dragon in 12:1–17, the spatial interaction between heaven and earth is perhaps at its most intense. The sequence here resembles the vision in Daniel 7–8 of parallel heavenly and earthly conflict, rather than the more usual Old Testament tradition of conflict *between* the heavenly host and human foes, as in Isaiah 24:21 and Judges 5:19–20.[60] This, then, is a classic example of the expansion of spatial horizons. By expanding his vision to include heaven and to unmask the demonic, John shows that the community has heavenly support in its conflict, which is not simply with human foes. But there is more to it than that: this episode is in fact a critical one in the spatial development of the entire text. The dragon, the ultimate eschatological adversary, suffers a defeat *which is expressed in spatial terms* (12:8, 'there was no longer any place – οὐδὲ τόπος εὑρέθη – for them in heaven'). In a sense, the casting down of the dragon and his restriction to earth (12:12) is one of the precursors to the eventual descent of the New Jerusalem. The downward dynamic of divine judgement/salvation has the effect of gradually limiting the areas of the cosmos within which the just rule of God can be challenged. It is therefore especially interesting that in the final preparation for the appearance of the new heaven, new earth and New Jerusalem, the disappearance of the old heaven and old earth is described in a way which echoes 12:8: 'no place was found – τόπος οὐχ εὑρέθη – for them' (20:11).

In the third of the three visions (the two beasts in 13:1–18) the spatial horizon is expanded downwards, to below the earth and sea, revealing

---

[59] Bauckham (1993a, ch. 9) argues in detail, using parallels in Daniel and Zechariah, that the often puzzling passage in 11:1–2 about the measuring of the inner court of the temple is in fact a representation of the two sides of martyrdom: the outward apparent defeat, and the inner reality of vindication. One might add that the measuring of only part of the city here contrasts with the measuring of the *whole* of the city in some detail in 21:15–17, stressing the contrast between the present, almost hidden preservation of God's people and their future manifest protection.

[60] See the discussion in Collins (1983a).

the ultimate origin of the two beasts who ascend from the sea and the land. The usual interpretation of the first beast, from the sea, is that it represents the imperial power of Rome. The mysterious saying which ends the vision of the first beast (11:9–10) can certainly be read as a condemnation of the violence of Roman rule and a call for the patient endurance of the saints, confident in the assurance that they will ultimately prevail. O'Donovan suggests that the beast of 13:1ff. represents more generally 'the pretensions of evil to provide a positive focus for social unity and cohesion'.[61] In other words, the beast offers the vision of a society which is the antithesis of that for which the church is called to strive. The most convincing explanation of the identity of the second beast is that it represents the imperial cult in the province of Asia. The advent of this beast clearly raises to a new level of intensity the pressure on the church to compromise. At about this time, a great altar and temple was erected to Domitian in Ephesus on a large terrace (100m × 50m), with a statue four times life size.[62] Price concludes: 'it is in principle quite likely that the establishment of the cult of Domitian at Ephesus, which involved the participation of the whole province, as attested by the series of dedications by numerous cities, led to unusually great pressure on the Christians for conformity'.[63] Hence John could possibly have perceived the cult as a powerful threat as early as the 90s CE, even though, as we have seen, widespread persecution of Christians at this point seems to have been unlikely.[64]

Spatial ambiguity and expectation (14:1–20)

14:1–5 looks forward in important ways to the New Jerusalem. It is of particular interest because the site of the Mount Zion upon which the Lamb and the 144,000 stand is ambiguous. Previously the 144,000 were mentioned as being sealed upon earth (7:4–8). Yet 14:2ff. suggests a location in heaven.[65] The most convincing explanation is offered by Fiorenza,

---

[61] O'Donovan (1986), p. 80.   [62] Description in Yamauchi (1980), pp. 84ff.
[63] S. R. F. Price (1984), p. 198.   [64] See chapter 3, pp. 57–61.
[65] There is an understandable divergence of view among commentators about the location of Mount Zion in this vision. Those favouring a heavenly setting include Mounce (1977, p. 267), Sweet (1979, p. 221), and Harrington (1993, pp. 146ff). Swete (1906, p. 174) and Roloff (1993, pp. 169ff.) suggest an earthly setting. Aune (1998a, pp. 803–4) and Bauckham (1993a, p. 230) argue that Mount Zion in 14:1 is an earthly location, and that the action shifts to heaven in 14:2. Bauckham suggests that, as in *4 Ezra* 13, the reference to Mount Zion is primarily an allusion to Ps. 2:5, which depicts the triumph of the messianic king over the hostile nations. Until 19:11 and the opening of heaven, manifest divine triumph is seen only in heaven, not on earth; hence the shift from earth to the immediate portrayal of triumph in heaven in 14:2.

who suggests a location which is neither heavenly nor earthly, but rather 'an eschatological place of protection and liberation'.[66] As such, it is an important link between the earthly sealing of the 144,000 in 7:3–8 and their promised home in the city, which belongs neither to the old heaven nor to the old earth. The 144,000 are identified with the Lamb (14:4; cf. the New Jerusalem as the wife of the Lamb, 21:9). Yet in comparison with the New Jerusalem there is still a sense of penultimacy about the vision. In 14:4 the 144,000 follow the Lamb wherever he goes (an image of movement)[67] whereas the faithful live constantly in the New Jerusalem (a more settled, stable image, suggesting that an ultimate destination has been reached). Moreover, 14:4 describes the 144,000 as first fruits, possibly in relation to the greater multitude in 15:2ff. (just as the 144,000 of 7:3–8 relates to a greater multitude in 7:9–17).

The remainder of this chapter (14:6–20) is also of importance in the spatial development of the book. The three angels uttering messages of final judgement, which will be implemented in the succeeding chapters, do so in midheaven (μεσουράνημα), one of the spatial indicators which John uses to signify communication between heaven and earth. It is fitting that this announcement is made from a point in the cosmos where it can be seen and heard by all. Moreover, the scene of preparation for ultimate judgement (14:14ff.) envisages the one like a son of man seated on a cloud (νεφέλη), another sign of movement between spatial planes.

The outworking of divine initiative on earth (2) (15:1–19:10)

The spatial focus of this section begins in heaven, with the appearance of the seven bowl angels in 15:1, and the scene of heavenly praise in 15:2–8, then switches almost entirely to earth, as judgement is executed upon those who worship the beast, and upon Babylon. Just as the appearance of the Lamb in heaven in 5:6 acted as a means of beginning to bridge the gap between heaven and earth, and as the descent of the strong angel in 10:1ff. introduced the visions of the church's tribulations within a heavenly perspective, so now, as the seven bowl angels prepare to execute final judgement by pouring their bowls down onto earth, there is a scene which begins in heaven but is orientated towards forthcoming

---

[66] Fiorenza (1991), p. 87. Beasley-Murray (1974, p. 222) also believes that the location is not simply heaven or earth.

[67] Aune (1998a, pp. 812–14) suggests that following the Lamb wherever he goes (14:4) is a metaphor for martyrdom. If correct, this would reinforce the sense of penultimacy, given that martyrdom in Revelation does not of course belong to the ultimate future.

activity on earth.[68] On the one hand, the angels are preparing to deliver terrible judgement, which does not lead to repentance, but rather blasphemy on the part of those affected (16:9, 11, 21). On the other hand, the 'song of Moses' envisages that all nations will come and worship before God (15:4). This apparent paradox in the seer's vision between separatism and universalism is never fully resolved, even in the New Jerusalem. As Bauckham argues, this is deliberate: final judgement and universalism have to coexist in the seer's vision, so that the text can achieve its aim of focusing the need for a human response to the divine initiative.[69]

The sequence of bowl judgements is followed by the description of the demise of Babylon. Babylon (an image of course from prophetic and apocalyptic tradition, but here clearly referring primarily to Rome) functions as a contrasting image to that of the other city, the New Jerusalem.[70] Politically, Babylon's fall is envisaged in 17:15–18. This is a difficult passage, but as has often been suggested, some kind of conflict within the Empire may be envisaged, perhaps a reaction by provincial rulers against the centre.[71] In any case, it seems clear that the passage is proclaiming that the political order established by Rome, founded on domination and violence, is inherently unstable, in comparison with the alternative polity of the New Jerusalem which does not end (22:5).

In parallel, 18:1–24 offers an economic critique of Babylon, and an account of the final fall of the great city in language which makes striking use of spatial movement. The announcement of the fall of Babylon is made by an angel with great authority (18:1–2), repeating the cry of 14:8: ἔπεσεν ἔπεσεν Βαβυλὼν ἡ μεγάλη.[72] The final fall of the city is strikingly symbolized by the casting down of the stone like a great millstone in 18:21. It is significant that the action is accomplished by an ἄγγελος ἰσχυρός, an expression which I have previously noted in connection with

---

[68] The pouring of bowls onto the earth is of course a graphic instance of downward movement from the heavenly to the earthly plane. The image of the outpouring of God's wrath is a common Old Testament device: cf. Ps. 69:25; Jer. 10:25; 42:18; 44:6; Zeph. 3:8.

[69] Bauckham (1993a), pp. 238–337.

[70] For a helpful list of the contrasts between the two cities, see Deutsch (1987), pp. 122–4.

[71] See, for example, Aune (1998b), pp. 250–61.

[72] The angel is described as making the earth bright with his splendour. Several commentators suggest a reference here to the return of the glory of God to the temple in Ezek. 43:2; see Caird (1984), p. 222; Mounce (1977), p. 322–3; Roloff (1993), p. 204. Beasley-Murray argues that the combination of this reference with the actual content of the angel's message serves to stress that divine judgement and redemption are intertwined (1974, p. 264).

key moments of downward orientation of the action from heaven to earth (5:2; 10:1).[73]

The outworking of divine initiative on earth (3) (19:11–20:15)

This passage represents the culmination of the process of judgement which began back in ch. 6 of the text. It begins with the striking image of heaven opened (19:11). The downward dynamic of divine judgement upon the earth is graphically illustrated. Not only does judgement originate in heaven with earthly effect, as in the three sequences of seals, trumpets and bowls, but the very boundary between heaven and earth is now removed to allow the final outworking of divine judgement.[74]

A detailed treatment of the complex history of interpretation of the millennial kingdom (20:4–6) is beyond the scope of this study.[75] However, it is important to note the role that the millennium plays in the spatial development of the text. It is the first point in the text at which the sovereignty of God is openly manifest on earth.[76] The enemies of God have been defeated, and the justice of God can be dispensed openly by his servants. Caird comments in relation to the millennium:

> like the Old Testament prophets before him, [John] really believed in the importance of the life men lead and the history nations fashion on this earthly scene. God is the Creator, and he has a purpose, not merely for isolated individuals of the human race . . . but for his creation as a whole. His purpose is worked out

[73] The economic critique of Rome in Rev. 18 has been analysed in detail by Yarbro Collins (1980) and Bauckham (1993a, pp. 338–83). The impression of provincial prosperity built on economic subservience is consonant with the results of historical investigation. There is little doubt that contemporary Asia Minor was generally prosperous, especially the cities; see Magie (1950). Yet this prosperity was built on dependence: Macro (1980) describes the attempts at social climbing by local élites in Asia Minor in the 90s CE. See also Kraybill's detailed analysis of the Roman patronage system as it operated in Asia Minor, and his comments on the relationship between maritime trade and the imperial cult (1996, chs. 2–3). The sense of economic exploitation running through the critique of Babylon in 18:1–24 contrasts strongly with the picture of the society of the New Jerusalem.

[74] The opening of the heavens is a common apocalyptic image. In contrast to the image of the door opened in heaven in 4:1, it tends not to accompany the idea of human ascent into heaven, but rather divine descent from heaven, or at least the manifestation of heavenly realities (cf. Ezek. 1:1; Matt. 3:16 and parallels; John 1:51; 2 *Bar.* 22:1).

[75] For a brief discussion of the significance of the millennium for the temporal dimension of the text, see chapter 5, pp. 134–5.

[76] Many recent commentators assume the millennium to be set on earth; see, for example, Beasley-Murray (1974), pp. 287–92; Caird (1984), p. 248–58; and Roloff (1993), p. 227. An alternative view, that the kingdom should be understood as heavenly, is suggested by Beale (1999), pp. 991ff.

in history and must be vindicated in history. There must come a
time on earth when it is true to say: 'the sovereignty of the world
has passed to our God and to his Christ'.[77]

The millennium is also a symbol of God's vindication of the martyrs,
who are specifically named as sharing in the rule of the kingdom. As
Bauckham comments: 'those whom the beast put to death are those who
will truly live – eschatologically, and . . . those who contested his right to
rule and suffered for it are those who will in the end rule as universally
as he – and for much longer: a thousand years!'[78] As an affirmation of
God's sovereignty over human history and the vindication, on earth, of his
people, the symbol of the millennium therefore provides support for the
idea that the text is offering not an escapist view of an alternative reality,
but a glimpse of an *encompassing* reality, within which the earthly present
is included.

The reach of God's judgement is extended to the utmost bounds of
the cosmos, as the eschatological enemies lying behind earthly reality are
finally conquered one by one and consigned to destruction, the two beasts
and the dragon in 20:10 and Death and Hades in 20:14. In addition, the old
heaven and earth flee in 20:11, so that the way is cleared for the descent
of the New Jerusalem in 21:1ff.[79] With the judgements of 16:1–18:24
and 19:11–20:15 the spatial dimensions of the text are broadened to such
an extent that all things – not just the visible realities of everyday life
but also the invisible realities which the text has revealed as underlying
them – are seen to be ultimately under God's control.

The New Jerusalem and the epilogue (21:1–22:21)

The resolution of spatial dissonance

The spatial setting of the book was established in 1:1–20 as the seer began
to expand the spatial horizons of the text beyond the visible realities of
this world. 4:1–5:14 saw the posing of the key problem – how could divine
rule be restored on the spatial plane of earth? – and the beginning of a
solution, with the appearance of the Lamb and the consequent earthward
orientation of divine activity. 5:1–14; 10:1–11 (the strong angel with the
scroll); and 16:1–21 (the bowl judgements) – all mark descents (either
actual descents, as in 10:1, or downward orientation, as in 5:1ff.) from
the heavenly plane to the earthly, as part of the process of the restoration
of divine rule. The descent of the New Jerusalem is the culmination of

---

[77] Caird (1984), p. 254.   [78] Bauckham (1993b), p. 107.
[79] Literally, no place is found for them: see above, p. 101.

this process.[80] It confirms the abolition of the spatial separation between the planes of heaven and earth. It sets the seal on the defeat of earthly and eschatological enemies. It fills the void left by the flight of the old earth which was subject to the ravages of God's enemies. But although there is discontinuity with the old earth, there is clearly also continuity, for example in the references to the nations in 21:24–6, and 22:2. Thus the culmination of Revelation reaffirms the unitive nature of the seer's vision.[81] For John, the vision of divine reality which asserts itself in the face of a distorted earthly picture is ultimately the encompassing paramount reality.

Also of importance for understanding the spatial significance of the New Jerusalem is its situation on a great, high mountain (21:10). The symbol of the mountain where God is encountered reaches far back into Old Testament tradition and beyond, and its history has been well covered.[82] Here, I shall simply draw out briefly those elements in the tradition which are especially relevant to my argument. First, the Old Testament symbol of Zion clearly goes back to the ancient tradition of the mountain as a cosmic meeting place. The theme of encounter with the divine is at the heart of Revelation 21–2. Second, the symbol of Zion has particular characteristics: for example, it expresses the extension of Yahweh's sovereignty from heaven to earth (e.g. Isa. 66:1); it is eternally secure (e.g. Ps. 125:1; cf. Rev. 22:5); the river of paradise flows from it (e.g. Ps. 46:5; cf. Rev. 22:1);

---

[80] The symbol of the New Jerusalem does of course occur widely elsewhere, either as a restored, earthly city (e.g. Tobit 13:9–18) or as a celestial city to which the just ascend (e.g. *2 Bar.* 4:1–7), but only in Revelation in this period does the city descend from heaven. See the discussion in Rissi (1972), pp. 41–51.

[81] Attempts to rationalize the apparent contradictions between 20:15 and 21:8 (in which those who do not follow the Lamb are thrown into the lake of fire) and 21:24 and 22:2 (in which life outside the city is still envisaged) are generally misguided. The danger is that interpreters seek to resolve the issue by taking those elements which agree with their theology as normative and discarding the others. For example, Mounce, in defence of a traditional evangelical understanding of the eschaton, takes 20:14–15 (the second death) at face value but urges against placing too much weight on the references to continuing life outside the city: he seems to regard these as awkward borrowings from the language of Jewish earthly eschatological expectation. He gives little justification for making this distinction (1977, pp. 367, 384–5). In contrast, Rissi tries in a rather unconvincing manner to harmonize logically the whole of 21:1–22:21 into one seamless account; this leads him to the strange conclusion that the nations who walk by the light of the city, and the kings of the earth who bring their glory into it, are situated in the lake of fire (Rissi, 1972, p. 68). It is surely wiser to acknowledge the ambiguities of the text, and to remember that the seer's aim is not to provide a neatly packaged historical survey, but rather an expanded perspective within which to view the present. Wilcox (1980) points out that a similar unclarity appears in 11QT from Qumran (the Temple Scroll), and that this may indicate that a common pre-existent tradition lies behind both texts. See also Aune (1998b, pp. 1171–2), who draws attention to the similarities with *Sibylline Oracles* 3:657–731.

[82] See Clifford (1972), Brueggemann (1978), R. L. Cohn (1981), Levenson (1985), Ollenburger (1987).

Yahweh triumphed there over the flood of chaos waters (e.g. Ps. 46:3; cf. Rev. 21:1). Third, these characteristics combine to provide a transcendent perspective on the world.[83]

The intensification of spatial dissonance

Thus the text has the effect of locating the present earthly experience of the reader within a framework of ultimate reality. It also, however, refocuses back to the hard realities of earthly experience, now seen in the light of that ultimate perspective. This refocusing back to the reader's earthly experience is evident from the epilogue (22:6–21), with its admonitions to the faithful to stand firm and 'keep the words of the book of this prophecy', and promises of imminent divine intervention, which echo 1:1–8. As in 1:1–8, reference is made to an angelic intermediary sent by God to show his servants what must soon take place. The prophetic nature of the book is affirmed (22:6, 6, 7, 10, 18–19; cf. 1:3) as is John's standing as a prophet (22:8–10; cf. 1:1, 9–10); the book is to be read in the churches (22:18; cf. 1:3, 11) to encourage the faithful (22:7, 12, 14).

I have argued that with the juxtaposition of 2:1–3:22 and 4:1–11 a fundamental dissonance is established between the vision of the all-embracing sovereignty of God expressed in the throne vision and the earthly reality of life for John's communities, alluded to in the seven messages. At one level, this tension is resolved with the descent of the New Jerusalem. But at another level, the tension is, if anything, intensified for the reader. As the narrative of the text unfolds, the reader sees the effective establishment of the sovereignty and justice of God and the vindication of his people, so that God's rule is acknowledged not only in heaven, but also explicitly on earth. And the extension of God's rule to the earthly plane is graphically represented by the descent of the New Jerusalem. Yet in the earthly present, that rule still appears to be partial or limited. So contradiction or dissonance remains, despite the ultimate perspectives opened up by the text. The text does not advocate escape, but holding to the vision of the all-embracing sovereignty of God in dialectical relationship with the tribulations of earthly experience, both of which are parts of a single, ultimate, spatial reality.

---

[83] Levenson (1985, p. 101) argues that the promises relating to the Davidic possession of Zion in 2 Kings 8:19 and elsewhere 'are a sign that beneath and beyond the pain and chaos of the realm we call history, there is another realm, upheld by the indefectible promise of God'.

5

THE TEMPORAL DIMENSION OF THE BOOK OF REVELATION

5.1   Introduction

In this chapter I attempt to illustrate that the text offers a view of reality which is irreducibly temporal, without giving a chronological account of history. My aim is to show how John seeks to set the present experience of his readers within ultimate temporal horizons in order to provide a deeper understanding of reality, while at the same time focusing on the present situation of the communities to which he writes.

In chapter 4 I used a heavily modified version of a method adopted by Elizabeth Struthers Malbon in her analysis of the Gospel of Mark. By categorizing the spatial references in the text into groupings relating to ancient conceptions of the arrangement of the cosmos, I sought to map out the development of the spatial dimension of the text. I discussed at length how the text uses spatial categories to establish in 2:1–4:11 a dissonance between the way things appear to be on earth and the way things really are in the cosmos created by God. In 5:1ff., with the appearance of the Lamb, a long process begins in which this dissonance is intensified and finally resolved, in 21:1ff., in the vision of the New Jerusalem, where spatial distinctions between heaven and earth are removed, transforming the cosmos. I also commented that the New Jerusalem operates not only as a point of resolution but also as a starting point, from which the readers of the text must work as they face once again the present reality portrayed in the earlier visions. As the analysis in this chapter shows, the temporal development of the text mirrors this pattern strikingly. In 2:1–4:11 a fundamental dissonance is established between the way things appear to be in the time of John's communities and the way things are within the everlasting reign of God. In 5:1ff., this dissonance begins to be broken down, and it is again finally resolved in the New Jerusalem, where the everlasting reign of God is manifested explicitly.

5.2   The temporal categories of the text

Temporal categories

The method I have adopted in analysing the temporal dimension of Revelation has been to categorize the temporal references in the text in relation to five different categories: present, primordial past, historical past, penultimate future and ultimate future. These are categories which suggested themselves as I examined the text: I did not start out with them as a preconceived framework. Of course, whether certain passages should be taken as referring to the past, present or future is in itself a matter of considerable debate among commentators, and inevitably I have had to come to judgements in these cases. I have drawn attention to such passages in the course of the exegesis.

The category of 'present' includes all those references which I take to relate to the present from the point of view of John and the communities to whom he writes. This covers both references of a punctiliar nature, such as the injunction to hear (ἀκουσάτω, aorist imperative) in each of the messages to the seven churches, and also references which may be taken as describing a current state of affairs, such as Οἶδα ποῦ κατοικεῖς in 2:13. It covers references both to the earthly present and to the present in heaven as it is conceived by John. The category of 'primordial past' is, I think, self-explanatory: it includes, for example, references to the creation of the world. The category of 'historical past' includes references both to the distant past (e.g. the song of Moses in 15:3) and to the recent past (e.g. the martyrdom of Antipas in 2:13).

More comment is needed about the division of future temporal references into penultimate and ultimate. In the category of 'penultimate future' I have included all those references to circumstances which, although envisaged by John as occurring at some point in the future, are not seen by him as enduring permanently into the everlasting state described in 21:1–22:5. The category includes references to a variety of different circumstances, such as judgement (e.g. 2:16) and tribulation (e.g. 2:10). Other future references, which *do* relate to that everlasting state are included in the category of 'ultimate future'. At first sight, this may appear to be an unusual course to have taken. Other possibilities would have been to categorize episodes in the text in some kind of chronological order, or to distinguish between those which are envisaged as imminent and those which are not. However, such an approach would have been misconceived, for two main reasons. First, as early as 1:1, all the contents of the visionary sections of the book are referred to generally as ἃ δεῖ γενέσθαι ἐν τάχει. Therefore, although certain references are specifically described as imminent (see 22:7), there is no reasonable way of disentangling these from the contents of the text as a whole. Rather, the clearer distinction is between those future circumstances which John envisages as enduring and those which he envisages as temporary. Second, there is in any case no real basis for constructing a chronological pattern out of the visions. For example, most commentators reject the idea that the sevenfold visions of seals, trumpets and bowls should be seen as following on from one another in a linear sequence, in favour of seeing them as recapitulating the same circumstances from different perspectives. Hence my basic argument that while the text has irreducibly temporal elements within it (the basis of my five categories of temporal reference), it is misguided to seek to construct a chronological scheme out of it.[1] Analysing the text by means of temporal categories, rather than attempting to discern chronologies, enables distinctions to be made between the *narrative* sequence of the text and the *temporal* sequence envisaged by the seer. My analysis of the temporal dimension of the text therefore relies on examining the interplay between the temporal categories and the narrative, or, to put it another way, between the eschatological and narratological development of the text.

Textual markers

My decision to divide future temporal references into those dealing with the penultimate future and those with the ultimate future is also based on an examination of the way in which John uses particular words and groups of words to signal these two categories.

Expressing the penultimate future

In the case of the penultimate future, John makes extensive use of a small number of key words in his treatment of the expected tribulation of the church and the associated need for faithfulness and endurance. Three examples of this are especially important.

(1) νικάω (conquer, overcome) occurs fifteen times in the text. Of these, seven (2:7, 11, 17, 26; 3:5, 12, 21) are related to exhortations and promises to each of the seven churches. As an example, 2:7 states: τῷ νικῶντι δώσω αὐτῷ φαγεῖν ἐκ τοῦ ξύλου τῆς ζωῆς, ὅ ἐστιν ἐν τῷ παραδείσῳ τοῦ θεοῦ. In each of the seven messages, the one who overcomes, or conquers,

---

[1] See my discussion above of attempts to relate the text to human history (section 3.2).

in the testing which lies ahead is offered a subsequent, and permanent, reward. In a further three references (12:11; 15:2; 21:7) νικάω is again used in the context of the saints' overcoming: in 12:11 they overcome the dragon through the blood of the Lamb; in 15:2 it relates to their overcoming the beast; and 21:7 is a final climactic reference embedded in the promises associated with the New Jerusalem – the one who overcomes in the penultimate future will inherit in the ultimate future. Two references relate to Christ himself: in 5:5 the Lion of Judah is said to have conquered (it can be argued that part of the reason νικάω is used here is to stress the exemplary role of Christ for the church in its expected tribulation); in 17:14 the Lamb conquers the ten kings, in one of the episodes marking the penultimate future.[2]

(2) τηρέω occurs eleven times in the text (1:3; 2:26; 3:3, 8, 10 (twice); 12:17; 14:12; 16:15; 22:7, 9), always in the context of the need for faithfulness and endurance in the time before the ultimate future. Three of these references occur in the introduction and epilogue, where the exhortation to keep the words of the prophecy of the book (by implication, during a coming time when such a stance will be threatened) is combined with a warning that the 'time is near'.[3] In 2:26 τηρέω is used together with νικάω in the context of the need to do the works of Christ to the end (ἄχρι τέλους), and in 3:3 the church in Sardis is urged to keep (τηρέω) that which they received and heard. In 3:8 and 3:10 the Philadelphians are commended for the way in which they have kept Christ's word to date, and this is linked with a promise that in return they will be 'kept' during the coming tribulation. In 12:17 the dragon makes war on the children of the woman, the ones who keep (τηρέω) the commandments of God, and in 14:12 they are called to persevere. The final reference, 16:15, is the only instance of τηρέω being used to mean literally 'keep' (an object), rather than 'observe', but here also the idea is linked to behaviour in the present and penultimate future. Christ is coming soon: blessed is the one who keeps his garment so that his nakedness is not exposed. I have noted that in 2:26 τηρέω is used together with νικάω (see above). It is

---

[2] The remaining three uses of νικάω relate neither to Christ nor to the saints. Bauernfeind (1967, pp.944–5) argues that while the other twelve references should be taken as relating to the prelude to a final, unlimited victory, these three relate to earthly, provisional victories. This may be so, but it does not get us very far. It is important to note the ironic content of two of the references (11:7 and 13:7), which relate to conquest by the beast: the point is that what appears to be conquest will eventually be shown to be defeat. The one remaining reference, in 6:2, comes in the description of the rider who appears with the breaking of the first seal.

[3] 1:3; 22:7, 9. Although the form is slightly different in each case, all three references link τηρέω, λόγος and προφητεία closely.

important also that in two of these references, 3:10 and 14:12, τηρέω is closely associated with a third term, ὑπομονή.

(3) At the outset (1:9) John uses ὑπομονή to describe his own position, sharing in Jesus the tribulation, the kingdom and the ὑπομονή (NRSV: 'patient endurance'). It is used in 2:2, 3; 2:19; and 3:10 to commend the qualities of the churches at Ephesus and Thyatira. At 13:10, in the midst of the persecution by the beast, comes the exhortation: 'Ὧδέ ἐστιν ἡ ὑπομονὴ καὶ ἡ πίστις τῶν ἁγίων; and at 14:12 there is a similar exhortation, this time in the context of encouragement through the proleptic vision of judgement over the beast's followers, and now associated with keeping (τηρέω) the commandments of God. The repetition of this exhortation, first in the context of persecution and second in the context of subsequent deliverance from persecution is not just for emphasis: it carries with it the sense of temporal progression, as faithful endurance characterizes the saints through the present and the penultimate future. More generally, ὑπομονή always bears the connotation of temporal progression, whether one judges it to mean 'endurance' or 'expectation'.[4]

Thus, John's use of νικάω, τηρέω and ὑπομονή is one example of his consistent use of key expressions to indicate the penultimate future. Another example is apparent in his sophisticated use of number.[5] It has often been commented that part of John's purpose in using the number seven so frequently is to express a sense of completeness in the activity of God. It seems to be noticed less often that he uses the number three and a half, exactly half of seven, to express incompleteness or limitedness.[6] In this context, the connection made by the use of the formula of three and a half years (= 42 months = 1260 days = 'time and times and half a time') in the visions of the two witnesses (11:2, 3), of the dragon and the woman (12:6, 14) and of the beast (13:5) acquires new significance. Not only are the visions (as is often noted) covering the same period of time, but they are also describing events which are of an inherently limited duration, and therefore circumstances which will not ultimately prevail.

---

[4] Hauck (1967, p. 588) takes 1:9 and possibly 3:10 to mean expectation, and the rest of the references to mean endurance. He cites Lohmeyer's comment, in relation to Revelation, that 'ὑπομονή is an endurance which is grounded in waiting, a waiting which expresses itself in endurance'.

[5] See Bauckham (1993a), pp. 1–37, for a detailed discussion of John's use of number.

[6] Roloff (1993) is an exception, remarking that John uses halves of symbolic whole numbers (such as three and a half) to indicate a 'situation of crisis and transition' (p. 102). The symbolic number three and a half is of course drawn from the apocalyptic tradition reflected in Daniel; see the discussion below, pp. 129–31.

Expressing the ultimate future

John uses the term καινός to relate solely to concepts associated with the ultimate future. It occurs three times in the seven messages (2:17, the promise of a new name; 3:12, again a new name, and the New Jerusalem), twice with reference to new songs in heaven (5:9 and 14:3) and then four times in 21:1–5, with the descent of the New Jerusalem and the climactic statement from the one seated on the throne: 'Ιδοὺ καινὰ ποιῶ πάντα. Καινός is being used to express the new, the unprecedented, the marvellous, and that which will have permanent validity.[7] As Behm comments, 'καινός is the epitome of the wholly different and miraculous thing which is brought about by the time of salvation. Hence "new" is a leading teleological term in apocalyptic promise.'[8]

Activity across temporal boundaries

Of course, many temporal references in the text cannot be pinned down as relating only to the historical past or the present or the penultimate or ultimate future. There is inevitably much blurring of the edges, especially since, as I have argued, one of the the the seer's central aims is to illuminate the present situation by referring to the future and the past.

In particular, as will become clearer in the detailed examination of the text, there is an interplay between references to restricted periods of time, usually present, and unlimited time. This is shown especially in the frequent use of formulae involving αἰών in the heavenly scenes, often in a doxological context.[9] I shall try to demonstrate, as the examination of the text proceeds, the role which these formulae play in the expansion of the temporal horizons of the text.

The analysis which follows therefore treats the text in a way which preserves a temporal sense by setting it in a framework which includes past, present, penultimate future and ultimate future. However, this framework is sufficiently flexible to accommodate the temporal dimension of the text without forcing it into a chronological straitjacket. I shall attempt to show how the development of the temporal horizons of the text expands backwards from the present through the historical and primordial past, and forwards from the present into the penultimate and ultimate future. I

---

[7] Compare the use of καινός elsewhere in the New Testament to convey such qualities, for example, new creation in 2 Cor. 5:17 (which Aune (1998b, p. 1125) describes as 'a microcosmic application of the apocalyptic notion of the recreation or renewal of the world'), and the new commandment in John 13:34.

[8] Behm (1965), p. 449.   [9] See 1:6; 4:9, 10; 5:13; 7:12; 10:6; 11:15; 15:3?, 7; 22:5.

shall also attempt to show that with this expansion comes a renewed and sharpened focus on the present, through the dynamic dissonance evident between the vision of the New Jerusalem and present earthly historical reality in which the reader has to live.

5.3   Analysis of the text

Patmos and divine epiphany (1:1–20)

In my analysis of the spatial dimensions of 1:1–20 I remarked that the action takes place in a clearly earthly setting, Patmos, but that the seer is already beginning to intertwine the everyday context of Asia Minor with a wider, encompassing, spatial reality. A similar process is at work in the temporal dimension. On the one hand, there are clear indications that the text is anchored in the present. John is addressing seven churches which are situated in contemporary Asia Minor (1:4), and he shares with them common experiences of suffering in relation to faith in Christ (1:9). The time of his visionary experience is located as ἐν τῇ κυριακῇ ἡμέρα, on the Lord's Day (1:10).

Yet, at the same time, the seer is beginning to expand the temporal horizon beyond the present. In the very first verse, attention is directed to the imminent future: John has been shown ἃ δεῖ γενέσθαι ἐν τάχει. The precise scope of this reference is much debated. It certainly indicates divine foreknowledge of, and sovereignty over history.[10] But can anything further be said? What exactly does John expect to come quickly? This has caused considerable difficulty to commentators, especially to those whose instinct is to take such references at face value, but who find problems in accommodating John's imminent expectation with the fact that, 1900 years later, the parousia has not happened. Caird's distinctive response that John is referring not to the parousia at all, but to persecution, is one solution, but not a particularly plausible one, since it evades the natural sense of the reference in 1:1, which must surely refer to the text in general.[11] More convincing is the kind of solution put forward by Ladd, who argues that the note of imminence sounded in 1:1 stands in the

---

[10] Hence Mounce (1977), p. 64: 'The express purpose of God in giving the revelation is to show his servants the things which must shortly come to pass. History is not a haphazard sequence of unrelated events but a divinely decreed ordering of that which must come to pass. It is a logical necessity arising from the nature of God and the revelation of his purpose in creation and redemption.' See also Roloff (1993), p. 19.

[11] Caird (1984), p. 12. His conclusion fits with his overall interpretation of the text as not looking to the end as such, but rather using eschatological language to speak of things (persecution, conversion etc.) which John consciously knows not to be end-time

prophetic tradition which always tended to see the future as imminent, and which had little regard for chronology.[12] The point of the imminence of the expectation thus becomes, as much as anything, a spur to the reader to live in an attitude of expectation and watchfulness. The repetition of ἃ δεῖ γενέσθαι ἐν τάχει in the epilogue (22:6) underlines the importance of imminent expectation on the part of the readers in their present context.

Also relevant here is my earlier discussion of Rayner's findings about the tendency of small, tightly knit groups to collapse the future into the present, and of Malina's argument that New Testament writers saw the future as growing organically out of the present.[13] This is helpful in interpreting ὁ γὰρ καιρὸς ἐγγύς (1:3), which Beasley-Murray describes as a 'foreshortening – one might call it telescopic – view of history'.[14] Note that the time is not merely imminent: most commentators interpret καιρός here as referring to the events of the whole book, rather than simply their onset. Thus 1:3 represents a conviction that the ultimate deliverance described in 21:1ff. is close at hand. In order to attain that deliverance, it is necessary to remain faithful through the penultimate tests ahead: in 1:3 John uses τηρέω to convey this.[15] The effect of 1:1–3 is both to begin to expand temporal horizons into the future and to begin to distinguish between the ultimate and the penultimate future.

1:4 contains the first appearance of the formula describing God as ὁ ὢν καὶ ὁ ἦν καὶ ὁ ἐρχόμενος. This formula also occurs in 1:8, and in slightly different forms in 4:8; 11:17; and 16:5.[16] The use of ὁ ἐρχόμενος has been seen by several commentators as emphasizing God's relationship to the world. Beasley-Murray writes that 'God not only transcends the ages, and awaits us from the future. It is of his nature that he "comes" from the future

events. See also Caird (1980), ch. 14. However, this seems to me to beg various hermeneutical questions. The challenge of interpreting Revelation for today comes from acknowledging that, on a natural reading of the text, John did indeed expect the end to come quickly.
[12] Ladd (1972), p. 22. Also Mounce (1977), pp. 64–5. Beale (1999) suggests an alternative: 'The focus of "quickness" and "nearness" in vv. 1–3 is primarily on inauguration of prophetic fulfillment and its ongoing aspect, not on nearness of consummated fulfillment, though the latter is secondarily in mind as leading from the former' (p. 182).
[13] See chapter 3, p. 54.   [14] Beasley-Murray (1978), p. 52.
[15] See above, pp. 112–13. Roloff comments in relation to John's use of τηρέω here: 'It is John's conviction that the hearers can withstand the afflictions of the end time that are coming to them only if they adhere, in thought and behavior, to the firm basis of the message that is declared to them' (1993, p. 21).
[16] At 4:8 the same components are present, in a different order: ὁ ἦν καὶ ὁ ὢν καὶ ὁ ἐρχόμενος. In 11:17 and 16:5 it is shortened to ὁ ὢν καὶ ὁ ἦν. It may be that ἐρχόμενος is dropped in these later references to make the point that divine initiative is now no longer awaited, but is under way.

and works his gracious and powerful will.'[17] The immediate context of a greeting to the seven churches is interesting: John is juxtaposing a primarily present temporal reference (the seven churches which are in Asia) with a reference to everlasting reality (the one who was and is and is to come). There is a clear focus on the present in the light of the everlasting. This juxtaposition of the present moment and the continuity of God is an important instance of the time threshold described by Wheelwright as calling forth the use of tensive language.[18]

The succession of statements in 1:5–6 about the work of Christ also serves to expand the temporal horizons of the reader. The designation ὁ πρωτότοκος τῶν νεκρῶν (1:5) has caused much debate. While some see πρωτότοκος as referring primarily to Christ's sovereignty,[19] others, I think rightly, want to preserve the temporal element in the meaning of the word, so that it carries the dynamic implication that resurrection from the dead is a process over time, with Christ as the pioneer, whom the faithful will follow in due course.[20] Thus the text introduces interplay between the present and the future, with the sense that a dynamic process of redemption is at work, still awaiting its resolution. In addition, this process is anchored in the historical past of the Christ event, a point underlined by the description of Christ as Τῷ ἀγαπῶντι ἡμᾶς καὶ λύσαντι ἡμᾶς ἐκ τῶν ἁμαρτιῶν ἡμῶν ἐν τῷ αἵματι αὐτοῦ (1:5).[21] The statements about Christ are then rounded off by a doxology which stretches the temporal horizon to the utmost past and the ultimate future, using the formula εἰς τοὺς αἰῶνας [τῶν αἰώνων] (1:6). Once again in 1:7 attention is focused on the future, with the use of the traditional apocalyptic material, ᾿Ιδοὺ ἔρχεται μετὰ τῶν νεφελῶν. With many commentators, I take this to be primarily a proleptic reference to the parousia,[22] although the present tense of ἔρχεται also suggests to some commentators a reference to the present lordship of Christ as experienced in the church, thus again linking present and future together, and seeing the present in the light of future consummation.[23]

---

[17] Beasley-Murray (1978), p. 54. Giblin suggests that John uses this formula in a polemical fashion, to emphasize the interventionist nature of God, over against ἐγώ εἰμι πᾶν τὸ γεγονὸς καὶ ὢν καὶ ἐσόμενον in the inscription on the statue of Isis at Sais (1991, p. 41).

[18] See chapter 3, pp. 68–9.

[19] Charles (1920), vol. I, p. 14; Mounce (1977), pp. 70–1.

[20] Beasley-Murray (1978), pp. 56–7; Caird (1984), pp. 16–17; and the fuller discussion in Aune (1997), pp. 38–9. Also Bartels (1975), pp. 668–9.

[21] Swete (1906, p. 7) comments on the present tense of ἀγαπάω here as implying a distinction between the past act of redemption and the continuing love of Christ.

[22] See, for example, Aune (1997), pp. 53–6.

[23] See in particular Caird (1984), pp. 18–19.

Of particular importance in this opening section is 1:8: Ἐγώ εἰμι τὸ Ἄλφα καὶ τὸ Ὦ, λέγει κύριος ὁ θεός, ὁ ὢν καὶ ὁ ἦν καὶ ὁ ἐρχόμενος, ὁ παντοκράτωρ. This is one of only two instances in the book when God himself speaks. The other is 21:5–8, of which I shall have more to say in due course. For now, it is worthy of note that both statements have a strongly temporal content (see particularly 21:5, Ἰδοὺ καινὰ ποιῶ πάντα; and 21:6, ἐγώ [εἰμι] τὸ Ἄλφα καὶ τὸ Ὦ, ἡ ἀρχὴ καὶ τὸ τέλος). God defines himself in relation to the world by using temporal categories; this is of great importance for understanding the overall temporal frame-work within which the seer understands earthly reality. The time-frame within which God operates is infinitely greater than the present moment, yet he is also intimately involved in human time. Beasley-Murray makes the point that the phrase A to Ω would probably have carried the connota-tion not just of the beginning and the end but also all points in between, so that God is sovereign at all times, even when other forces apparently have the upper hand.[24] This relationship between the everlasting time of God and human history is reinforced in 1:17–18, where Christ declares: ἐγώ εἰμι ὁ πρῶτος καὶ ὁ ἔσχατος καὶ ὁ ζῶν, καὶ ἐγενόμην νεκρὸς καὶ ἰδοὺ ζῶν εἰμι εἰς τοὺς αἰῶνας τῶν αἰώνων καὶ ἔχω τὰς κλεῖς τοῦ θανάτου καὶ τοῦ ᾅδου. Affirmations of a very high Christology are combined with allu-sions to the death and resurrection of Jesus: the infinite temporal perspec-tive of God (ὁ πρῶτος καὶ ὁ ἔσχατος ... εἰς τοὺς αἰῶνας τῶν αἰώνων) with events in the historical perspective of human history (ἐγενόμην νεκρὸς καὶ ἰδοὺ ζῶν εἰμι).

Finally, in this opening section, it is necessary to turn to a verse which has provoked a great deal of debate, 1:19: γράψον οὖν ἃ εἶδες καὶ ἃ εἰσὶν καὶ ἃ μέλλει γενέσθαι μετὰ ταῦτα; literally, 'write then those things which you see and those things which are and those things which are about to come after these'. Previous generations of commentators sought in this verse some indication that the text as a whole could be divided into different parts, corresponding to the different components of the verse. Hence, for example, Swete sees ἃ εἶδες as referring to the vision of Christ in 1:12–20; ἃ εἰσίν to 2:1–3:22, as the present situation of the church; and ἃ μέλλει ... as referring mainly to the rest of the text.[25] However, a critical consensus now seems to have emerged to the effect that the verse should be taken as referring to the text as a whole, mainly because it is simplistic to regard parts of the text as referring only to the past, or the present, or

[24] Beasley-Murray (1978), p. 59.
[25] Swete (1906), p. 20. Charles (1920), vol. I, p. 33, adopts a similar line, as – in a modified form – does Ladd (1972), p. 34.

the future.[26] The seer's treatment of time is more complex than that: there is a constant interplay between different temporal categories through the whole text.

To sum up this first section: the seer anchors his experience and his message firmly in the present. Yet already, the reader is aware of a wider temporal context, embracing the primordial and historical past, and the penultimate and ultimate future. The scene has been set, upon which the action of the book is to take place.

The messages to the seven churches: present realities in ultimate perspective (2:1–3:22)

In chapter 4 I argued that although the setting of the seven messages is primarily earthly, the spatial horizon of the narrative is stretched to encompass a wider reality: the messages demonstrate the solidarity of the one like a son of man (who transcends spatial boundaries) with the communities of his followers, whatever their situation. My contention here is that a similar process occurs in respect of the temporal dimension of the text. Each message is firmly rooted in the present situation of the church; at the same time, each message places the church's experience in the perspective of ultimate temporal horizons. As Bauckham comments in relation to the messages: 'The Spirit's prophetic ministry is both to expose the truth in this world of deceit and ambiguity, and to point to the eschatological age when the truth of all things will come to light. To live faithfully and courageously according to the truth of God now requires a vision of that eschatological future.'[27]

In my previous chapter I noted the similarities in the structure of the seven messages: each includes an instruction to write to the angel of the relevant church, a prophetic utterance of the risen Christ prefaced by the formula τάδε λέγει; an eschatological promise, sometimes linked with a warning; and an exhortation to hear what the Spirit says to the churches. I also noted that this structure followed an important spatial pattern, not to my knowledge observed by commentators. The same is true in the temporal dimension. In each of the messages there is a fivefold temporal structure.

---

[26] See Mounce (1977), pp. 81–2; Caird (1984), p. 26; Roloff (1993), p. 38. Beale (1999) gives an overview of different interpretations of this verse, arguing also that it should be taken as referring to the whole of the text. In addition, he postulates a specific dependence on Daniel 2 (pp. 152–70).

[27] Bauckham (1993b), p. 125.

First, at the beginning of each message there is a self-reference to the risen Christ. One function of these references is to set what follows in the widest possible temporal context. Christ has just stated: ἐγώ εἰμι ὁ πρῶτος καὶ ὁ ἔσχατος καὶ ὁ ζῶν, καὶ ἐγενόμην νεκρὸς καὶ ἰδοὺ ζῶν εἰμι εἰς τοὺς αἰῶνας τῶν αἰώνων (1:17b–18). Therefore, by implication, the references to Christ at the head of each of the messages suggest the widest temporal perspective: they relate to one whose existence is everlasting. This is explicitly underlined in the message to Smyrna: Τάδε λέγει ὁ πρῶτος καὶ ὁ ἔσχατος, ὃς ἐγένετο νεκρὸς καὶ ἔζησεν (2:8). It is, I think, also strongly suggested in the messages to Philadelphia and Laodicea.[28] The idea is less immediately present in the designations used of Christ in the other four messages, but in each case the description of Christ refers explicitly back to the vision of 1:12–18, and therefore to the one who is ὁ πρῶτος καὶ ὁ ἔσχατος.[29] Moreover, all four descriptions use a construction of definite article and present participle (e.g. ὁ κρατῶν... ὁ περιπατῶν in 2:1), which suggests a continuous state.

The second temporal component in each message is a reference to the current situation of the church. This takes the form of encouragement or criticism in relation to the present conduct of each community, always introduced by οἶδα, I know. In the cases of Ephesus (the testing of false apostles), Pergamum (the martyrdom of Antipas) and Philadelphia (the keeping of Christ's word), this reference explicitly takes in the conduct of the community in the recent past as well as the present. The emphasis is, however, firmly on the present context. I argued in chapter 4 (pp. 89–92) that the seven messages begin to develop a sense of spatial tension between the reality of God and Christ, to which 1:1–20 points, and the earthly situation of the church in its difficulty and complexity. This spatial tension is both heightened and paradoxically gradually resolved through the remainder of the book until it is finally removed with the descent of the New Jerusalem and the abolition of the distinction between heaven and earth. The seven messages play a similar role in respect of the temporal dimension of the text. As I noted in the previous paragraph, each message begins with a reference to the figure of Christ, which is set

---

[28] In the message to Philadelphia, Christ is described as ὁ ἀνοίγων καὶ οὐδεὶς κλείσει καὶ κλείων καὶ οὐδεὶς ἀνοίγει (3:7). This carries the implication that the actions of Christ have an everlasting validity. In the message to Laodicea, Christ is described as ἡ ἀρχὴ τῆς κτίσεως τοῦ θεοῦ (3:14); most commentators take this to refer to the idea of Christ as the origin and source of creation (cf. Swete, 1906, pp. 58–9; Charles, 1920, vol. I, pp. 94; Ladd, 1972, p. 65; Mounce, 1977, p. 124). Beale (1999, p. 301) argues that the reference is to Christ's inauguration of the new creation.

[29] 2:2 (Ephesus) refers back explicitly to 1:13 and 1:16. 2:12 (Pergamum) refers to 1:16. 2:18 (Thyatira) refers to 1:14–15; and 3:1 (Sardis) to 1:4 and 1:16.

in the present, while also locating what follows in an ultimate temporal context (Christ is ὁ πρῶτος καὶ ὁ ἔσχατος). In each case, this is then juxtaposed with a reference to the present situation of the church. Although the sovereignty of Christ is a present reality which stretches back and forward to ultimate temporal horizons, there is a sense in which it is not yet fully manifest in the present experience of the church. In the church's present there are still persecutors, false prophets and the internal enemies, lukewarmness and lack of love. Yet the text constantly urges that this state of affairs is not permanent.

The third temporal element in each message is a reference to the penultimate future. This can include references to the need to withstand coming tribulation (e.g. 2:10; 3:10) as well as warnings about impending divine judgment (2:5, 16; 3:3, 16). I mentioned above (pp. 111–13) the important role played by the terms νικάω, ὑπομονή and τηρέω in John's portrayal of the penultimate future: all three feature in the seven messages. In each message, an eschatological promise is made to ὁ νικῶν (2:7, 11, 17, 26; 3:5, 12, 21). It is those who overcome in the forthcoming, and penultimate, test who will inherit in the ultimate future. This is made particularly clear in the message to Thyatira, in which ὁ νικῶν is described as ὁ τηρῶν ἄχρι τέλους τὰ ἔργα μου (2:26). Τηρέω occurs also in 3:10, in the context of Christ's preserving the faithful through the tests to come. Ὑπομονή is mentioned in 2:2, 19 and 3:10; while in each case the immediate reference is to Christ's commendation of the church's demonstration of patient endurance in the past leading into the present, the nature of the quality of ὑπομονή and the context of coming tribulation also suggest the relevance of ὑπομονή to the penultimate future. The one who overcomes will be the one who endures.

Fourth, in each message, following the references to the everlasting Christ, the present situation of the church and the penultimate future, there come references to the ultimate future. In the last four messages (Thyatira, Sardis, Philadelphia, Laodicea) this reference precedes a final exhortation to listen to what the Spirit says to the churches, while in the first three messages, this order is reversed. Either way, the reference to eschatological blessing for the one who overcomes serves to place each message in the widest temporal framework. The dissonance between these promises and the present situation of the church produces a sense of eschatological tension which will be resolved only with the descent of the New Jerusalem. I noted in my previous chapter the strong connections between the promises in the messages and the New Jerusalem. The promises are not conceived of only in the spatial dimension, but also temporally. They are explicitly eschatological.

Finally, the repetition in all the messages of the exhortation ὁ ἔχων οὖς ἀκουσάτω τί τὸ πνεῦμα λέγει ταῖς ἐκκλησίαις brings the focus explicitly back to the present. One of my main contentions about the text is that while its temporal horizons extend to the ultimate future (and the primordial past), it remains focused on the present, so that, for example, the New Jerusalem represents a starting point as much as a *telos*. In a sense, each of the messages reproduces this pattern in microcosm. The references to the penultimate and ultimate future in each message are there to enable the community to see the present in wider perspective.

The revelation of the heavenly perspective (4:1–11)

The vision of the heavenly court in 4:1ff. is one of the pivotal points of the whole text. Seen in the context of the messages to the seven churches, it provides a stark contrast between the way things are in heaven, under the manifest sovereignty of the creator, and the way things appear to be in the earthly present, represented by the situations of the seven churches. This juxtaposition produces tension at a spatial level (the apparent limitation of God's sovereignty in the earthly sphere) and also at a temporal level (is this discrepancy permanent?). The tension is in fact reinforced by the recurrence in 4:1–11 of features from the promises in seven messages, suggesting that resolution of the dissonance may be possible, although it is not manifest on earth.

The vision of heaven is introduced by a voice saying to John: Ἀνάβα ὧδε, καὶ δείξω σοι ἃ δεῖ γενέσθαι μετὰ ταῦτα (4:1). This formulation has caused disagreement among commentators about the temporal setting of the vision. Some, taking the introduction rigidly to refer to what follows, assume therefore that the vision of heaven in 4:1–11 must be located at a point in the future.[30] This approach seems to me, however, misguided. As I argued earlier, it is simply not possible to assign large sections of the text solely to the past, present or future: its treatment of time is more complex than that. Following a second group of commentators,[31] I take the vision in 4:1–11 to possess a timeless quality, which suggests that the scene of worship is continuous in heaven. Elements of the description clearly imply that it is a glimpse of a continuous picture of heavenly worship. John says that the living creatures ἀνάπαυσιν οὐκ ἔχουσιν ἡμέρας καὶ νυκτός in their worship (4:8).[32] They praise God as ὁ ἦν καὶ ὁ ὢν καὶ

---

[30] See Swete (1906), pp. 65–6; Charles (1920), vol. I, p. 109.

[31] E.g. Beasley-Murray (1978), p. 111; Roloff (1993), p. 69.

[32] Note the ironic contrast with the punishment of the worshippers of the beast: καὶ οὐκ ἔχουσιν ἀνάπαυσιν ἡμέρας καὶ νυκτός ... (14:11).

ὁ ἐρχόμενος in 4:8, and in 4:10 the elders worship the one who lives εἰς τοὺς αἰῶνας τῶν αἰώνων. Yet this continuous (and present) reality is yet to be manifested explicitly on earth.

God is everlasting and his sovereignty is permanent. Yet this appears to be contradicted by the state of affairs in the earthly present. The seven messages have promised to the faithful a share in God's kingdom made manifest, but in the present situation of the churches the hand of God may appear hidden. How is this tension to be resolved? The appearance of the Lamb in 5:6ff. begins to point to a solution. As I discussed in chapter 4 (pp. 94–6), it is misleading to drive a wedge in the narrative between 4:1–11 and 5:1–14: there are important features common to both. Perhaps the most helpful way of conceiving of the relationship between them is that, with the appearance of the Lamb, a new element is introduced into the existing scene as described in 4:1–11. However, this does not imply *chronological* progression from one to the other. Rather, as Hurtado suggests, the progression is a *logical* one, between complementary scenes in the same vision.[33]

The Lamb: the possibility of divine intervention in human history (5:1–14)

The appearance of the Lamb begins to answer the problem posed at the end of the previous section. He is deemed to be worthy to open the scroll in 5:5, from which flow the events associated with the opening of the seven seals, trumpets and bowls and the visions of the church's struggle in 11:1–13:8.[34] Spatially, this is significant, as I noted in my previous chapter, because at this point the spatial coverage of the narrative begins to reach downwards from heaven to embrace earth. In the same way, the appearance of the Lamb begins the process of the resolution of the *temporal* (now–not yet) dissonance, caused by the juxtaposition of, on the one hand, the description of the earthly present and, on the other hand, the future promises to the faithful in 2:1–3:22 and the vision of heaven in 4:1–11. For while 4:1–11 is essentially a timeless vision of heaven, the appearance of the Lamb in 5:6ff. brings with it references to events in the historical past, which represent divine intervention in human history. Thus the Lamb is described as ὡς ἐσφαγμένον (5:6) and τὸ ἀρνίον τὸ ἐσφαγμένον (5:12), a clear reference to the death and resurrection of

---

[33] Hurtado (1985), p. 117. See the discussion above (pp. 94–6), in relation to the different views of this question put forward by Hurtado and Rowland (1982).

[34] See the discussion on pp. 94–6.

Christ. And it is through his death that Christ has overcome (ἐνίκησεν, 5:5).[35] This resonates with the promises in the seven messages to ὁ νικῶν. Christ has overcome as a pioneer: the faithful are called to follow him, to death if need be. In 5:9–10, the four living creatures and the twenty-four elders sing a new song, praising Christ as worthy to break the seals of the scroll, because of his redemptive death.

The death of Christ is therefore seen not only as an event in earthly history, but also an event in the wider cosmic drama. As the one able to open the seals of the scroll, the Lamb triggers the whole process of judgement and salvation which now forms the substance of 6:1–20:15, in preparation for the consummation in 21:1–22:5. The hymns of 5:9–10, 12, 13 illustrate this point, with their references both to the historic death of Christ and – proleptically – to ultimate eschatological triumph.[36] As I shall argue in chapter 6 (pp. 185–6), there are striking parallels here with the role of prolepsis in the theologies of both Pannenberg and Moltmann.

---

[35] The death of the Lamb is elsewhere seen in a perspective which goes beyond simply the historical past. See especially the much-debated reference in 13:8: καὶ προσκυνήσουσιν αὐτὸν πάντες οἱ κατοικοῦντες ἐπὶ τῆς γῆς, οὖ οὐ γέγραπται τὸ ὄνομα αὐτοῦ ἐν τῷ βιβλίῳ τῆς ζωῆς τοῦ ἀρνίου τοῦ ἐσφαγμένου ἀπὸ καταβολῆς κόσμου. The debate revolves around whether the verse should be read with 17:8 and interpreted as meaning that it is the writing of the names in the book of life which is from the foundation of the world (thus Ladd, 1972, p. 181; and Aune, 1998a, pp. 746ff.) or whether the word order in 13:8 should be followed closely, so that it is the slaughtering of the Lamb which is from the foundation of the world (thus Charles, 1920, vol. I, p. 354; Beasley-Murray, 1974, pp. 213–14; Caird, 1984, p. 168; Giblin, 1991, pp. 133–4). The second solution is preferable on grammatical grounds. It need not, however, lead to the kind of interpretation suggested by L. L. Thompson, that the crucifixion should not be seen as a specific event, but as a recurring element in the deep structure of the text (1990, p. 85). It may simply suggest a sense of fore-ordination in the death of the Lamb (Charles, 1920, vol. I, p. 354; Sweet, 1979, pp. 211–12).

[36] See Jörns (1971, p. 168). In the context of discussion of eschatological tension in the text, the variant readings of βασιλεύ[σ]ουσιν (5:10) are of interest. Nestle–Aland[26] and UBS[4] both decide in favour of the future tense, and the manuscript evidence suggests that this judgement is probably right. However, many commentators have preferred the harder reading of the present tense. Swete (1906, p. 80), Sweet (1979, pp. 130–1) and Beale (1999, pp. 362–4) prefer βασιλεύουσιν as the harder reading, describing the reign of the saints begun in the present, in the life of the Spirit, although yet to be fully manifested. Charles (1920, vol. I, p. 148) also opts for βασιλεύουσιν, albeit as a proleptic reference to the millennial kingdom. In contrast, Beasley-Murray (1978, p. 128) agrees with Nestlé–Aland, preferring the future tense. Whatever the correct textual conclusion, it seems to me that the concept is difficult to pin down temporally with precision. Given the context of redemption through Christ's death and resurrection, and the reference earlier in 5:10 to the creation (ἐποίησας, aorist, implying that it is already achieved) of a kingdom and priests, it is difficult to assign the concept purely to the future. This is certainly the view of Caird (1984, pp. 76–7), who argues that whatever reading is adopted, the sense is of a present reality, extending into the future.

The outworking of divine initiative in earthly history (1) (6:1–9:21)

The appearance of the Lamb in 5:6ff. begins to build bridges between the spatial planes of heaven and earth and also to indicate a possible resolution of the now–not yet temporal tension in the text. The central sections of the book, 6:1–20:15, now recount the process of judgement, persecution and vindication through which the ground is laid for the eschatological resolution in 21:1–22:5. The way in which the whole of this section deals with temporal categories is of great importance. John interweaves references to the penultimate future with references to the ultimate future and references to ultimate (past and future) temporal horizons. John is describing a process of judgement, persecution and vindication. Yet this is not to be taken as a chronological account; rather, it is the interrelationship of different temporal categories which underlies the temporal development of the material in 6:1–20:15.

In my previous chapter I argued that the section 6:1–9:21 juxtaposes material in two spatial categories: first, material describing action which takes place on the earthly plane as a result of divine initiative (the first four and the sixth seals in 6:1–8; 6:12–17; and the first six trumpets in 8:6–9:21); and second, material which spreads its spatial coverage across both heaven and earth (the fifth seal in 6:9–11; the visions of the 144,000 and the great multitude in 7:1–17; the opening of the seventh seal in 8:1–5). The juxtaposition of these two spatial categories is designed to herald forthcoming divine judgement on the earth while providing assurance to the faithful. The faithful suffer on earth, but divine protection, applicable in both heaven and earth, catches them up into the ultimate positive purposes of God, to be consummated at the descent from heaven to earth of the New Jerusalem. By contrast, the enemies of God will be subject to divine judgement which originates in heaven with earthly effect. Similarly, at a temporal level, the text oscillates between different temporal categories in order to reinforce its message. An important feature is the juxtaposition of references to the penultimate future and references to the ultimate future. Warnings of forthcoming judgement are intertwined with assurances that the faithful will be preserved through it, and ultimately vindicated.

The section begins with the opening of the first six seals (6:1–17). I take the first four seals to refer primarily to the present. In so doing, I am accepting the consensus among many commentators, who have followed Swete in seeing in the first four seals 'the condition of the Empire as it revealed itself to the mind of the seer'.[37] The tribulations of the present – war, economic distress, death – are placed in the context of ultimate divine control. While the fifth seal (the martyrs under the altar) also seems to be set in the present, the material contains within it a clear forward dynamic. The martyrs demand vengeance, and are told to rest for a limited period: the passage therefore anticipates further divine action. The sixth seal, with its description of cosmic judgement, drawing on traditional prophetic and apocalyptic motifs relating to the day of the Lord, is best understood as a reference to the penultimate future.[38] The overall effect of the first six seals is to expand the temporal horizon of the reader forwards into the penultimate future (and in 6:9–11, with its sense of vindication, implicitly into the ultimate future). This is achieved not through the tracing of a chronological account, but through the juxtaposition of references to the present and the penultimate future.

With the account of the two groups of the faithful in ch. 7, the focus shifts away from divine judgement to the related, and intertwined, theme of the preservation of the faithful. In terms of temporal categories, the action at first continues to deal with the penultimate future with the account of the sealing of the 144,000 in 7:1–8, but then presses on to the ultimate future with the vision of the numberless multitude in 7:9–17. The question of the identity of the two groups in ch. 7 and their relationship to one another has caused much discussion among commentators. On balance, the most convincing explanation is that both groups represent the entire church, first before the final tribulation, and then seen in the perspective of the ultimate future.[39] The point is that the assurance to the

---

[37] Swete (1906), p. 87. See also Caird (1984), pp. 78ff.; Sweet (1979), pp. 136ff.; Roloff (1993), p. 87; and Beale (1999), pp. 370–1.

[38] Compare, for example, Isa. 2:10, 19, 21; 13:10; 34:4.

[39] There are broadly three positions on the identity and relationship of the two groups. First, some have argued that the two groups are distinct, with the 144,000 representing the final generation of Christians on the eve of the final tribulation, and the great multitude of vv. 9ff. representing the entire church across all generations; see Mounce (1977), pp. 164ff. Aune (1998a, pp. 439–50) offers a variant on this view: the first group are those Christians who are living when the great tribulation begins, and who are protected through it; the second group are all other Christians, of all ages, not including the first group. The first group are therefore on earth, the second in heaven (p. 447). A second interpretation is that each of the two groups represents the entire church, from two viewpoints, before and after the final tribulation (or, in our terms, in the penultimate and ultimate future). This interpretation is held by, among others, Ladd (1972, pp. 116–17), Beasley-Murray (1978, pp. 139ff.) and Roloff (1993, pp. 97–8). Third, some commentators, including Caird (1984, pp. 94ff.), have argued that while the two groups are certainly identical, they should be taken as representing the martyrs only, and not the entire church. The first solution is the weakest of the three, since a distinction between a final generation of Christians and the church across the ages is surely alien to John's scheme. As Beasley-Murray (1978, p. 140)

faithful that they will be preserved through judgement and persecution is traced through the penultimate to the ultimate future. The subsequent accounts of tribulation, persecution and judgement in 8:1–20:15 are therefore placed in perspective. The faithful have been promised in 2:1–3:22 that they will have a place in God's ultimate future, and 7:9ff. offers a vision of this, in confirmation that they will ultimately be vindicated. The close textual links between 7:15–17, the description of the condition of the great multitude, and the accounts of the New Jerusalem in 21:1–22:5 are therefore highly significant.[40]

The section recounting the sounding of the first six trumpets (8:6–9:21) raises the question of the temporal relationship between the sequences of sevenfold actions in the text (seals, trumpets and bowls). These three sequences are not to be considered as a chronological progression. Rather, in some sense, they represent progressively intensifying accounts of the end-time events. Several commentators have detected a pattern in which the trumpet visions are to be seen as somehow comprehended within the seal visions, and the bowl visions within the trumpet visions.[41] As Bauckham argues, 'each series represents the same end, but from starting-points progressively closer to the end'.[42] The apocalyptic imagery of the trumpets sequence suggests that the seer is envisaging the penultimate future, characterized by divine judgement. This judgement should not, however, be seen in a completely deterministic context. 9:20–1 appears to envisage an opportunity for repentance, albeit one which is not taken.[43]

---

rightly comments, 'So far as John is concerned the Church of his day is the Church of the last day.' Both of the other solutions are plausible, but, on balance, it seems to me that Beasley-Murray is again right to argue (pp. 145ff.) that there is no clear evidence in the passage to suggest that only martyrs are in view.

[40] Note the following parallels between 7:15–17 and 21:1–22:5:

καὶ λατρεύουσιν αὐτῷ ἡμέρας καὶ νυκτός (7:15); καὶ οἱ δοῦλοι αὐτοῦ λατρεύσουσιν αὐτῷ (22:3). (These are the only two occurrences of λατρεύω in the text.)

ὁ καθήμενος ἐπὶ τοῦ θρόνου σκηνώσει ἐπ' αὐτούς (7:15); ἰδοὺ ἡ σκηνὴ τοῦ θεοῦ μετὰ τῶν ἀνθρώπων, καὶ σκηνώσει μετ' αὐτῶν (21:3).

οὐ πεινάσουσιν ἔτι οὐδὲ διψήσουσιν... καὶ ὁδηγήσει αὐτοὺς ἐπὶ ζωῆς πηγὰς ὑδάτων (7:16, 17); ἐγὼ τῷ διψῶντι δώσω ἐκ τῆς πηγῆς τοῦ ὕδατος τῆς ζωῆς δωρεάν (21:6).

ἐξαλείψει ὁ θεὸς πᾶν δάκρυον ἐκ τῶν ὀφθαλμῶν αὐτῶν (7:17); ἐξαλείψει πᾶν δάκρυον ἐκ τῶν ὀφθαλμῶν αὐτῶν (21:4).

[41] See, for example, Lambrecht (1980).   [42] Bauckham (1993b), p. 40.

[43] The οὐ μετενόησαν of 9:20 and 21 is later repeated in respect of the fourth and fifth bowls of judgement (16:9, 11). See the earlier discussion about the genre of Revelation in chapter 3 (pp. 76–9), and the support which elements of conditionality in the text may be held to give the view that the work is at least partly a prophecy.

The scroll brought down from heaven (10:1–11)

I remarked in chapter 4 (pp. 99–100) on the importance of this passage in terms of the development of the spatial dimension of the text. The descent of the ἄγγελος ἰσχυρός from heaven to earth marks an important new phase in the resolution of the spatial tension between the manifest sovereignty of God, represented by the vision of heaven in 4:1–11, and its apparent limitation in the immediate earthly situations of the seven churches.[44] The passage (especially vv. 5–7) is also of great importance in the *temporal* structure of the book, for two reasons.

First, the angel proclaims on earth the rule of God in ultimate temporal terms:

> Καὶ ὁ ἄγγελος, ὃν εἶδον ἑστῶτα ἐπὶ τῆς θαλάσσης καὶ ἐπὶ τῆς γῆς,
> ἦρεν τὴν χεῖρα αὐτοῦ τὴν δεξιὰν εἰς τὸν οὐρανὸν
> καὶ ὤμοσεν ἐν τῷ ζῶντι εἰς τοὺς αἰῶνας τῶν αἰώνων,
> ὃς ἔκτισεν τὸν οὐρανὸν καὶ τὰ ἐν αὐτῷ καὶ τὴν γῆν καὶ τὰ ἐν αὐτῇ καὶ τὴν θάλασσαν καὶ τὰ ἐν αὐτῇ…

Just as the descent of the angel to earth symbolizes the ultimate spatial compass of divine power, so the proclamation of God's everlasting power and the reference to his acts of creation stress the ultimate temporal compass of his sovereignty. Thus the expansions of spatial and temporal horizons are closely intertwined at this point. The sealing of the 144,000 in 7:4–8 and their reappearance later in the chapter beyond the tribulation, as the great multitude before the throne, offered assurance about divine protection during the trials of the penultimate future. The message is implicitly repeated here. The scroll delivered to John is the call of the church to the task of witness, to be discharged in 11:1–13:18. The persecution into which that witness will lead the church is to be seen – despite outward appearances in the penultimate future – in the context of the ultimate faithfulness of God, proclaimed by the strong angel.

Second, the passage includes an important statement about the temporal dimension of the book. In 10:6 the strong angel says ὅτι χρόνος οὐκέτι ἔσται. In the early centuries of the church it was popular to interpret this

---

[44] Following Bauckham (1993a, pp. 243–57), I take the βιβλαρίδιον of 10:2 to be the same scroll as the βιβλίον of 5:2, which the Lamb alone is worthy to open. Thus the appearance of the strong angel in 10:1ff. is linked closely with the beginning of the process of spatial and temporal integration begun with the appearance of the Lamb in ch. 5.

statement as signifying the end of time itself.[45] Most modern commentators, however, take the statement to be an expression of the imminence of God's forthcoming action, translating χρόνος as 'delay'. Sweet and others link the statement to Habakkuk 2:3: 'For there is still a vision for the appointed time; it speaks of the end and does not lie. If it seems to tarry, wait for it; it will surely come, it will not delay.' Sweet also rightly argues that the statement is more plausibly seen as an answer to the cry of the martyrs under the altar in 6:9–11 (Έως πότε, ὁ δεσπότης ὁ ἅγιος καὶ ἀληθινός...), rather than as a kind of metaphysical proclamation about the nature of eternity.[46] Thus the episode offers a double reassurance: God's sovereignty is everlasting, and he is poised to intervene decisively and imminently to vindicate the faithful.

The witness of the church on earth (11:1–13:18)

There now follows a triptych of visions: the two witnesses; the dragon and the woman; and the two beasts. Each deals with the witness and resultant persecution of the church in the penultimate future; each involves the period of three and a half years.[47] As many commentators have noted, the idea of three and a half units of time is a reference back to Daniel 7:25 and 12:7 ('a time, times and a half').[48] Swete therefore argues: 'The time-limit serves of course no further purpose than to synchronize the several periods, and to compare them with the greatest crisis through which the Jewish people passed between the Exile and the Fall of Jerusalem

---

[45] Swete (1906, p. 126) cites Bede as an example of this interpretation. As I explain in chapter 6, both Pannenberg and Moltmann curiously adopt this interpretation, in the face of the weight of the contrary opinion among contemporary biblical scholars.

[46] Sweet (1979), p. 179; see also Mounce (1977), pp. 210–11.

[47] The idea of three and a half appears at several points in chs. 11–13:

The nations are to trample over the holy city for μῆνας τεσσεράκοντα δύο (42 months, i.e. $3\frac{1}{2}$ years) in 11:2.

The two witnesses have authority to prophesy for ἡμέρας χιλίας διακοσίας ἑξήκοντα (1260 days = 42 months = $3\frac{1}{2}$ years) in 11:3.

The witnesses are dead for ἡμέρας τρεῖς καὶ ἥμισυ ($3\frac{1}{2}$ days) before God raises them (11:9, 11).

The woman is nourished in the wilderness for ἡμέρας χιλίας διακοσίας ἑξήκοντα in 12:6. In 12:14 that same period is referred to as καιρὸν καὶ καιροὺς καὶ ἥμισυ καιροῦ.

The beast from the sea is allowed to exercise authority for μῆνας τεσσεράκοντα δύο in 13:5.

[48] As Mounce (1977, p. 221) comments, it became 'a conventional symbol for a limited period of time during which evil would be allowed free rein'.

[i.e. the persecution under Antiochus].'[49] However, in the context of the temporal structure of the text, the duration of this period of activity in the penultimate future surely has an additional purpose: the use of three and a half must be seen as in contrast to the perfection and completeness of the divine action in the text, so often delineated by the figure seven. Roloff notes that the duration of three and a half is connected in Daniel with the reign of the oppressing prince for the first half of the final week of the seventy weeks of history, at the end of Daniel 9:

> [in Daniel] the persecution is not only limited in time, it does not complete the time period provided and planned by God but rather is surrounded by it. In this sense John also uses the mysterious number: the three and a half years (and its equivalents) symbolize an epoch of affliction, limited by God and surrounded by his plan of salvation.[50]

Thus the period within which the three visions are for the most part encompassed is inherently characteristic of the penultimate future.[51] Moreover, as Sweet perceptively comments, the time period also conveys the paradoxical situation of the church, being assured of salvation in the ultimate future and at the same time vulnerable in the penultimate future to the effects of persecution.[52] It is also worth noting the appearance of τηρέω, νικάω and ὑπομονή, words which, as I mentioned earlier, are characteristic of John's handling of the penultimate future.[53]

Just as the appearance of the great redeemed multitude in 7:9–17 served to provide the assurance of salvation in the ultimate future in the midst of the divine judgements associated with the seven trumpets, so there are glimpses of the ultimate future, embedded in the penultimate context

---

[49] Swete (1906), p. 131. [50] Roloff (1993), p. 130.

[51] Beale (1999) also argues that 'the duration of the period [of $3\frac{1}{2}$ years/42 months] spans the time from Christ's death and resurrection to the culmination of history ... the events of 11:2–3; 12:6, 14b; and 13:5 are parallel in time' (p. 695). That is not to say that there are not also references to other temporal categories in these chapters. For example, 12:1–4 recalls the primordial myth of divine victory over the chaos monster, while the defeat of the dragon in 12:7–9 appears to be closely linked to the death and resurrection of Christ; see Bauckham (1993a), pp. 185–98.

[52] Sweet notes that in the story of the two witnesses, the figure of three and a half is used to denote both invulnerability (11:3–6) and eclipse (11:7–9). The implication is that both are of the church's essence: 'There can be *no* period at which the church is simply at peace in the world, much less simply triumphant, or simply crushed' (1979, p. 183).

[53] In 12:11 the saints are said to have overcome (ἐνίκησαν) the dragon through the blood of the Lamb and the word of their testimony. In 12:17 the dragon makes war on those who keep (τηρούντων) the commandments of God. In 13:10 there is a call for the endurance (ὑπομονή) of the saints.

of the visions of the church's witness. The clearest is in the passage in 11:15–19, where the action switches to heaven. Loud voices proclaim:

'Εγένετο ἡ βασιλεία τοῦ κόσμου τοῦ κυρίου ἡμῶν καὶ τοῦ
Χριστοῦ αὐτοῦ,
καὶ βασιλεύσει εἰς τοὺς αἰῶνας τῶν αἰώνων.   (11:15)

And the twenty-four elders sing:

Εὐχαριστοῦμέν σοι, κύριε ὁ θεὸς ὁ παντοκράτωρ, ὁ ὢν καὶ ὁ
ἦν,
ὅτι εἴληφας τὴν δύναμίν σου τὴν μεγάλην καὶ ἐβασίευσας.

(11:17)

Many commentators rightly take this passage as a proleptic vision of the ultimate triumph of God. Charles, for example, comments that the proclamation from 11:15 is celebrating the ultimate divine conquest as though it is already achieved, and heralding the advent of the everlasting kingdom of 21:1ff.[54]

The Lamb and the 144,000 on Mount Zion (14:1–20)

In both spatial and temporal terms, the location of the vision in this passage is ambiguous. Interpreters have, however, often attempted to pin the vision down to a particular temporal and spatial location. One position is to see the vision of the Lamb and his followers as a proleptic vision, looking forward to the ultimate victory and the New Jerusalem.[55] Others have argued that the vision is best understood as representing the present, earthly church, in a way which emphasizes its ultimate divine protection in the midst of persecution.[56] In other words, in the temporal categories which I am adopting, it is arguable whether this is a vision of the present,

[54] In fact, although Charles's comments in respect of this passage *per se* are correct, he sets it in a misleading overall context of a chronological progression in the narrative of the text as a whole. 11:15–19 should not be seen as proleptic in the sense of looking forward from one point in a continuous, chronological narrative sequence to a later point, but rather in the sense of looking forward from the midst of one temporal *category* (the penultimate future) to another (the ultimate future). Caird's argument that in 11:15–19 'futurity is caught up in the eternal present' (1984, p. 141) dissolves too far the distinctions between temporal categories which the text preserves.

[55] See, for example, Ladd (1972), pp. 188ff., who locates the vision in the New Jerusalem, and Mounce (1977, pp. 266ff.), who sees the 144,000 as corresponding to the great multitude in the second half of ch. 7, standing secure in heaven, beyond the final tribulation. A variant on this proleptic view is to see the vision as pointing forward to the millennium (e.g. Charles, 1920, vol. II, p. 4).

[56] See, for example, Swete (1906, p. 174) and Roloff (1993, pp. 169ff.), who link the vision to that of the 144,000 sealed on earth in 7:4–8.

the penultimate future or the ultimate future. Some have tried to get round this ambiguity by locating the vision outside the categories of space and time used in the rest of the text. Thus Giblin speaks of 'a metahistorical, supra-historical place equivalent to heaven itself'.[57] It is possible that the setting is deliberately ambiguous. The triumphant nature of the scene and the fact that the 144,000 are in the physical presence of the Lamb, having been redeemed from humankind (14:4), suggest a setting in the ultimate future.[58] Yet the textual situation of the passage (immediately following the visions of persecution in 11:1–13:18, and within a section of the book where much of the concern is with the penultimate future) tends to pull its significance back towards the present. At the same time, the passage also seems to stand within a forward dynamic, including the 144,000 of 7:4–8, sealed on earth out of the twelve tribes of Israel in advance of the tribulations of the trumpets; the 144,000 here, standing in an ambiguous spatial and temporal location; and the New Jerusalem, upon whose gates are inscribed the names of the twelve tribes (21:12), and which symbolizes the ultimate spatial and temporal resolution of the book.[59]

If the exact sense of 14:1–5 in terms of spatial and temporal categories is ambiguous, the visions of the two eschatological harvests in 14:14–20 are clearly references to the imminent parousia. The message is that God's ultimate eschatological act is now at hand.[60]

The outworking of divine initiative in earthly history (2) (15:1–19:10)

This section of the text recounts the fulfilment of divine judgement on earthly history, with the sequence of the seven bowls of judgement (16:1–21), the demise of Babylon (17:1–18:24) and the subsequent rejoicing in heaven (19:1–10). For the purposes of my analysis of the text,

---

[57] Giblin (1991), p. 137. In a similar vein, Fiorenza (1991) describes the setting as neither historical nor heavenly, but rather 'an eschatological place of protection and liberation'.

[58] Note in this context the use of καινός to describe the song sung by the 144,000 in 14:3. I suggested on p. 114 that in Revelation καινός is always associated with the ultimate future.

[59] This sense of a forward progression is emphasized by the description of the 144,000 as ἀπαρχή (first fruits) in 14:4.

[60] There are differing views of the significance of the two eschatological harvests of grain and the vintage. Bauckham (1993a, pp. 283–96) argues that the imagery of the grain harvest should in this instance be regarded in a positive light, as the conversion of people from the nations, whereas the harvesting of the vintage is a sign of eschatological judgement. Aune (1998a, pp. 801–3, 844–5) rejects this view, arguing that both harvests represent judgement, as does Beale (1999), who gives a detailed critique of Bauckham's view (pp. 776–8).

the spatial features of this section (such as the pouring down from heaven to earth of the contents of the bowls, and the casting down of Babylon in 18:21) are perhaps of more immediate significance than its temporal features. Nonetheless, a few points are worth noting here.

In considering questions of history and temporality, it is important to examine the role played by the opening of the sequence, the vision of heaven and the singing of the 'song of Moses' in 15:1–8, and its relationship to the visions of judgement which follow in 16:1–18:24. The song is important in continuing to set the narrative in a wide temporal framework. In 15:7 God is described as the one who lives for ever and ever.[61] And although the 'song of Moses' recorded here does not tally with any particular passage from the Pentateuch, the reference to Moses serves to establish resonances with redeeming works of God in the historical past. The description of the song as the song of Moses and the song of the Lamb is noteworthy in this respect, as it ranges across divine actions in different historical periods. Especially important in the overall temporal shape of the text is that such expressions of a very wide temporal frame, which have been noted throughout the text, are now explicitly combined with a specific statement that, in respect of the seven bowls of God's wrath held by the angels, ἐν αὐταῖς ἐτελέσθη ὁ θυμὸς τοῦ θεοῦ (15:1). In other words, 15:1 asserts that the penultimate future, characterized by the judgement of God and the persecution of the church, is shortly to end; the promised ultimate future is therefore at hand. The temporal tension caused by the dissonance between 'what is', in the eternal purposes of God, and 'what appears to be', in the earthly present, is soon to be finally resolved.[62]

A second important role played by 15:1–8 relates to the *content* of the song of Moses and the Lamb, and in particular the statement in 15:4 that πάντα τὰ ἔθνη ἥξουσιν καὶ προσκυνήσουσιν ἐνώπιόν σου. Bauckham argues that the song of Moses in 15:3–4, with its echoes of Jeremiah 10 and Psalm 86, stands in 'the most universalistic strain in Old Testament

---

[61] The emphasis on the widest possible temporal frame would be strengthened by the alternative reading of ὁ βασιλεὺς τῶν αἰώνων in 15:4, although on balance the manuscript evidence suggests that the reading of ἐθνῶν, preferred by Nestle–Aland, is correct.

[62] Sweet writes perceptively about the way in which the penultimacy of the power represented by the beast and its allies is described in this section. His view of the mysterious number 666 in 13:18 is that it should be taken in contrast to the perfect, complete number seven (or 777), so that it represents 'penultimacy intensified, and "the penultimate claiming ultimacy"'(1979, p. 215). He argues that the sixth king, now reigning, in 17:10 should similarly be taken to represent the 'penultimate moment', given that the seventh is to last only a short time.

hope', and 'the effect is to shift the emphasis in the significance of the new exodus, from an event by which God delivers his people by judging their enemies to an event which brings the nations to acknowledge the true God'.[63] This anticipation of universal praise to be offered to God seems to be in tension with the visions of apparently final and uncompromising judgement which follow in 16:1–18:24. Some commentators have argued that this section of the text provides evidence that the view of history espoused by John is marked to some extent by conditionality rather than by determinism.[64] Bauckham suggests that John deliberately sets ideas of universal conversion (15:4) and universal judgement (the bowls sequence) side by side. Thus the choice facing humankind in response to the divine initiative (mediated through the witness of the church) is posed starkly, but that choice is a real one.

The outworking of divine initiative in earthly history (3) (19:11–20:15)

This section represents the culmination of the process of judgement which begins in 6:1ff. I suggested in chapter 4 (pp. 105–6) that, spatially, the reach of God's judgement is now extended to the utmost bounds of the cosmos, as the eschatological enemies lying behind earthly reality are finally conquered and consigned to destruction, and as the old heaven and earth flee, clearing the way for the descent of the New Jerusalem in 21:1ff.

On the temporal plane, the section also plays a pivotal role in preparing for the resolution in 21:1ff., in two respects. First, the final defeat of the eschatological enemies marks the end of the penultimate future. The removal of the beasts, the dragon, Death and Hades from the scene removes the source of persecution of the church, as well as marking the completion of the judgement of God. The key features which have characterized the penultimate future are hence at an end, and the way is open for the resolution of the temporal dissonance between heaven and earth in 21:1ff.

Second, if the defeat of the eschatological enemies in 19:11–20:15 suggests an element of *discontinuity* between the penultimate and the ultimate future, then the much-discussed episode of the millennium (20:4–6) may

---

[63] Bauckham (1993b), p. 101.

[64] As I argued in chapter 3 (pp. 73–6), the use of a contrast between determinism and conditionality as a means of distinguishing between the outlooks of Revelation and Jewish apocalyptic can be overplayed. Nonetheless it remains the case that elements of conditionality can be found in Revelation, not least here in chs. 15–19.

provide an element of *continuity*. These three verses have probably occasioned more debate than any others in the text, far beyond their importance in the context of the rest of the book. I do not propose here to venture into the various detailed attempts to interpret these verses.[65] My purpose is simply to argue that John uses the traditional idea of the messianic kingdom to make a theological point which relates in important ways to the temporal framework of the text as a whole. Although the idea of the millennium *per se* is absent from the Old Testament, the general expectation of the fulfilment of divine promises within history is a basic component of prophetic hope, and one of the features which distinguishes it from apocalyptic. The picture in 20:4–6 is clearly an earthly one, since the city is still open to attack by Satan and the nations in 20:7–9. The old earth and heaven do not disappear until 20:11. To that extent, the millennium is still part of earthly history. At the same time, the situation has clearly moved on from the long description of the present and penultimate future in chs. 6–19, characterized by judgement and persecution. The beasts are in the lake of fire: the saints are ruling with Christ, and are in fact no longer vulnerable to attack (in 20:9b fire consumes their enemies before they can attack the beloved city). Hence the use of the idea of a preliminary messianic kingdom is particularly apt, standing as a bridge between the penultimate and the ultimate future.[66] Moreover, the status of the millennial kingdom, as part of earthly history and yet also marking a move beyond the penultimate future, enables it to serve the important purpose in the narrative, of reflecting God's judgement upon history as a whole.[67]

---

[65] A good survey of different approaches is in Mealy (1992), chs. 1–3. Elsewhere, I have developed the argument that while the symbol of the millennium in Revelation 20 is clearly set in the future, its relevance for theology lies not in the expectation of a literal transitional kingdom, but rather in emphasizing the this-worldly dimension of the eschatological consummation (Gilbertson, 1997). See also now Bauckham (1999), pp. 123–47.

[66] Compare the prophecies relating to an intermediate messianic kingdom in *4 Ezra* 7:28ff. Beasley-Murray (1978, pp. 288–9) suggests that the period of a thousand years may be derived from the idea of a sabbath of history, before the onset of a timeless age. He refers in particular to *2 En.* 32–3 and the *Epistle of Barnabas* 15, both of which appear to work with a scheme in which the overall frame of history is represented by a week, consisting of days each lasting a thousand years. There are clearly similarities with 20:4–6, though any direct linkage is difficult to determine, especially in the case of *2 Enoch*, given the obscurity of its date.

[67] It is this theological importance of the millennium in John's overall temporal scheme which makes Mealy's reassessment of the significance of the millennium rather unsatisfying. Essentially, he argues that the parousia and the descent of the New Jerusalem should be seen as different views of the same event. This leaves no space for an intermediate role for the millennium.

The New Jerusalem and the epilogue (21:1–22:21)

In this chapter I have sought to explore two important and dynamic aspects of the temporal dimension of the Book of Revelation. First, the text seeks to enable readers to perceive their present situation in the light of a wider context of God's sovereignty over the whole of time. Second, the text operates in a framework moving from dissonance to resolution. It establishes in 1:1–4:11 a powerful degree of temporal tension between God's sovereignty, which is always valid, and the present (which ought to be manifestly subject to God's rule, but appears not to be); chs. 5–20 are a sustained description of the process of divine judgement and vindication in the midst of persecution, necessary to resolve this tension; the resolution itself now takes place in 21:1ff.[68] In the following section I shall examine the ways in which these two processes culminate in the New Jerusalem. I shall also try to show that the interaction of these two crucial processes means that there is more to this apparent resolution than may at first appear. On one level, the New Jerusalem represents a culmination of the expansion of temporal horizons – into the ultimate future – and the resolution of the dissonance between 'what is' and 'what appears to be'. But this should not be taken to mean that the text offers an escapist, future vision. The whole point of revealing ultimate temporal horizons is to equip readers to live in the present; and while the New Jerusalem appears to be the *culmination* of the argument of the book, it is also a *starting point*, posing, if anything, the dissonance between 'what is' and 'what appears to be' all the more sharply, as readers seek to assimilate the message of the book into their understanding of present experience.

The passage with which this section opens, 21:1–8, is arguably the most important in the entire text. O'Donovan suggests that in hearing the words of God, in 21:3–8, 'we stand in the sanctum sanctorum of history'.[69] In a detailed and careful study of the literary structure of Revelation, Hellholm concludes that the words of God himself, in 21:5–8, represent the deepest level of communication in the text. He argues that the importance of this text is emphasized by the observation that it is central not only to the pragmatics (i.e. communication embedment) of the text, but also to the semantics (i.e. positive and negative propositions) of the text. God himself is speaking words which are πιστοὶ καὶ ἀληθινοί,

---

[68] This process should be seen as working in parallel with the *spatial* dynamic in the text, in which the initial dissonance between 'what is', represented by the rule of God in heaven, and 'what appears to be' in terms of earthly reality is resolved, culminating in the abolition of the old heaven and earth and the descent from heaven of the New Jerusalem.

[69] O'Donovan (1986), p. 94.

and which summarize the consequences of the choices facing humanity.[70] And in terms of the temporal categories with which I have been analysing the text, the passage is of great significance. I argued above (p. 114) that John adopts the term καινός when referring to the ultimate future. Four of the nine instances of this word in the text of Revelation occur in 21:1–5, describing the new heaven and new earth (21:1), the New Jerusalem (21:2), and in the climactic word of God in 21:5, Ἰδοὺ καινὰ ποιῶ πάντα. The message could not be clearer: with the descent of the New Jerusalem we have moved from description of the penultimate future to description of the ultimate future.[71] But this is an ultimate future of profound significance for the present. Several commentators have remarked on the use of the present tense ποιῶ, arguing that it should be taken to refer to God's re-creating activity in the present, as well as in the future.[72]

The resolution of temporal dissonance

In the New Jerusalem the dissonance between the everlasting sovereignty of God and its apparent contradiction in the earthly present and penultimate future is resolved. In the ultimate future of 21:1–22:5 the life of God and the life of humankind are brought into a unity in which such discrepancies cannot exist. The background of the traditions surrounding Mount Zion is important here. Passages such as Ezekiel 28:13–14 draw clear links between the mountain of God and the paradise of Eden, with

---

[70] Hellholm (1986, pp. 43–4). Hellholm's argument has much to commend it, despite the reservations of Yarbro Collins in her introduction to the same *Semeia* volume (pp. 1–11).

[71] In this context, it is interesting to compare the description of the New Jerusalem in Revelation with the various other surviving traditions of the New Jerusalem, from the Old Testament and from Jewish apocalyptic. It is possible to detect three main strands of eschatological expectation associated with the appearance of a new or renewed Jerusalem. The first strand involves the restoration of the existing earthly Jerusalem in the end-times (see, for example, Isa. 62; Tobit 13:9–18; *2 Bar.* 32:2ff.). The second envisages a perfect heavenly Jerusalem, to which the just ascend (see, for example, *2 Bar.* 4:1–7; *4 Ezra* 8:52; *4 Bar.* 5:35; Heb. 12:22). Neither of these traditions corresponds exactly to Rev. 21:1ff. Closer perhaps is a third strand of tradition, also present in *4 Ezra*, which describes the building on earth of a New Jerusalem by divine agency (*4 Ezra* 7:26, 10:25–54, 13:36), but this has no mention of the city's *descending* from heaven, a central feature of the account in Revelation. Moreover, the assumption behind this section of *4 Ezra* appears to be that the New Jerusalem represents a complete break with the past (*4 Ezra* 10:54: 'no work of human construction could endure in a place where the city of the Most High was to be revealed'). The view of Revelation at this point appears to affirm an element of *continuity* with what has gone before; see, for example, 21:24–6, in which the glory of the nations is brought into the city. The overall image seems to be one of transformation.

[72] See especially Caird (1984), pp. 265–6.

the implication that the restoration of Jerusalem will mean a return to a different plane of temporality. As Levenson writes: 'at the cosmic mountain, the axis of the world, the act of creation is shielded from the ravages of time and of the decay time measures. On that mountain the divine creative energy remains intact.'[73] The link with the primordial past is explicit in Revelation; see especially 22:1–5. In her study of the symbol of the New Jerusalem in Revelation, Deutsch concludes that in this passage 'End time has become primeval time, assuring communities under crises of the ultimate meaning of life and order.'[74]

In rhetorical terms, the effect of the vision of the New Jerusalem is partly to reassure the reader of God's ultimate purposes, and therefore to enable a greater understanding of the realities underlying the crises of the present and the penultimate future. To an extent, therefore, the conclusion of the text offers a resolution for the present, given the possibility of anticipating the splendour of the New Jerusalem now. Thus Rissi argues that for John the parousia enables the manifestation of the true nature of the church at present: 'the church can demonstrate the reality neither of her kingship nor of her priesthood during the time of her pilgrimage. Only the great moment of Christ's revelation will bring what she really is to light.'[75] The expansion of temporal horizons, a key feature of the text as a whole, has reached its culmination in the vision of the ultimate future: all other times, including the present, are therefore now seen in that perspective.

The intensification of temporal dissonance

However, to regard the New Jerusalem merely as a means of *resolving* temporal tension would be to oversimplify the complexity of the role which the image plays in the structure of the text. In addition to the dynamic in the text pushing outwards towards an ultimate temporal horizon, there is a countermovement back into the present. An important role of the New Jerusalem is therefore in a sense to *intensify* a sense of tension in present experience, by revealing all the more clearly the dissonance between the reality of God's sovereignty and its apparent contradiction

---

[73] Levenson (1985), p. 127. In his discussion of the relationship between the earthly and heavenly Jerusalem in Old Testament tradition, Levenson concludes that 'it is clear that we are dealing with a world picture which is composed essentially of two tiers. The upper tier represents ultimate reality; it is the realm of God and his retinue. The lower tier is that of mundane reality, which is vulnerable to time, change, and flux, in short, open to history' (p. 141). For other examples of traditions linking the expected New Jerusalem with paradise, see *2 Bar.* 4:1ff., *1 En.* 90:33ff., *4 Ezra* 8:52.

[74] Deutsch (1987), p. 117.   [75] Rissi (1972), p. 34.

in present experience. This feature of the operation of the text is one of the main reasons why the interpretation of Revelation as an escape from history is so inadequate.

I have discussed earlier the ways in which images and symbols in the text lead from the present through the penultimate future towards the ultimate future. However, in the epilogue the reverse process is clearly also present. The focus shifts from the ultimate future in 21:1–22:5 back to the penultimate future and the present in 22:6–21, with the stress on instruction, encouragement and warning about the community's behaviour and the imminence of the coming of Christ. This transitional quality of the epilogue is emphasized by the way in which it is connected both to the vision of the ultimate future in the New Jerusalem of 21:1–22:5 and also to the description of the present in 1:1–3:22.[76] Thus the epilogue forms a bridge between the ultimate future of 21:1–22:5 and the present. Its function is to turn the reader's attention back to the present situation, but now in the light of the vision of the New Jerusalem.

This move back from the ultimate future to the present occurs of course not merely within the text itself, but also in the context of the implied rhetorical situation in which the text operates. The communities to whom John wrote were still situated in the turbulence and impending crisis of the present, and reading the book would not have altered that.[77] So the

---

[76] The links back to 21:1–22:5 include:

> the designation of God and Christ in temporal terms, as τὸ Ἄλφα καὶ τὸ ᾽Ω, ἡ ἀρχὴ καὶ τὸ τέλος (22:13 and 21:6);

> the two, similar, lists of those forbidden from entering the New Jerusalem, in 22:15 and 21:8;

> the promise of the gift of living water in 22:17 and 21:6.

> The links back to chs. 1–3 include:

> the statement of the imminence of the events of the book: δεῖξαι τοῖς δούλοις αὐτοῦ ἃ δεῖ γενέσθαι ἐν τάχει in 22:6 and 1:1; and ὁ καιρὸς γὰρ ἐγγύς ἐστιν (22:10; cf. 1:3);

> the imminence of Christ's coming (ἔρχομαι ταχύ) in 22:7, 12, 20 and in 2:16 and 3:11;

> the warning of impending judgement: ἀποδοῦναι ἑκάστῳ ὡς τὸ ἔργον ἐστὶν αὐτοῦ (22:12); cf. δώσω ὑμῖν ἑκάστῳ κατὰ τὰ ἔργα ὑμῶν (2:23);

> again, the designation of Christ in temporal terms, ὁ πρῶτος καὶ ὁ ἔσχατος, in 22:13 and 1:17;

> the promise of the eschatological gift of the morning star, linked to the person of Christ himself (22:16 and 2:28).

[77] Böcher (1983, pp. 164ff.) brings out quite clearly the sense in which although the eschatological hope represented by the New Jerusalem offers hope, it must also be seen in the present context of unfulfilment and persecution.

city symbolizes the 'not yet' as well as the 'now', and provides a focus for tension between hope and unfulfilment.

One way of setting this in context is to refer to the ideas relating to the possession of the land in Israel. In his seminal study of the land Brueggemann notes:

> The Bible is the story of God's people with God's land. It is the agony of trying to be fully in history but without standing ground in history. To be in history means to be in a place somewhere and answer for it and to it. But Israel's experience is of being in and belonging to a land never fully given, never quite secured.[78]

It can be argued that in Revelation the New Jerusalem plays this role of the place reserved for the faithful, in the light of which they live, and in respect of which God makes promises to them, but which they do not yet fully possess.[79] Brueggemann's basic thesis with regard to the land in scripture is that it is always to be seen as divine gift, and never to be taken for granted: hence, for example, the tendency in the settled kingdoms to forget the great works of Yahweh (Deut. 6:12ff.; 8:11–17). Thus Israel rightly understands its true position when it knows simultaneously the sense of belonging and yet also the sense that the land is not fully its own, but rather a divine promise, to be fulfilled.[80] This background helps to explain why the element of irreducible temporality in the Book of Revelation is so important, and why interpretations which assume either an attempt to escape from history or an attempt merely to convey timeless principles will not do.

5.4   Conclusions

At the end of chapter 3 I concluded that John's primary aim was to encourage his readers to live faithfully and to avoid damaging compromise with the prevailing political, economic and religious climate of their

[78] Brueggemann (1978), p. 13. He later argues that '[apocalyptic] rhetoric rejects seeing land as free space and insists that land is seen as gift, as arena for holy intervention, transformation, and the keeping of promises' (p. 164).

[79] Compare the combination in Hebrews of the sabbath rest which remains for the people of God (4:9) and the idea that the church on earth has no lasting city, but rather looks for the city that is to come (13:14).

[80] In a trenchant attack on a Bultmannian approach, with its stress on existential encounter, Brueggemann states: 'The central problem is not emancipation but *rootage*, not meaning but *belonging*, not separation from community but *location* within it, not isolation from others but *placement* deliberately between the generation of promise and fulfilment' (1978, p. 187).

times. In order to achieve this rhetorical impact, John uses the device of first enabling his readers to place the earthly present within an ultimate perspective, and then refocusing attention back onto the earthly present.

In chapters 4 and 5 I have sought to demonstrate how this twofold dynamic actually operates in the spatial and temporal dimensions of the text. The symbol of the New Jerusalem acts to resolve spatial and temporal dissonance, reinforcing the message of divine judgement and the assurance of salvation which runs through the text. At the same time, as we have seen, the symbol serves to intensify dissonance because the readers now see the ambiguity and anticipated tribulation of their current position within an ultimately salvific context. The cry of the martyrs under the altar – how long, O Lord? – is intensified because the resolution has been glimpsed in the foretaste of the New Jerusalem, but still not yet attained. The rhetorical impact of the text is thus to inspire hope and to guard against complacency.

John is not interested in the categories of time and space for their own sake: he uses them as a framework within which to make theological, ethical and pastoral points about the judgement of God on his enemies, the need for the faithful to avoid compromise, the expectation that this will lead to persecution, and the ultimate assurance of God's vindication of his people. The spatial and temporal categories which I have used in analysing the text are therefore of course heuristic, designed to enable clarification of John's message. It is most important not to separate the dimensions of space and time artificially. I have treated them separately in chapters 4 and 5 for the sake of clarity, but their interrelatedness is shown by the striking parallels which I observed in those two chapters between the development of spatial and temporal dimensions in the text. This leads me to make two further comments before turning back to contemporary theology in the next chapter.

First, the interrelatedness of the spatial and temporal dimensions of the text serves to reinforce the unitive nature of the seer's vision. In a particularly important passage Thompson seeks to show how these two dimensions, spatial and temporal, interrelate to guard against dualism:

> A radical transcendence which could sever heaven from earth is tempered by the future transformation of earthly into heavenly existence; and a radical transcendence which could sever this age completely from the age to come is tempered by the presentness of the age to come in heaven. *Thus, the presence and interplay of spatial and temporal dimensions in transcendence prevent a*

> *thoroughgoing dualism in which the revelation of transcendence*
> *would become a separate set of forces without present effect on*
> *everyday human activity.*[81]

So the treatment of each dimension, spatial and temporal, serves to guard against tendencies towards dualism in the other. The anticipation that the New Jerusalem will descend out of heaven, and that the current radical distinction between earth and heaven will ultimately be transformed, prevents the vision of sublime worship in heaven in 4:1–11 from being seen as ultimately separate from the earth. Similarly, the vision of continuous present worship in heaven prevents the promise represented by the New Jerusalem from being seen as purely in the future. Thus there is a sense in which the promise associated with the ultimate future is also present, precisely because it is ultimate.[82]

Second, in the narratalogical and eschatological dynamic of the text, space and time are interdependent. The spatial dissonance suggested by the contrast between earthly reality and the heavenly scene in 4:1–11 is resolved in the ultimate future: spatial dissonance is resolved by the activity of God over time. The temporal dissonance suggested by the juxtaposition of the reality of the earthly present and divine claims to everlasting sovereignty is resolved when the New Jerusalem descends from heaven, transforming the spatial distinctions between heaven and earth.[83]

---

[81] L. L. Thompson (1990), p. 31 (my italics). See also Howard-Brook and Gwyther (1999), pp. 120ff.

[82] Lincoln (1981) makes some interesting parallel points about Paul's contrast between ἡ νῦν Ἰερουσαλήμ and ἡ ἄνω Ἰερουσαλήμ in Gal. 4:25–6. The 'present' Jerusalem is not only present but also by implication earthly, since it is contrasted with the Jerusalem 'above'. The Jerusalem 'above' is not only heavenly but also by implication future, since it is contrasted with the 'present Jerusalem' (p. 21).

[83] Ellul suggests that Revelation 'seeks to disclose to [the reader] the "mysterious riches" of the present, the hidden dimension of this world in which he finds himself . . . there is . . . a more profound, more essential reality than that which we see immediately, and this reality can be comprehended only starting from a consideration of the end time' (1977, p. 24).

6

PANNENBERG, MOLTMANN, AND THE BOOK OF REVELATION

6.1   Introduction

In 1972 an influential book by Klaus Koch, the German Old Testament scholar, appeared in English as *The Rediscovery of Apocalyptic*. Koch charted the way in which theologians from different disciplines – both biblical studies and systematics – had begun to rediscover apocalyptic texts as a resource for contemporary theological reflection. He paid particular attention to two German systematicians, Wolfhart Pannenberg and Jürgen Moltmann, both of whom had worked extensively on the relationship between theology and history, using apocalyptic texts as exegetical support. The work of Pannenberg and Moltmann has often been characterized as a reaction against a dehistoricizing tendency evident in the dialectical theology of a previous generation of theologians, represented most clearly by Rudolf Bultmann. In fact, the original German title of Koch's book, *Ratlos vor der Apokalyptik* (which may be loosely translated as 'At a Loss over Apocalyptic'), indicates something of the awkwardness and embarrassment apocalyptic had caused this earlier generation. In the face of the Bultmannian stress on the overwhelming importance of the present moment, and its dismissal of historical fact as a basis for faith, both Pannenberg and Moltmann have reaffirmed the centrality of history in theological understanding, and have used interpretations of apocalyptic in so doing.

Although the work of Pannenberg and Moltmann has important common features (for example, their interest in apocalyptic, their reaction against dialectical theology, and the strong orientation of their theology to the future), there are also important differences of emphasis. Pannenberg is concerned to emphasize the overall unity and coherence of history as the self-revelation of God. Therefore, apocalyptic is a useful resource for him because of its postulation of ultimate horizons within which all events should be seen. Moltmann, on the other hand, is concerned to stress the *contradiction* between the coming reality of God and present historical reality. For him, therefore, the attraction of apocalyptic lies in its vision of a new inbreaking of God's sovereignty which contradicts the present reality of suffering and injustice. Bauckham brings out well this essential distinction between Pannenberg and Moltmann:

> [For Moltmann] it is not simply the *unconcluded* nature of present reality which requires God's self-revelation to be escha-tological, as is the case for Pannenberg. Rather it is the suffering and godforsakenness of present reality which makes it incapable of revealing God. In distinction from Pannenberg, Moltmann holds the revelation of God to be not only eschatological, but dialectical.[1]

The purpose of this chapter is to examine the contributions which Pannenberg and Moltmann have continued to make in this area, and to re-late their conclusions to my reading of the Book of Revelation. Their early published work provoked vehement discussion in the 1960s and early 1970s, some of which consisted of fairly negative assessments by biblical scholars of the use they had made of apocalyptic.[2] Much of this criticism was based on the assumptions that apocalyptic writers were not interested in human history for its own sake at all and that the central premise of Pannenberg and Moltmann was flawed. These assumptions have been questioned by more recent apocalyptic scholarship,[3] and it is therefore an opportune time to re-examine the extent to which Pannenberg's and Moltmann's conclusions can be justified from the apocalyptic tradition. The Book of Revelation is of particular importance in this regard. It rep-resents by far the most sustained piece of apocalyptic writing in the New Testament. It is the paradigmatic example of the transformation of the Jewish apocalyptic tradition in the light of the Christ event; as such, it is of prime significance for considering the relevance of apocalyptic for contemporary Christian theology. Yet, perhaps surprisingly, no detailed attempt appears to have been made so far to assess the work of Pannenberg or Moltmann in the light of the Book of Revelation.[4]

I begin with two preliminary questions, which have arisen particu-larly in Pannenberg's writing: the nature and the appropriation of divine revelation. I then turn to consider the contributions of both Pannenberg

---

[1] Bauckham (1987), p. 36.

[2] See for example Murdock (1967), Betz (1969), J. Barr (1975), Laws (1975).

[3] Among others, Rowland (1982) and Bauckham (1993b) have both sought to stress the interest of apocalyptic in the present as well as the eschatological future. My analysis of the treatment of space and time in the Book of Revelation in my previous two chapters took close account of recent scholarly study of the text.

[4] Laws (1975) is an exception, albeit on a small scale; her conclusions are fairly negative.

and Moltmann in the areas of the dynamics of history, proleptic revelation, eschatological consummation, and the relationship of the present to the eschatological horizon.

6.2 Preliminary questions: the nature of divine self-revelation and its appropriation

Revelation as history: the nature of divine self-revelation

The proposals of the 'Pannenberg circle'

The book *Revelation as History*, which is often considered to have represented the manifesto of the so-called Pannenberg circle, included an important section by Pannenberg himself, entitled 'Dogmatic Theses on the Doctrine of Revelation'.[5] These seven theses provided a framework within which to consider the proposals of the group, and have continued to form the basis of Pannenberg's own thinking on the question of faith and history. He has returned to them again in his most recent work, in which it is clear that, three decades later, he still regards them as central to his argument.[6] The first thesis concerns the nature of revelation: 'The Self-Revelation of God in the Biblical witnesses is not of a direct type in the sense of a theophany, but is indirect and brought about by means of the historical acts of God.'[7] In arguing that the locus of divine self-revelation is the events of history, the Pannenberg group is seeking to rehabilitate the idea of the realm of events as divine communication, over against the stress in certain strands of dialectical theology upon a distinction *between* the plane of faith commitment and the world of historical events.

Pannenberg and his colleagues provided a considerable amount of scriptural evidence for their position. In support of his first thesis, Pannenberg used the exegetical conclusions from elsewhere in the volume to trace an overall development in scripture of the idea of indirect divine self-revelation through the events of history.[8] This begins with references to God's revelation through the specific event of the Exodus: Pannenberg cites Exodus 14:31 as an example, of which he comments: 'faithful trust was effected by the evidence of historical facts that brought about salvation and revealed Jahweh's deity and power'.[9] Later, the tradition moved from concentration on single events to the Deuteronomic concern with the occupancy of the land and the close linkage between the

---

[5] The original German, *Offenbarung als Geschichte* (Göttingen: Vandenhoeck and Ruprecht), appeared in 1961.
[6] Pannenberg (1991), pp. 243–50.   [7] Pannenberg (1969a), p. 125.
[8] Pannenberg (1969a), pp. 125ff.   [9] Pannenberg (1969a), p. 126.

obedience of Israel and the subsequent faithfulness of God demonstrated in history; Pannenberg gives Deuteronomy 4:37–40 and 7:7–11 as evidence. The ultimate development of this tradition in the Old Testament is the dramatic shift in the later prophetic literature, notably Deutero-Isaiah, towards an expectation of the *future* demonstration of divine glory, in an eschatological perspective.[10] This tradition is intensified and heightened in the apocalyptic literature, in such passages as *4 Ezra* 7:37–42.

Turning to the New Testament, Ulrich Wilckens's essay in *Revelation as History* sought to demonstrate a Pauline emphasis on a balance between past, present and future, illustrated by the threefold stress in 1 Corinthians on the past event of Christ's death and resurrection, the present authority of Paul to proclaim the gospel as Christ's apostle, and the future eschatological hope.[11] For Wilckens, this synthesis began to fragment with the second generation of New Testament writers, who provided a less balanced account, Luke concentrating on the life of Christ in the past, John on the present experience of the believer, and Hebrews on the future. Pannenberg used Wilckens's conclusions to argue that the overall shape of the New Testament witness served to guard against any gnosticizing overemphasis purely on the present, which would have led to a dissolution of the temporal dimension of reality.[12]

Critiques of Pannenberg's position

Pannenberg's original formulation of the nature of revelation as history has attracted a good deal of criticism, partly on the grounds that it appears to make divine communication much less direct than the biblical witness often seems to assume, and partly on the grounds that it was too crudely drawn and failed to recognize the variety of different ideas within scripture about the nature of revelation.[13] Ironically, the

[10] In this respect, Pannenberg cites Isa. 40:5 and 66:18–19 (1969a, p. 128). On pp. 27ff. of *Revelation as History* Rendtorff offers a more detailed consideration of the development of the idea of revelation in the Old Testament.

[11] Pannenberg (1969a), pp. 87–8.

[12] Pannenberg (1969a), pp. 128–31. Although, as we shall see, Moltmann's view of the relationship between faith and history is markedly different from that of Pannenberg in certain important respects, he too has been concerned to stress the importance of history as a medium of revelation. His particular concern has been to emphasize the dynamic of promise and fulfilment in the biblical idea of revelation. He sets this in opposition to a more static, 'epiphanic' view of revelation, which depends on self-revelation of the divine in the present moment. See, for example, Moltmann (1967), pp. 40–2.

[13] Brown (1988, pp. 70–1) attacks Pannenberg's earlier writings for their tendency to regard word and event as mutually exclusive media of revelation. He argues that a coherent account of *both* is required. As I argue below, pp. 147–51, Pannenberg has now refined his arguments to deflect the force of this line of criticism.

very genre to which Pannenberg attaches particular weight – apocalyptic literature – appears to call his original scheme into question. To take the Book of Revelation as an example: it may be true that revelation is still expected to take place through the future events of history, in the sense that God's action will be seen in the expected events of judgement and his glory will be definitively revealed with the descent of the New Jerusalem. Yet what of the communication to the seer on Patmos? Surely this must be seen as revelation in some sense, and yet how far can it really be seen as revelation as *history*?

Thus, in a particularly trenchant critique of Pannenberg's approach, W. R. Murdock argues that, far from supporting the idea of revelation in history, apocalyptic literature in fact provides evidence to the contrary, in two main respects.[14] First, the typical view in apocalyptic literature was that the eschaton would represent a *terminus* of history, not its *telos*. Its view of history was an essentially pessimistic one, looking forward to the destruction of this age, and of the godless powers who were in conflict with God. I will consider this criticism in more detail in the section on universal history. For the moment, Murdock's second criticism is more relevant: given its pessimistic view of this age, apocalyptic would hardly locate God's self-revelation in the events of history. Rather, apocalyptic revelation came through *visionary experience*, with the communication of secrets and mysteries. So, although Murdock accepts that the apocalyptic writers envisaged continuity between the revelation of secrets granted in this age and the eschatological revelation to come, any revelation in the present took the form of a literary report of visionary experiences, not historical events.

Murdock's critique opens up the whole question of the relationship between word and event in revelation. If Murdock is correct, would it not be appropriate to conclude that revelation in apocalyptic literature is a matter of verbal communication from God to the seer, rather than God's self-revelation in the events of history? For a defence of Pannenberg's position on this question, we need to examine some of his most fundamental thinking about the nature of history.

A defence of Pannenberg's position

A consistent theme in Pannenberg's whole approach has been his rejection of the Neo-Kantian bifurcation between fact and value which had so influenced dialectical theology. One of the ways in which this emerges

[14] Murdock (1967).

in Pannenberg's thought is his assertion that events and their meaning are inextricably entwined. On the one hand, history cannot be seen as mere brute facts: events always occur within a wider context of meaning. On the other hand, the meaning of events must be sought in the events themselves and the context within which they occur: it cannot be imported from elsewhere.[15] Pannenberg is therefore highly critical of the approach of, for example, Kähler and Bultmann, for whom reports of historical facts are accompanied by testimony to their revelatory value, which is *supplementary* to the events in themselves, and which exists for faith alone.[16] He is strongly influenced by the work of von Rad and, in particular, his idea of history as the transmission of traditions, in which Israel understands its faith to be firmly based on historical facts, but open to reappraisal and development as God's hand is perceived at work in subsequent acts. At work is 'a hermeneutical process involving the ceaseless revision of the transmitted tradition in the light of new experiences and new expectations of the future'.[17]

This is a significant point of difference between Pannenberg and Moltmann. The latter is also indebted to von Rad's idea of the transmission of traditions, but whereas Pannenberg emphasizes the role of historical experience in reshaping the tradition, Moltmann uses von Rad differently, arguing instead that promises within the tradition continue to apply, but are simply reactualized in each new present, so that old promises may be fulfilled in new ways.[18] For my immediate purposes, however, the important point to note is that Pannenberg is not satisfied with any hermeneutic which assumes a self-revelation of God in the form of a verbal or other means of communication floating free from the world of historical events.[19] But the challenge of Murdock's critique remains. Even if Pannenberg's approach could be held to fit the process by which past events in the history of Israel are interpreted, does it not fail to explain the particular genre of apocalypse, with its future orientation, coupled with its apparently pessimistic view of human history? I believe that Pannenberg's

[15] See Pannenberg (1969a), pp. 152–3.
[16] Pannenberg (1970), pp. 85ff.; see also Pannenberg (1991), p. 250.
[17] Pannenberg (1970), p. xviii.
[18] Moltmann (1967), pp. 109ff. For a discussion of the different uses which Moltmann and Pannenberg make of von Rad, see Meeks (1974), pp. 64–76.
[19] See Pannenberg's strong critique of various ways in which God's self-revelation has been understood as the Word of God (1991, pp. 241ff.). As an example, he cites the appearance of Christ as the Word of God in Rev. 19:13, arguing that 'the rider on the white horse, Jesus Christ, is called the Word of God *as the one who fulfils the prophetic words of promise* . . . The world order that is manifest in Jesus Christ is thus a historical order, the order of the divine plan for the redemption of the world which is revealed in him. The actualization of the order also takes place through historical events' (1991, p. 255; my italics).

position can be defended, to an extent, against this criticism. Part of this defence needs to relate to the content of apocalyptic attitudes towards history (are they positive or negative?).[20] Part of the defence relates to the question of whether divine self-revelation in apocalyptic can be said to be linked inextricably to historical events – albeit future ones – or whether it must simply be regarded as visionary experience (in other words, a kind of verbal revelation, divorced from history).

In this respect, Pannenberg's return to the subject in his *Systematic Theology* is important. He provides a considerably more complex account of the biblical concept of revelation, without, however, conceding ground on his fundamental point that revelation is through history. He remains committed to the importance of revelation through events: 'the fact of an experience of revelation does not guarantee the reality of the God from whom it is received or to whom it is ascribed . . . above all it depends on whether what is revealed, or what follows therefrom, is broadly confirmed in the realm of experience'.[21] However, his analysis of the variety of different modes of revelation in scripture is more sophisticated than his previous attempt. Pannenberg now detects five forms of revelation in the Old Testament tradition: intuitive manticism, involving divine inspiration rather than the seeing or hearing of God; occasions on which God is seen, such as the patriarchal theophanies or Isaiah 6:1ff.; the revelation of the divine name to Moses; the revelation of the will of God in the law at Sinai; and the prophetic word of demonstration. But events remain the primary source of God's self-revelation. Pannenberg argues that the first four forms of revelation listed above do not represent instances of God revealing himself for the first time. Rather, they function as God communicating knowledge on the basis of *prior* acknowledgement of who he is on the part of the recipient. Thus, argues Pannenberg, God's identification of himself to Moses in Exodus 3:6 as 'the God of your father, the God of Abraham, the God of Isaac, and the God of Jacob' is not 'a basic self-declaration but an identification by appeal to prior events that were known from the tradition'.[22] Nor do these different modes of revelation represent *definitive* divine self-revelation. Even in the case of the imparting of the divine name in Exodus 3, which Pannenberg concedes is a self-declaration of God in a general sense, the actual focus of revelation continues to be in the historical acts of God, through which his statement that 'I am who I am' (or, as Pannenberg prefers, following von Rad: 'I will be who I will be') will actually be verified.[23] It is the fifth category, the

---

[20] See the discussion on pp. 73–5 and 164–6. [21] Pannenberg (1991), p. 191.
[22] Pannenberg (1991), p. 204. [23] Pannenberg (1991), p. 205.

prophetic word of demonstration – and its subsequent development into apocalypticism – which is particularly relevant for this study.

Pannenberg repeats his argument that apocalyptic represents a development from classical prophecy, in which the experience of exile and the lack of a glorious restoration of the fortunes of Israel led to the development of an eschatological expectation of a final actualizing of the kingdom of God at the end of time. He argues that the focus of God's revelation remains in historical events, although the events to which prophecies refer often lie in the future. Although in apocalyptic the focus shifts from anticipation of earthly events to eschatological expectation, there are basic similarities with the prophetic hope. Both forms consist of 'a word which points toward future events as a self-demonstration of the power and deity of God . . . For as all that happens in the world has its beginning in the word but a manifest end, so are the times of the Most High. Their beginning takes place in word and sign, their end in acts and wonders.'[24] Pannenberg suggests that apocalyptic texts speak of revelation in two ways:

> First there is the disclosure of the eschatological future (and the way to it) by the vision which is communicated to the seer. This aspect corresponds to the experience of revelation in intuitive manticism and also to the prophetic reception of the word. But then there is the future occurrence of what is seen, the final manifestation of what is as yet still hidden in God. As in the expectation that comes to expression in the prophetic word of demonstration, this will also involve a knowledge of God. With the end-time revelation of what is now hidden in God will come a manifestation of God's own glory (Syr. Bar. 21:22ff.; cf. Isa. 60:19–20; *4 Ezra* 7:42). The material basis here is the idea of a self-revelation of God by future events.[25]

Pannenberg goes on to show how the New Testament writers take up this twofold framework of present provisional and future universal disclosure, adapting and transforming it in the light of the Christ event; this will be discussed in more detail in the section on prolepsis.[26] For the moment, I want to note the way in which Pannenberg has now sought to defend his view of revelation as history in a way which gives a more convincing role to verbal communication within his overall scheme. In developing this line of approach, Pannenberg draws on Ebeling's work

---

[24] Pannenberg (1991), p. 208.   [25] Pannenberg (1991), p. 208.
[26] See below, pp. 179–86.

in seeking to elucidate the concept of the 'Word of God'. According to Ebeling, the word is characterized by 'an ability to make what is hidden present, especially what is past and future. By making what is not there present, it frees us from bondage to what is there.'[27] To this insight, Pannenberg adds the idea (developed also by Ebeling) that 'talk about God has the totality of the world as its theme as well as God's own existence ... the Word makes both the past and the future present by setting them in relation to the totality of human life and the world through the connotative references which the spoken Word brings with it'. The word therefore 'articulates the hidden link that connects things and events'. It performs an essential mediatory role in anticipating the totality of truth which will be complete only in the future.[28] It can be properly understood only in this light. For these reasons:

> we do not make the concept of revelation more precise by means of the concept of the Word of God. We do so when we use revelation for the manifestation of the future which was announced by the prophets and the apocalyptic seers and which the prophetic word of demonstration related to the thought of the self-demonstration of God. This is a revelation of the contents of the end-time event which is now hidden, and also of the glory of God. In this light we may then define mantic experience of revelation as provisional disclosures of that which will be made manifest at the end.[29]

With this line of argument, Pannenberg has, I believe, gone some considerable way to defend his position against Murdock's criticism that revelation in apocalyptic is purely a matter of visionary experience rather than anticipation of future divine action. He has transcended the critique by incorporating a role for verbal communication, including visionary experience, within a framework which remains true to his original concept of revelation as history.[30]

Reflections in the light of the Book of Revelation

Pannenberg is now offering a formal mechanism, in which the word may be considered to be the essential means of mediating the reality of historical events as a whole. This provides a stimulating framework within which to consider the Book of Revelation. In my analysis of the

---

[27] Pannenberg (1991), p. 252.   [28] Pannenberg (1991), p. 253.
[29] Pannenberg (1991), p. 256.   [30] This is also the view of Grenz (1990), p. 37.

temporal dimension of the text I have sought to emphasize that the text relates the present to the horizon of the ultimate future. Thus the text plays a role which mediates to the reader the hidden linkages between past, present and future: linkages which for the moment remain hidden in God, but which are ultimately to be manifested at the consummation of history with the descent of the New Jerusalem.

A striking feature of the text is the way in which God defines himself in terms with a strong temporal component. This feature is already evident in the opening few verses of the text, as the action is set in the context of an ultimate temporal horizon (1:8, ἐγώ εἰμι τὸ Ἄλφα καὶ τὸ Ω). This is one of only two instances in the book when God himself speaks; the other is 21:5–8. It is especially striking that both of these statements have a strong temporal content (see particularly 21:5, ᾿Ιδοὺ καινὰ ποιῶ πάντα; and 21:6, ἐγώ [εἰμι] τὸ Ἄλφα καὶ τὸ Ω, ἡ ἀρχὴ καὶ τὸ τέλος). It is also striking that on the two occasions when God speaks he identifies himself by reference to his involvement in the creation and the consummation of the cosmos. The divine word is being used precisely to reveal linkages within the totality of historical events. God is not defining himself in a way which diverges from the historical process.

I noted in section 5.4 the interdependence of the spatial and temporal dimensions in the development of the text. One key element in this is the way in which the seer looks forward to the final consummation by means of access to the heavenly plane.[31] For example, in the seven messages (2:1–3:22) eschatological promises are given by the Son of Man, who transcends the boundary between earth and heaven.[32] And the linkages in the text between those promises and the heavenly court scene of 4:1–5:14 suggest that the expansion of the spatial horizon heavenwards in the present reveals a guarantee of vindication at the ultimate temporal horizon.[33] In addition, worship, which has an important role in the text in transcending the spatial boundary between heaven and earth, has a powerful proleptic role, looking to the eschaton.[34] So visionary experience – the revelation of hidden dimensions of reality by the transcendence of spatial boundaries – is tied to future fulfilment in history. It is critically important that this link to fulfilment exists. Access to heavenly secrets would be gnosticism were it not linked to history. As Thompson comments in

---

[31] See my discussion of the idea of ascent to receive heavenly secrets (chapter 4, pp. 83–4).

[32] See my discussion of the Son of Man figure in chapter 4, pp. 88–9.

[33] See p. 92, n. 31.

[34] This is particularly clear in the sequence of hymns in 5:9–14, where ever-widening circles of praise look forward to the ultimate triumph of God and the Lamb. See p. 96.

respect of Revelation, 'A radical transcendence which could sever heaven from earth is tempered by the future transformation of earthly into heavenly existence.'[35]

A particular example of the linkage of verbal and visual revelation to future vindication is the proclamation made by the mighty angel in 10:6–7. This is an important episode, since the themes of expansion of the spatial horizon and of the temporal horizon are explicitly intertwined. Just as the descent of the angel to earth symbolizes the ultimate spatial compass of divine power, so the proclamation of God's everlasting power and the reference to his acts of creation stress the ultimate temporal compass of his sovereignty. The divine initiative to restore just rule to the cosmos started with the Lamb's enabling the process to begin by unsealing the scroll in 5:7, and continued with the contrasting accounts of judgement and eschatological preservation in chapters 6:1–9:21. 10:1ff. now introduces a new phase of the narrative. Just as the extension of the spatial coverage of the text from heaven to earth began with the appearance of the Lamb, and the introduction of earthly spatial references into the heavenly scene in 5:1–14, so now an actual descent by the strong angel from the heavenly to the earthly plane begins the new phase, in which the role of the church as God's witness becomes more prominent. In 5:1–14 the action was in heaven. Here, the strong angel is making a highly public proclamation to the whole of the cosmos: χρόνος οὐκέτι ἔσται, ἀλλ᾽ ἐν ταῖς ἡμέραις τῆς φωνῆς τοῦ ἑβδόμου ἀγγέλου, ὅταν μέλλῃ σαλπίζειν, καὶ ἐτελέσθη τὸ μυστήριον τοῦ θεοῦ, ὡς εὐηγγέλισεν τοὺς ἑαυτοῦ δούλους τοὺς προφήτας (10:6b-7).

Bornkamm argues that the term μυστήριον in the New Testament is drawn from Jewish apocalyptic ideas about the revelation of God's plan of salvation. He therefore suggests that 10:7 represents a proleptic invocation of the fulfilment of the hidden eschatological plan of God declared to his servants the prophets.[36] Assuming Bornkamm's assessment to be correct, the passage may be said to function on at least three different levels. First, it looks forward to the final consummation, the manifestation of the μυστήριον, which in 10:6–7 is still in the future. Second, the μυστήριον is anticipated in the proclamation of the angel (in Bornkamm's words a proleptic invocation). Third, the angel refers back to an earlier level of anticipation in the revelation of the μυστήριον to God's servants, the prophets. The reality which links together the three levels of proclamation

---

[35] L. L. Thompson (1990), p. 31.
[36] Bornkamm (1967), p. 824. See also Aune (1998a), pp. 568–70 and Beale (1999), pp. 541ff.

is the anticipation of the event of the eschatological consummation: the reality of this connection is mediated by the word of proclamation.

This section has dealt in general terms with Pannenberg's central contention that God reveals himself through the events of history. I have argued that there are important similarities between Pannenberg's model of revelation as history (as refined in his *Systematic Theology*) and the spatial and temporal development of Revelation as I have analysed it in chapters 4–5 of the study. I argued in chapter 3 that the apocalyptic character of Revelation is reflected in the way it relates present experience to ultimate spatial and temporal horizons. Pannenberg's arguments from *Revelation as History* onwards also rely on the use of an apocalyptic framework. And the interplay between the seer's vision and the ultimate horizons to which it relates has affinities with Pannenberg's model of the relationship between verbal proclamation and historical fulfilment. This brings us to the related question of the actual appropriation of revelation, an area in which Pannenberg's views have proved to be controversial.

The appropriation of divine revelation

Pannenberg's position

In this section I move from the question of the nature of revelation in the biblical text itself, to the question of the appropriation of that revelation by the reader. One of the most distinctive features of Pannenberg's theological enterprise is his wholehearted embrace of historical criticism. His response to the challenge laid down by Ernst Troeltsch at the turn of the century is not to seek (as many seem to have done) to insulate faith from the effects of historical criticism, but rather to accept many of Troeltsch's conclusions and incorporate them. Pannenberg rejects the idea that the world of reason, represented in this context by historical critical thinking, and the world of faith are somehow on two separate planes.[37]

The third of Pannenberg's Dogmatic Theses on the Doctrine of Revelation states: 'In distinction from special manifestations of the deity, the historical revelation is open to anyone who has eyes to see. It has a universal character.'[38] As scriptural evidence for this claim, Pannenberg refers to passages in the Old Testament which envisage the historical

---

[37] This reaction against Neo-Kantianism is of course shared by Moltmann (see, e.g., 1967, p. 65).

[38] Pannenberg (1969a), p. 135.

acts of God as manifesting his glory not merely to Israel, but also to all other peoples as well, regardless of faith background.[39] He also cites 2 Corinthians 4:2–4, in which Paul speaks of the truth being commended to the conscience (συνείδησις) of everyone in the sight of God, saying that some may be incapable of discernment because they have been blinded by the god of this world. Unless people have become blinded, the truth is in principle accessible to them through their natural reason.[40] Pannenberg accepts that this thesis was one of the most hotly debated parts of *Revelation as History*.[41] Since it relates to the whole question of the relationship between perception and reality, it is highly relevant to the interpretation of how the Book of Revelation seeks to reveal layers of reality beyond the appearances of earthly history.

It is important to be clear exactly what Pannenberg is saying at this point. He is not, as some critics have argued, claiming that faith is somehow superfluous, and that true knowledge of God is possible by the exercise of reason alone. Rather, he is arguing that since God reveals himself in the events of history, it is legitimate to stake one's faith in the future firmly on the basis of historical facts. His concern is to refute views that faith requires some form of supplementary inspiration, structurally separate from the historical events on which faith is based.[42] This is not to deny the role of faith or the inspiration of the Spirit: rather it is to say that the activity of the Spirit is inextricably bound up with the event, and is not to be regarded as separate from it.

If Pannenberg is saying that faith and knowledge are not the same thing, but that nonetheless they should not be separated, how then precisely do they relate to one another? He argues that trust (*fiducia*) is based on knowledge (*notitia*) and assent (*assensus*); together, these comprise the classical

---

[39] In fact, some of the references from Isaiah given to support this argument in Pannenberg (1969a, p. 136, n. 10), appear to bear little relevance to the matter. Pannenberg's more recent citation of Isa. 40:5 and Ps. 98:2–3 (1991, p. 246, n. 151) is more helpful. The tradition of the glory of God being made manifest to all nations certainly exists.

[40] Maurer (1971, p. 917) defines the Pauline use of συνείδησις as 'the central self-consciousness of knowing and acting man'.

[41] Pannenberg (1991), p. 249.

[42] Part of Pannenberg's concern here is to counter what he sees as an authoritarian streak in dialectical theology, which he sees as imposing an interpretation on events from outside. Interestingly, Moltmann, who shares some of Pannenberg's antipathy towards the Neo-Kantian inheritance of dialectical theology, accuses Pannenberg of simply substituting one unwarranted authority for another at this point. 'It is not a liberating change when belief in God's promise and pardon is replaced by a world view based on a Christian version of universal history which seeks to exact faith through pressure for a logical assent in the wake of information . . . Christian proclamation can neither set up authoritarian assertions and demand blind faith, nor can it offer "total" interpretations of the world and seek to compel agreement' (Moltmann, 1977, p. 215).

definition of faith.[43] To assume the priority of faith in the sense of *fiducia*, so that it becomes the basis upon which knowledge is grounded, is for Pannenberg 'only the perversion of a correct understanding of Christian faith'. On the other hand, he admits that trust can in a sense run ahead of knowledge, assuming that knowledge will subsequently become clearer, and he accepts that not every believer need or can prove the trustworthiness of knowledge.[44] Hence, 'psychologically speaking the decision of faith can well have the form of an anticipation of future insight, or of simply resting on the presupposition of the truth of what is believed. But logically, it must remain grounded upon possible insight'.[45] Knowledge is not a condition for participating in salvation (Pannenberg is anxious to avoid any charge of Gnosticism), but it has an indispensable role in assuring faith about its basis.[46]

Therefore, it is quite wrong, argues Pannenberg, to seek to insulate faith from the exercise of reason. In particular, faith cannot and should not be protected from the findings of historical criticism. Hence, with certain qualifications, Pannenberg accepts Ernst Troeltsch's principles of criticism and correlation, although he has more doubts about Troeltsch's principle of analogy.[47] He goes on to argue that faith is able to withstand revisions to our knowledge which emerge from advances in historical research:

> The knowledge of God's revelation in the history demonstrating his deity must... be the basis of faith. Faith does not need to worry that this knowledge has been altered because of shifts in historical research, just as long as this current image of the facts of history allows [the Christian] to reassess and to participate in the events that are fundamental to it.[48]

Thus, although faith springs out of knowledge, it also transcends it, looking as it does to the future. For Pannenberg, 'there is no essential contradiction in basing a sure trust on an event which we can know historically only with probability'.[49]

---

[43] Pannenberg (1971), pp. 30ff.

[44] It is important to grasp the subtleties of Pannenberg's position at this point. The critique by Fuller (1968, pp. 177–87) of Pannenberg's early writings appears to oversimplify matters. Fuller attacks Pannenberg for assuming that access to revelation can be attained only by the sifting of historical evidence, leading to the creation of a 'priesthood of historians'. This ignores the careful distinctions which Pannenberg makes between *fiducia* and *notitia*.

[45] Pannenberg (1971), p. 34.   [46] See Pannenberg (1967), p. 270–1.

[47] See my discussion of Pannenberg's view of Troeltsch in section 1.4.

[48] Pannenberg (1969a), p. 138.   [49] Pannenberg (1967), p. 273.

Pannenberg's desire to keep faith and reason together in this way makes him reject the distinction made by Bultmann and others between *Historie*, as the study of events in themselves, and *Geschichte*, as the study of the faith significance of events. For Pannenberg, *Historie* in this sense is inevitably concerned exclusively with the past, and therefore leaves open the question of the final meaning or essence of the realities it is investigating. Since the ultimate meaning of any event can be seen only in the context of the whole of reality, including the anticipated future, something more than a purely *historisch* approach is essential to make sense of an event.[50] On the other hand, Pannenberg is certainly not seeking to reimport a supernaturalist understanding of divine action, which would undermine his commitment to historical criticism: 'if religious or theological elements are to be reintroduced into the reconstruction and re-presentation of history, that cannot be done in terms of authoritative statements of faith that would not be open to critical historical examination'.[51]

An influential alternative: Van Harvey

This leads us into what Van Harvey termed 'that swampy ground which borders both theology and the philosophy of history', relating to 'systematic reflection on the nature of historical judgement itself'.[52] Harvey's book *The Historian and the Believer*, though published over thirty years ago, is still an important point of departure for considering the relationship between faith and history. The book's dedication to Rudolf Bultmann and Harvey's acknowledged debt to Schubert Ogden illustrate the influences which shaped his arguments. His views represent a clear and sustained challenge to those of Pannenberg. Harvey certainly shares Pannenberg's openness to historical criticism. However, his conclusion is different from that of Pannenberg. While Pannenberg regards faith and reason as inextricably bound together, Harvey aims to keep them distinct. It is crucially important for Harvey that, regardless of one's beliefs, honest and open debate can take place at the level of the assessment of warrants (or justifications) for historical explanations. He argues that the intrusion of faith into this debate often merely clouds the issues. Faith is legitimate, but it 'has no function in the justification of historical arguments representing fact'.[53] He comments provocatively that 'the basic but unspoken issue between the historian and the believer is a difference concerning intellectual integrity, the morality of knowledge'.[54] This leads him to argue

---

[50] Pannenberg (1976), pp. 69–70.   [51] Pannenberg (1977), p. 87.
[52] Harvey (1967), p. xiii.   [53] Harvey (1967), p. 112.   [54] Harvey (1967), p. 47.

in favour of an approach he terms 'soft perspectivism'. By this, Harvey means that the Christian historian uses the same tools as other critical historians, but unlike them is committed to discerning the deeper meaning events have for faith.[55] Therefore, it is possible to hold meaningful dialogue at the level of historical warrant because everyone is playing by the same rules, even though the believer may want to detect a deeper meaning in the events themselves. In this connection, Harvey refers to H. Richard Niebuhr's distinction between external and internal history.[56] Niebuhr seeks to escape from having to resort to two different realities (natural and supernatural) in analysing religiously significant historical events. Niebuhr's conclusion is that we are in fact dealing with the *same* event seen from two different perspectives (the external, dealing with ideas, objects, relationships, effects, etc.; and the internal, dealing with the inner impact the event has on human selves and communities). Harvey is ultimately attracted to this kind of solution since it allows open discussion according to the canons of the morality of knowledge, at the level of external history, leaving faith to explore the meaning of internal history.[57]

However, Pannenberg rejects any attempt to divide history into internal and external elements: 'The events in which God demonstrates his deity are self-evident as they stand within the framework of their own history. It does not require any kind of inspired interpretation to make these events recognizable as revelation.'[58] In a sense, Pannenberg transcends Harvey's alternatives of soft and hard perspectivism. By rejecting the fact–value distinction which lies at the heart of Harvey's position, Pannenberg is turning his face against the soft perspectivism which Harvey supports.

---

[55] Harvey contrasts this with the approach of 'hard perspectivism', which assumes that all historical judgement is a matter of interpretation, bound up with the historian's presuppositions. For Harvey, the problem with hard perspectivism is that its thoroughgoing relativism makes open debate about the warrants for historical explanations impossible (1967, pp. 205–8).

[56] Harvey (1967), pp. 234ff., drawing on Niebuhr's *The Meaning of Revelation* (New York: Macmillan, 1946).

[57] The problem with Harvey's approach is that it ultimately runs the risk of cutting the link between faith and particular historical events. He concludes that 'the significance of Jesus lies precisely in the relevance of his image for understanding that final reality which confronts men in all events. Christians turn to Jesus not in order to rehabilitate any exclusive claim that a defensive Christianity wishes to make but because it understands that human beings only seem to decide concerning the truth about life in general when they are confronted by a life in particular' (Harvey, 1967, p. 288). Cairns (1968) comments that Harvey's conclusions are very close to those of Bultmann's 'left-wing' critics, such as Schubert Ogden, in radically diluting the uniqueness of Christ.

[58] Pannenberg (1969a), p. 155. As Pannenberg explains (1970, pp. 90–1), part of his attraction to von Rad's model of history as the transmission of traditions is that it serves to remove the distinction between 'inner' and 'outer' history.

Yet Pannenberg is certainly not a hard perspectivist as defined by Harvey, since he is committed to the thoroughgoing use of the historical-critical method; and his emphasis on provisionality in making judgements – historical and otherwise – place him a long way from those who would flee into an insulated ghetto, despairing of the attainment of universal truth. Harvey ultimately argues that honest openness to debate on the basis of the morality of knowledge requires as a precondition the retention in some form of the Neo-Kantian distinction between fact and value. While Pannenberg shares Harvey's goal of openness, he regards the distinction between fact and value not as a necessary precondition but as an obstacle, which must be removed.

Other critiques of Pannenberg

Pannenberg's view of the relationship between faith and reason has been the subject of a wide variety of other critiques, from different – and sometimes contradictory – angles. Some critics have accused him of underestimating the importance of faith; others have claimed that despite his protestations he drives a wedge between faith and reason, and still others that he uses unwarranted presuppositions which derive from faith.

C. B. McCullagh has attacked Pannenberg for underestimating the importance of faith. For McCullagh, Pannenberg's insistence on using apocalyptic as the context for consideration of the resurrection of Christ is unhelpful, since apocalyptic categories hold little credibility today. As a result, his claim that historical revelation is open to anyone who has eyes to see is void. McCullagh actually prefers Oscar Cullmann's salvation-history approach, which assumes that a right interpretation of the biblical events requires faith, and is not self-evident: 'To Cullmann . . . biblical history is not of present significance as proof of God's existence and nature, as Pannenberg thought, but as offering an account of history in which people might well believe.'[59] McCullagh accepts the existence of Lessing's ditch between the accidental truths of history and the necessary truths of reason, although he also accepts that history might be able to show that faith in God and the divinity of Jesus is 'not entirely unreasonable'.[60] The ultimate importance of biblical history lies in its *theological* significance, not its historical or existential significance.

On the other hand, as I noted earlier, Pannenberg is *not* seeking to eliminate the need for faith. He does not simply equate faith and reason, and,

[59] McCullagh (1971), p. 517.
[60] McCullagh (1971), p. 517. For a brief discussion of the significance of Lessing for the area covered by this study, see section 1.3.

as we have seen, accepts that 'sure trust' may be based on historical judgements, which in themselves can deal only in probabilities.[61] However, this distinction between faith and reason in appropriation leaves Pannenberg open to attack from another angle. Is he not simply reintroducing by the back door a variant of the fact–value distinction he has fought so hard to repel from the front door? Holwerda argues that Pannenberg's position here is essentially incoherent, since he never resolves the question of how faith can be built upon foundations of historical probability.[62] He concludes that either Pannenberg must think that faith knows more than reason, or that he lapses into subjectivism: if either of these charges could be made to stick, Pannenberg would indeed be seen to have contradicted his basic position. Holwerda suggests the possibility of a third way lying between the opposite poles of subjectivism (which he describes as Pannenberg's 'ultimate fear') and reliance on reason alone (into which he argues that Pannenberg flees to escape subjectivism). This would seek to correlate faith and reason together, in a way in which Pannenberg cannot, because, under the influence of the Enlightenment, he has wrongly assumed that reason is autonomous.[63] Holwerda's argument certainly has force. His conclusion is that Pannenberg is open to attack on two grounds: first, that he reintroduces a bifurcation between faith and reason which contradicts his basic position; and second, he lapses into a kind of subjectivism, in which faith commitment comes to dominate reason.

Indeed, in a sharp critique of Pannenberg's views, Iain Nicol argues that Pannenberg *does* rely on faith presuppositions in a way which undermines his professed commitment to the historical-critical method.[64] Nicol identifies two principles underlying Pannenberg's treatment of theology and history, which represent presuppositions derived from faith. The first is that humanity's innate openness to the future (and hence to God) is the context within which the resurrection of Christ is to be seen. The second is

---

[61] Pannenberg (1967), p. 273.   [62] Holwerda (1983).

[63] It may in fact be the case that Pannenberg's position has the resources within it to surmount this difficulty. In an interesting article, Harder and Stevenson (1971) suggest that because of his rejection of distinctions between fact and value, his theology offers an opportunity to develop a holistic experience of reality, not limited solely to intellectual abstractions. They argue that behind Pannenberg's programme is 'nothing less than an effort to close the gap, which has existed at least since the time of Descartes, between phenomenal reality and our perception of that reality' (p. 34). They identify some key strengths of Pannenberg's theology in this respect. For example, he takes human entanglement in the process of history with a radical seriousness which unites form and content in history: God's presence in history enables us to apprehend events as they are in themselves, without the need to penetrate beyond them to some abstract principle in order to endow them with meaning.

[64] Nicol (1976).

that the framework of apocalyptic has a permanent and enduring validity. Nicol suggests, in relation to these two points, that while it is widely accepted that human beings characteristically hope beyond their immediate situation, it is less clear that this necessarily entails a hope for life beyond death, and less clear still that it is natural to formulate this orientation in apocalyptic terms. He therefore sets out two unclarities at the heart of Pannenberg's thought. First, it is not clear whether Pannenberg's case for the objectivity and universality of revelation rests more on facts or on meanings assigned to those facts deriving, for example, from an apocalyptic world-view. Second, it is not clear whether Pannenberg is genuinely using historical research to verify the claims of faith or whether, instead, history is being made to conform to the presuppositions of faith.[65] He certainly sets out to achieve the former, but, argues Nicol, appears to end by lapsing into the latter.[66]

Of these various criticisms of Pannenberg's view of the relationship between reason and faith, the one which carries the most force is the contention that Pannenberg may – despite his protestations to the contrary – be allowing faith presuppositions to dictate the outcome of historical investigation. It is on this particular point that I shall focus consideration of the Book of Revelation in this section. Clearly, Pannenberg's approach to the question of the relationship between reason and faith draws on many different resources apart from apocalyptic literature. Nonetheless, the central role he accords the apocalyptic tradition in underpinning his arguments suggests that it is at least reasonable to explore whether his conclusions are compatible with apocalyptic (for present purposes the Book of Revelation).

Reflections in the light of the Book of Revelation

As I explained above (pp. 149–51), Pannenberg's recent reformulation of the relationship between word and event gives a clear role to revelation

---

[65] For a more specific application of this criticism to Pannenberg's treatment of the resurrection, see Carnley (1987), pp. 81–95. Carnley argues that despite Pannenberg's apparent commitment to historical criticism, his insistence that the resurrection of Christ must be seen in the context of apocalyptic expectation amounts in fact to a prior faith commitment.

[66] A related problem in Pannenberg's thought which Nicol identifies specifically involves the use of apocalyptic. It is axiomatic for Pannenberg that all interpretations are provisional and open to modification. Yet he appears to give an unwarranted privilege to the apocalyptic world-view by exempting it from this openness to change (Nicol, 1976, p. 138). This is a fundamental criticism of Pannenberg's method from the standpoint of systematic theology. However, an analysis of this kind of criticism lies outside the scope of this study, which is concerned with the relationship *between* Pannenberg's theology and apocalyptic.

through word and vision, while retaining the controlling idea of revelation as history. My conclusion was that Pannenberg's use of apocalyptic literature to argue that God reveals himself in the events of history could be defended with reference to the Book of Revelation. Revelation comes to the seer through visionary experience, and he proclaims his message to the churches as a result; but the truth of his message will ultimately be vindicated only by *events yet to come*. In chapters 3–5 I noted that the rhetorical impact of the text is based on a twofold dynamic: an outward movement to ultimate spatial and temporal horizons, and an inward movement back to the earthly present. In examining Pannenberg's ideas of revelation as history (see pp. 145–54), I found considerable affinity with the outward movement of this dynamic.

However, the position is different when it comes to the *appropriation* of revelation. For this must be related more specifically to the present life of the believer. The events which ultimately prove the rightness of faith may indeed lie in the future, but the question of the *present* appropriation of the revelation by the believer remains. Therefore, in comparing Pannenberg's thought with Revelation at this point, we need to turn our attention not merely to the *outward* movement to ultimate spatial and temporal horizons, but also to the *inward* dynamic we have observed, the rhetorical impact which comes from the text's refocusing back to the earthly present of the reader.

One rather obvious potential difficulty in comparing the Book of Revelation with Pannenberg's formulation of the appropriation of revelation ('the historical revelation is open to anyone who has eyes to see') is that one of the fundamental features of the Book of Revelation is the expansion of the reader's spatial and temporal horizons to reveal dimensions of reality *which are not otherwise visible*. An ἀποκάλυψις reveals things to the faithful which are not visible to 'anyone' who has eyes to see. John has been shown the ultimate context within which the earthly present is to be seen. But as yet this is hidden from the perspective of the earthly present. In the meantime, the believer is to be sustained by faith and by worship in the context of the Christian community.

For example, the vindication which God brings about for his followers is as yet hidden from the perspective of the earthly present. It is ultimately assured, and will manifest itself in God's action in history, but as yet can be glimpsed only in anticipation. Meanwhile, the present and the expected tribulation in the penultimate future are characterized by the *apparent* victory of the church's enemies. One of the terms I have identified as marking the penultimate future in the text is νικάω. Generally, this term is applied to the church in exhortations to remain faithful in the present and the penultimate future.[67] In the three visions using the time-frame of three and a half (the two witnesses; the woman and the dragon; and the two beasts) νικάω is, however, used in a particular, ironic way, to underline the transient nature of the enemies' victory in the face of the ultimate vindication to be wrought by God. Thus, in 11:7 the two witnesses are killed by the beast: τὸ θηρίον τὸ ἀναβαῖνον ἐκ τῆς ἀβύσσου ποιήσει μετ' αὐτῶν πόλεμον καὶ νικήσει αὐτοὺς καὶ ἀποκτενεῖ αὐτούς. But the apparent triumph lasts only three and a half days (11:9), after which the two witnesses are raised to heaven, and judgement falls on the city in the form of an earthquake. In 12:11 it is said of the ἀδελφοί that they have conquered (ἐνικήσαν) Satan by the blood of the Lamb and by the word of their testimony, for they did not cling to life even in the face of death. In other words, they appeared to have been defeated by being killed, but ironically this actually represented their victory. In 13:5–7 the beast is given authority for forty-two months, during which time it is allowed to make war on the saints and conquer them (ποιῆσαι πόλεμον μετὰ τῶν ἁγίων καὶ νικῆσαι αὐτούς – note the similarity of wording to 11:7), but again, this is a limited and transient victory. The point here is that to the public eye the enemies' victory is indeed complete: it is only in the context of faith (admittedly on the basis of past divine action and anticipated future verification) that the transience of their triumph is discerned.

So the text calls for the believer in the earthly present to distinguish between the *apparent* nature of events and their *true* significance. The seer does not of course deal in the categories of faith and reason, or fact and value: they are modern currency, and it would be anachronistic to impose them on Revelation. But John's framework of apparent (visible) reality and true (as yet hidden) reality and his call to the believer to discern truth in events which apparently have the opposite meaning may be relevant to the discussion earlier in this section about the distinction between fact and value. In particular, it could be argued that the effect of the combination of apocalyptic and prophecy in Revelation is to create an epistemological division between historical events on the one hand and their faith-significance on the other. Are there formal similarities here, for example, with Van Harvey's use of fact–value or internal history–external history distinctions?

If this were the case, it would expose clear tensions between the text and Pannenberg's model. However, the position is more complex than it appears. I argued in chapter 3, following Thompson, that the seer is

[67] So 2:7, 11, 17, 26; 3:5, 12, 21; 12:11; 15:2; 21:7.

not seeking to offer a glimpse of a reality separate from the empirical world, but rather a vision of what the *whole* of reality is like. The seer's vision of reality is ontologically and cosmologically unitive, not dualistic (although epistemologically, there is clearly an implied distinction between the perception of appearances and the inspired perception of underlying truth). So the meaning of an event, such as the death of a martyr, can be discerned only within the vision of the *whole* of reality offered by the ἀποκάλυψις. Otherwise, the picture is partial – the spatial dimension of present divine sovereignty in heaven, and the temporal dimension of expected vindication are omitted – and the true nature of the martyrdom (victory) remains hidden. Ultimately, the true nature of the martyr's death will be manifest, and ultimately there will be no separation between its apparent meaning and its true meaning. Moreover, its true meaning will be seen to have been its true meaning all along.

Therefore, on one level, Pannenberg's model is parallel to that in Revelation: truth is as yet hidden and will be revealed. The difference is that, for John, the present hiddenness of truth is represented by the spatial distinction between heaven and earth. Pannenberg concentrates on the temporal dimension: God is the power of the future. I shall return to this question in my discussion of retroactive ontology (see pp. 171–6). However, some tensions remain in Pannenberg's thought here. Nicol's criticisms carry some force: there *is* a givenness about some of Pannenberg's assumptions, which sits uneasily with his radical commitment to historical criticism. Interestingly, that sense of givenness, in a context in which the true meaning of events is nonetheless obscured, is characteristic of apocalyptic literature, including Revelation. At its root, the residual tension in Pannenberg's thought at this point reflects the combination of his determination to operate as a modern theologian accountable to post-Enlightenment canons of rationality, and his equal determination to structure his theology within an apocalyptic framework. These two concerns are not incompatible, but there will probably always be a degree of tension between them.

6.3   The dynamics of history

Unity and coherence in history

Universal history

The concept of universal history, that is, the concept that history has an overall unity and coherence, is crucial to Pannenberg's argument. In one of his earliest published works he claims: 'History is the most comprehensive horizon of Christian theology. All theological questions and answers are meaningful only within the framework of the history which God has with humanity and through humanity with his whole creation – the history moving toward a future still hidden from the world but already revealed in Christ.'[68]

Pannenberg marshals scriptural evidence to support this conclusion. Once again, he traces the development of the Old Testament tradition which sees God revealed in the events of history, beginning with individual events, with the exodus as the paradigm (e.g. Exod. 14:31), moving through the more complex Deuteronomistic picture, in which God reveals himself through Israel's occupancy of the land, to the fall of Judah and the subsequent location of the decisive event of salvation in the future. This tradition is substantially sharpened in the apocalyptic literature:

> For apocalyptic thought, the present is filled with tribulation. It is only in the time of the eschatological inauguration of the new aeon that the meaning of the present time is revealed. The destiny of mankind, from creation onward, is seen to be unfolding according to a plan of God. The apocalyptic thought conceives of a universal history. Thus, the revelation of God and his glory is transferred to the end of all events. That the end will make manifest the secrets of the present is also the presupposition of primitive Christianity.[69]

---

[68] Pannenberg (1970), p. 15. The essay, 'Redemptive Event and History', in which the sentence appears, was originally published in German in 1959. This argument was repeated in Pannenberg's second thesis on the concept of revelation (1969a, p. 131). Pannenberg acknowledges Dilthey's influence here, citing his statement (from the *Gesammelte Schriften*, vol. VII: *Der Aufbau der geschichtlichen Welt in den Geisteswissenschaften* (Leipzig and Berlin: Teubner, 1927): 'One would have to wait for the end of a life and, in the hour of death, survey the whole and ascertain the relation between the whole and its parts. One would have to wait for the end of history to have all the material necessary to determine its meaning.' Pannenberg returns several times to this same sentence (see 1970, p. 163, in a discussion of hermeneutics; and 1971, p. 61, in a discussion of faith and reason). From the perspective of the present study, it is interesting to note the argument of Finger (1991, p. 4) that the ultimate eschatological horizon posited by the New Testament, with the implication of ontological unity, justifies the quest of the discipline of systematic theology, which aims for coherence in the understanding of God.

[69] Pannenberg (1969a), pp. 132–3. Pannenberg's early thought on this point owes a considerable debt to a study of apocalyptic by his colleague at Heidelberg, Dietrich Rössler, *Gesetz und Geschichte: Untersuchungen zur Theologie der jüdischen Apokalyptik und der pharisäischen Orthodoxie* (1960). Rössler's study was based on a distinction between two supposed views of history and the law: the rabbinic (including the pharisaic), which atomized both, seeing history as a series of individual episodes, and the law as a matter of observing individual commandments; and the apocalyptic, which viewed history as a unity, shaped by

The idea that apocalyptic literature is concerned with seeing human history as a coherent whole has been roundly criticized from various quarters. A good example is the critique of Pannenberg offered by W. R. Murdock.[70] Murdock argues that apocalyptic is in fact characterized by determinism and ontological dualism, in which this age is seen in profoundly pessimistic colours. The emphasis is therefore not on detecting meaning in history, but in expectation of a new age which would destroy history. The apocalyptic attitude to history in this age is that it represents the expression of a demonic will in conflict with God, and it is therefore to be destroyed with the establishment of the eternal, unchallenged rule of God. So human history cannot be the medium of divine self-revelation.[71]

Murdock's view of the apocalyptic attitude to history as pessimistic is, however, open to challenge, as I explained in my discussion of the genre of apocalypse.[72] More recent scholarly discussion of the Book of Revelation tends to support the thesis that the seer is indeed interested in history.[73] My analysis of the text of Revelation has also served to underline that providing an overall vision of human history which is unified and coherent is crucial to the rhetorical aim of the seer. It provides an ultimate framework within which the true nature of the present can be seen.

Openness or determinism? Moltmann's challenge to Pannenberg

However, even if one accepts that it is legitimate to interpret apocalyptic texts such as the Book of Revelation as offering a view of history as a whole, which resonates with modern ideas of universal history, is Pannenberg's version of universal history the most appropriate one? Jürgen Moltmann thinks not. Moltmann certainly accepts of course that Christianity is future-orientated: his theological programme is built on that basic premise. His early statement that 'From first to last, and not

God's election of Israel, and viewed the law as a unity, with the stress laid on its overall role as national identity marker, rather than on the individual commandments which constituted it. Rössler has in fact been heavily criticized, both for his methods and his conclusions, and whatever one makes of the conclusions of the 'Pannenberg group' more generally, its reliance on Rössler's study has provoked hostile reactions. See, for example, Betz (1969). On the other hand, in returning in his *Systematic Theology* to the issues raised originally in *Revelation as History*, Pannenberg has continued to draw on apocalyptic without reference to Rössler.

[70] Murdock (1967).
[71] Murdock (1967), p. 187. Unease at a more general level with the use Pannenberg has made of apocalyptic has been expressed by Barr (1975). Barr's principal complaint is that both Pannenberg and Moltmann have imposed their own theological ideas onto the texts.
[72] See section 3.4.   [73] See section 3.2.

merely in the epilogue, Christianity is eschatology, is hope, forward looking and forward moving, and therefore also revolutionary and transforming the present' might be taken as a guiding principle throughout his
work.[74] He shares Pannenberg's distrust of theologies constructed on the
assumption that the present moment is of overriding importance.[75] However, his commitment to the concept of hope in the promise of God is
such that his vision of history is fundamentally dynamic, and this leads
him to distinguish his position from that of Pannenberg.

Moltmann agrees that Pannenberg is right to start with the basic Old
Testament insight that history is a process of promise and fulfilment, but
disagrees with the results arrived at by the 'Pannenberg group':

> the basic Old Testament insight that 'history is that which hap-
> pens between promise and fulfilment' – the insight from which
> Pannenberg and Rendtorff set out – is ultimately abandoned in
> favour of an eschatology which is expressed in terms of univer-
> sal history and which proves itself by reference to 'reality as
> a whole' in an effort to improve on Greek cosmic theology...
> the thought structures of Greek cosmic theology remain in prin-
> ciple, and are simply given an eschatological application.[76]

This is an important line of criticism. In effect, Moltmann is accusing
Pannenberg of rediscovering the importance of history in biblical faith,
only to reimpose a framework of understanding which is basically static
rather than marked by historical flux. Moltmann suggests that Pannenberg's commitment to the idea that history is moving toward a universal
telos imposes a false sense of order on the historical process. Moltmann's
objection at this point is that it is impossible for any human observer to
attain a vantage point from which the concept of universal history can be
verified. In other words, to view history from Dilthey's projected moment
at the end of history would actually involve viewing history from a point
outside history, and that is impossible.[77] This is a common philosophical
and historiographical objection to the idea of universal history, and in
my view reflects a fatal weakness of attempts to provide comprehensive
explanations of the historical process.

---

[74] Moltmann (1967), p. 16.

[75] See Moltmann's criticism of Barth, Althaus and Bultmann in this regard (1996,
pp. 13–22).

[76] Moltmann (1967), pp. 78–9. Moltmann's own alternative is to argue for a different
interpretation of apocalyptic, in which the cosmos is actually taken up into history and
is rendered eschatological, so that eschatological movement, rather than a destination, is
primary (1967, pp. 136ff.).

[77] Moltmann (1985), p. 128.

However, Pannenberg's account of universal history avoids many of the difficulties associated with speculative philosophies of history, since he does not pretend to have reached an Archimedean point from which all events can be understood. That lies in the ultimate future, and until it is reached, all judgements are provisional. Moltmann's criticism of Pannenberg is not therefore well-founded.[78] Pannenberg responds further to Moltmann's criticism by reinforcing his argument that history should not be seen as a self-contained construct representing the sum of human finitude, but rather as the self-revelation of God himself. Pannenberg is therefore not postulating a static vision of reality, onto which divine action is overlaid. Rather, the dynamic activity of God constitutes history.[79]

In a related argument, Moltmann suggests that Pannenberg's view of universal history is too simple. History is not merely one process: rather, different historical events have different pasts, presents and futures. Thus, the 'present present' is different from how it appeared in the past when it was still in the future.[80] Moltmann is absolutely right to draw attention to this level of complexity in the historical process, although in fact Pannenberg's scheme can absorb such complexity relatively readily, because of his stress on the provisionality of judgement.

This leads us to one of the crucial areas of difference between Pannenberg and Moltmann: how far is the future genuinely open? Both are clearly committed to the idea of an open future, but Moltmann argues that Pannenberg's scheme is tinged with determinism. Pannenberg is at pains to argue that the future is open. Yet it is sometimes difficult to reconcile this apparent radical openness with his conviction that there will be a consummation at which the whole of history will be seen to be a meaningful unity. David Polk considers whether Pannenberg's idea of God as the power of the future entails 'soft' determinism, in which the future *ascertains* the true character of reality and decides what history means, or 'hard' determinism, in which 'the power of the future is a genuine force of creativity out of which history is fully and concretely constituted'.[81] Polk's conclusion is that Pannenberg's concern to protect

---

[78] Tupper also defends Pannenberg against Moltmann's criticism at this point (1974, p. 259). In fact, it is possible to accuse Moltmann of falling into the same trap as he claims Pannenberg does. For example, Otto argues that Moltmann's idea that God 'pulls' history from the future by opening up possibilities actually reintroduces a sort of Barthian transcendentalism, albeit rotated by 90 degrees so that it becomes a horizontal, future, not vertical, present, phenomenon. Otto goes as far as to say that Moltmann's God becomes essentially a Platonic construct, never involved in history because he is always ahead of it (1991, pp. 114ff.).

[79] Pannenberg (1967), pp. 253ff.   [80] Moltmann (1985), p. 128.

[81] Polk (1988), p. 160.

the sovereignty of God leads him to tilt inexorably towards 'hard' determinism, even though Pannenberg himself ostensibly favours an open future. Part of the problem here lies in a tension between two fundamental principles in Pannenberg's theology. On the one hand, he is committed to the contingency of an open future. On the other hand, the future is God's revelation of himself, and Pannenberg is not a process theologian: he sets his face decisively against any notion of development in God.[82]

Moltmann perceives this problem, and traces it partly to the use which Pannenberg has chosen to make of apocalyptic. Moltmann regards Pannenberg's view of apocalyptic as essentially an 'unveiling' of an existing reality, or an understanding of an existing reality. For Moltmann, this operates as a *limiting* framework, which rules out potentialities, and which therefore tends towards determinism rather than openness.[83] In this context, Moltmann expresses reservations about the way in which Jewish apocalyptic can be seen as transmitting some overall divine plan of history, since this would call into question his basic conviction of the need to emphasize a sense of divine contradiction of present reality, rather than continuity:

> The Christian consciousness of history is not a consciousness of the millennia of all history, in some mysterious knowledge of a divine plan for history, but it is a missionary consciousness in the knowledge of a divine commission, and is therefore a consciousness of the contradiction inherent in this unredeemed world, and of the sign of the cross under which the Christian mission and the Christian hope stand.[84]

He has recently reinforced this by making an important distinction between an apocalyptic world-view, which sees eschatology as 'the last things', and what he sees as the Christian eschatological view

---

[82] Pannenberg's own answer to this apparent incoherence in his thought is a highly complex argument based on the identity yet distinctiveness of the Immanent Trinity and the Economic Trinity. Essentially he argues that God is not bound to the historical process, because the eternal reality of God, the Immanent Trinity, governs the events of history; but at the same time, what is ultimately true of God is only decided by the unfolding of history due to the work of the Economic Trinity in the world, which then determines reality retrospectively. Pannenberg's doctrine of God lies beyond the scope of this study; for a good discussion of the point, see Grenz (1990), ch. 2. See also the discussion below (pp. 171–6) of the related issue of retroactive ontology.

[83] Moltmann (1967), pp. 277ff.

[84] Moltmann (1967), p. 195. His suspicion of schemes which appear to limit future potentialities leads Moltmann to reject philosophies of history which rest on the idea that there is some kind of immanent principle underlying historical development (1967, pp. 246ff.).

(represented, he argues, by the Book of Revelation), which stresses instead the idea of new creation, not necessarily limited to the end-times.[85]

Ultimately, however, it is difficult to sustain Moltmann's case that Pannenberg's theology is necessarily deterministic, because of the central role which Pannenberg accords the idea of an ontology from the future (see below, pp. 171–6). Pannenberg's scheme is designed precisely to protect the sovereign freedom of God as the power of the future, and to avoid any sense that the future is predetermined by the past.

Reflections in the light of the Book of Revelation

The question of the extent to which the Book of Revelation envisages an open or determined future is complex, and has produced varying reactions among scholars who have sought to assess its theological message. One view is that the text is essentially determinist, and cannot therefore be legitimately used to support the kind of approach favoured by either Pannenberg or Moltmann, with their emphasis on an open future.[86] In chapter 3 I discussed at some length the opposing view, adopted by Mazzaferri.[87] He concludes that the determinism which commentators often detect in the Book of Revelation is only surface-deep, and that in fact the view of history in the text is strongly marked by conditionality. This is part of his more general thesis that Revelation does not stand in the tradition of apocalyptic at all, an argument which in the end fails to convince.[88]

A more promising explanation of the balance between openness and determinism is offered by Bauckham, in his discussion of the role of chapters 15–19 in the text. He argues that the juxtaposition of the universalist song of Moses in 15:3–4 with the visions of judgement in 16:1–18:24 implies a fundamental choice for humankind.[89] This element of conditionality also runs through the messages to the seven churches, which, as we have seen, play a critical role in the rhetorical structure of the text. The commands in the messages require responses (such as repentance); the nature of the responses will be decisive in determining whether the

---

[85] Moltmann (1996), p. xi.

[86] Laws (1975) considers the use which Pannenberg, Moltmann and Braaten have each made of apocalyptic. One of her conclusions is that New Testament apocalyptic (she uses Mark 13 and Revelation as particular examples) stresses the imminence of the end, and a definite consummation, to the extent that Moltmann's radically open scheme cannot legitimately be based on these texts.

[87] Mazzaferri (1989).   [88] See my critique on pp. 77–8.

[89] See chapter 5, pp. 133–4.

community is blessed or punished.[90] These features would suggest a considerable element of conditionality in the theology of the text, albeit still within an overall framework which envisages an ultimate consummation brought about by the sovereign action of God. The balance between openness and determinism in the text would therefore be closer to that struck by Pannenberg (a contingent future within an overall perspective of universal history) than to the more radical openness postulated by Moltmann.

This is also the assessment of Stephen Travis, who regards Pannenberg's approach as the only substantial example currently available of a systematic theology which manages to assimilate apocalyptic. He regards the deterministic strand in the apocalyptic tradition as less marked than is sometimes claimed, but still sufficiently strong to make Moltmann's interpretation difficult to accommodate.[91] Travis is right that Pannenberg's position offers a stimulating framework, from within systematic theology, for accommodating apocalyptic. Apart from anything else, it ensures that the element of openness (which Bauckham and others have demonstrated to exist in Revelation) is not overlooked. However, the interpreter must beware of imposing an anachronistic framework onto the text. John appears to believe that the question of whether God's initiative will result in judgement or salvation in particular cases depends on human response. But that is not the same thing as a radically open future. As we shall see in the section on provisionality (pp. 193–5), John regards the restoration of divine sovereignty over the earthly plane as non-negotiable.

Retroaction and anticipation

For both Pannenberg and Moltmann the orientation of theology to the future leads to radical results in the way they conceive of reality. Even though Moltmann's criticism of Pannenberg's emphasis on unity at the expense of openness may have some justification, Pannenberg's view of the way reality is constituted is in fact extremely radical. In a crucial passage in *Jesus – God and Man*, Pannenberg explains that his view of the future orientation of theology has implications which are not merely epistemological but ontological. Seeing history against a universal eschatological horizon does not just mean that at the eschaton the whole of reality will

---

[90] Thus the calls to repent: 2:5 (Ephesus), 2:16 (Pergamum), 3:3 (Sardis), 3:19 (Laodicea). The other three messages also include commands to hold fast, or to be faithful, with the implication that to do otherwise will bring judgement. See also the opportunities given for repentance amid judgement at 9:20–1 and 16:9, 11.

[91] Travis (1980), p. 59.

be *understood* in a way that it cannot be understood before then. Rather, universal history has profound implications for the way in which reality is actually *constituted*. Pannenberg begins his argument by claiming that the resurrection has retroactive power: 'the resurrection has retroactive force for Jesus' pre-Easter activity, which taken by itself was not yet recognizable as being divinely authorized and its authorization was also not yet definitively settled. However, this has been revealed in its divine legitimation in the light of Jesus' resurrection.'[92]

Pannenberg argues that this retroactive effect in the ministry of Jesus is in fact not unique, but 'involves a matter of basic ontological relevance':

> for thought that does not proceed from a concept of essence that transcends time, for which the essence of a thing is not what persists in the succession of change, for which, rather, the future is open in the sense that it will bring unpredictably new things that nothing can resist as absolutely unchangeable – for such thought only the future decides what something is. Then the essence of a man, of a situation, or even of the world in general is not yet to be perceived from what is now visible. Only the future will decide it.[93]

Thus the historical process is marked not by an organic, teleological development, driven forward by an immanent principle (as in, for example, Hegel), but rather by a retroactive process, in which fresh backward links are constantly made and 'the continuity of history is constantly re-established'.[94]

Pannenberg's most radical application of the idea of retroactive ontology comes in its implications for his doctrine of God. He bases his argument on 'Jesus' understanding that God's claim on the world is to be viewed exclusively in terms of his coming rule'. Pannenberg goes on to suggest that therefore 'it is necessary to say that, in a restricted but important sense, God does not yet exist. Since his rule and being are inseparable, God's being is still in the process of coming to be.'[95] However, Pannenberg is not a process theologian, and rules out any notion of development in God. Although 'only in the future of his Kingdom come will the statement "God exists" prove to be definitely true... what turns out to be true in the future will then be evident as having been true all along'.[96]

---

[92] Pannenberg (1968), p. 135.   [93] Pannenberg (1968), p. 136.
[94] Pannenberg (1970), p. 76. See Galloway (1973), ch. 5 for a helpful discussion of this area of Pannenberg's thought.
[95] Pannenberg (1969b), p. 56.
[96] Pannenberg (1969b), pp. 62–3. See also Pannenberg (1998), pp. 531, 540–1.

The analogous concept in Moltmann is the distinction he draws between extrapolation and anticipation. Moltmann distinguishes between two different ways in which we speak about the future. On the one hand, it is possible to regard the future as that which emerges out of the present. He terms this *extrapolation*, and links it semantically to the German *Futur*. For Moltmann, the future in this sense cannot be the ground of Christian eschatology, since it tends merely to prolong the present and rule out the radically new.[97] On the other hand, one may speak of the future as *anticipation*, which Moltmann links to the German *Zukunft* and the Latin *adventus* – that which is coming. Because the dynamic of anticipation moves from the future into the present (unlike extrapolation, which moves from the present to the future), it cannot be dominated by the present. It is this sense of the future which Moltmann sees as the ground of Christian hope. In support of his argument, he cites the description of God in Revelation 1:4 as ὁ ἐρχόμενος. 'God's future is not that he will be as he was and is, but that he is on the move and coming towards the world.'[98] So God's being is in his coming, not in his becoming: his activity in history comes from the future, rather than growing out of the present. Unlike extrapolation, future in the sense of anticipation can never be overtaken so that it becomes the present and then the past. It always transcends the present. Moreover, it always transcends our present concept of what the future might be.[99] Moltmann therefore attaches fundamental importance to the category *novum*. God's action does not emerge from the past, but is a new creation (although it does also gather together the old). In this context, Moltmann claims exegetical support from Isaiah 43:18–19 and 2 Corinthians 5:17. He argues that the term καινός, which occurs both in 2 Corinthians 5:17 and at critical points in Revelation, notably in 21:1ff., has a fundamentally eschatological significance: 'The new thing, the καινός, the *novum ultimum*, is the quintessence of the wholly other, marvellous thing that the eschatological future brings.'[100]

Both Pannenberg and Moltmann therefore envisage the future in a radical way, seeking to avoid the possibility of the future being dominated by the present. In both cases, reality in effect comes from the future rather

---

[97] 'Fundamentally speaking, extrapolation is not knowledge about the future at all; it is the calculated continuation of the present into the future . . . Extrapolation sees the future as an extrapolated and extended present and it hence kills the very future character of the future' (Moltmann, 1979, p. 43). Moltmann also makes the point that this feature of extrapolation makes it the tool of those who wish to preserve the political and social status quo as opposed to those who seek the transformation of society.

[98] Moltmann (1996), p. 23.   [99] Moltmann (1985), pp. 132–5; (1996), pp. 22–9.

[100] Moltmann (1996), p. 28. See my discussion of καινός, with a similar judgement about its significance, in chapter 5, p. 114.

than developing out of the past. If there is a difference between them, it is that Moltmann, as elsewhere, has a harder-edged political motivation to his argument. His future confronts and contradicts the present, whereas Pannenberg's future constitutes the present.[101]

Reflections in the light of the Book of Revelation

How far might a reading of the Book of Revelation support this radical future orientation? In my analysis of the text I have sought to stress the way in which ultimate reality, as it is conceived by the seer both spatially and temporally, is juxtaposed with the earthly present. God, the coming one, brings about a transformation of the earthly present (chs. 6–19) in order to achieve the consummation of chs. 21–2. The process does not grow out of earthly reality: it comes from the ultimate to transform the earthly present. Thus, spatially, the process consists of the extension of manifest divine rule downwards from heaven to embrace the rest of the cosmos. Temporally, the process consists of the transformation of the present, via the penultimate future, to bring it into line with the peace and justice of God's kingdom in the ultimate future.

However, although this reading of Revelation implies the earthly manifestation of God's rule *in* the future, it is not immediately apparent that it implies a coming *from* the future in quite the way assumed by Pannenberg or Moltmann.[102] Hamerton-Kelly picks up this point in his discussion of Pannenberg. In particular, he finds difficulty with Pannenberg's argument that 'in a restricted but important sense, God does not yet exist'.[103] Hamerton-Kelly suggests that this position is in fact close to process theology, and that Pannenberg's attempt to distance himself from process theology leads to incoherence. Hamerton-Kelly concludes:

> It seems to us that the primitive conceptuality of apocalyptic is more adequate to Pannenberg's metaphysical proposal than his own structures. Apocalyptic recognizes God as 'the power of the future', whose rule is not yet established over the earth. It

---

[101] See pp. 195–9 on the ultimacy of divine justice.

[102] For example, I noted earlier in this section Moltmann's citation of the description of God as ὁ ἐρχόμενος (Rev. 1:4; 1:8; 4:8). This term is clearly connected to the coming of Christ (1:7; 2:5, 16; 3:11; 22:7, 12). And it certainly implies an interventionist picture of God, coming from heaven to earth. It is not clear, however, that it implies a coming *from* the future. On the other hand, at least one commentator does interpret ἐρχόμενος in something like Moltmann's sense (Beasley-Murray 1974, p. 54).

[103] The quotation is from Pannenberg (1969b), p. 56. See the discussion of Pannenberg's doctrine of God earlier in this section.

maintains, however, the distinction between God's power and His being. God is present to the world as the power of the future.[104]

Hamerton-Kelly's difficulty with Pannenberg's formulation is understandable, and he is right to draw attention to the distinction between apocalyptic and Pannenberg's idea of retroactive ontology. In Revelation God is certainly represented as present (although the manifest acknowledgement of his sovereignty is spatially limited, an obstacle which will be overcome in the course of the text). For Pannenberg there is a sense in which God is not yet present, since he comes from the future. Pannenberg's understanding of divine transcendence is expressed in predominantly temporal terms, whereas in Revelation divine transcendence is expressed in both temporal and spatial terms. I return to this question in the next chapter. There is therefore an important conceptual difference between Pannenberg and the text. However, I am not sure that Hamerton-Kelly's critique quite grasps the full implications of Pannenberg's thought here. Pannenberg is not actually saying that God does not exist in the present. As Pannenberg argues, the consequence of a thoroughgoing ontology from the future is that 'God was present in every past moment as the one who he is in his futurity. He was in the past the same one whom he will manifest himself to be in the future.'[105] Moreover, the eschatological work of God has implications for the church's *present* experience: 'The eschatological consummation itself is ascribed to the Spirit, who as an end-time gift already governs the historical present of believers. Conversely, then, eschatology does not merely have to do with the future of consummation that is still ahead; it is also at work in our present by the Spirit.'[106] As an interpretation of apocalyptic for use in modern theological debate, Pannenberg's proposal is perhaps closer in spirit to first-century apocalyptic than Hamerton-Kelly acknowledges.

Indeed, there are moments when Pannenberg finds himself expressing the tensions between the current realities of evil and the coming rule of God in terms which clearly incorporate some kind of spatial dimension. This is especially clear in his comments about the tension between the present reality of the exalted Christ and the continuing battle with evil: 'Already at the right hand of the Father the risen Christ has been invested with lordship (Phil. 2:9–10), but on earth the battle still goes on (Phil. 1:30), and only at Christ's return will it be concluded by the

---

[104] Hamerton-Kelly (1973, pp. 277–8).   [105] Pannenberg (1969b), p. 63.
[106] Pannenberg (1998), p. 553.

power with which he can subdue all things to himself (Phil. 3:21).'[107]
Overall, however, Pannenberg certainly describes eschatological tension
in predominantly temporal, rather than spatial, terms.

Moltmann's reinterpretation of apocalyptic cosmology

Moltmann has devoted considerable thought to the question of the relationship between heaven and earth, and how this might be expressed in
categories which are non-deterministic, and which make sense in contemporary terms. His arguments in this area are rather speculative, but do
possibly provide a helpful resource for examining the spatial and temporal
dimensions of the Book of Revelation.

For Moltmann, the traditional three-decker universe assumed by the
New Testament writers is no longer a tenable proposition for contemporary theology. Nonetheless, 'the experience of transcendence, the experience of the boundary, and religion in the general sense of the word are
just as relevant today as they ever were. It is just that we no longer find
them in the places where they used to be.'[108] Moltmann argues that the
breakdown of Cartesian subject–object dualism has led to an increasing
sense of helplessness on the part of men and women in the face of a
world they cannot control. Any sense of inward transcendence, which
previously could have been expressed in terms of powerful subjectivity
over against an objective world, now seems mere impotent escapism.
At the same time, human beings still experience a strong desire to transcend their particular situation, which manifests itself in an orientation
towards the future. This desire can be fulfilled only by the discovery of a
'qualitatively different, transforming and new future', which contradicts
the historical present. Moltmann characterizes this contradiction as that
between eschatology and history.[109] It is in this context that the idea of
heaven becomes particularly relevant to Moltmann's theology of history.

In discussing the relationship between heaven and earth, Moltmann rejects Barth's proposal that the relationship is a parable of
the divine–human relationship, on the grounds that this model is too
hierarchical.[110] This leads him to argue for a trinitarian view of the relationship, in which heaven is seen as the chosen dwelling place of the
Father, earth is seen as the chosen dwelling place of the Son, and 'the
chosen place of the Holy Spirit must be seen in the coming direct bond

---

[107] Pannenberg (1998), p. 605.   [108] Moltmann (1979), p. 5.
[109] Moltmann (1979), pp. 6–9.
[110] Moltmann (1985), p. 161, citing K. Barth, *Church Dogmatics*, vol. III/3, ed. G. W.
Bromiley and T. F. Torrance (Edinburgh: T. & T. Clark, 1960), p. 419.

between heaven and earth in the new creation, as whose energy the Holy Spirit already manifests himself now, in the present'. Hence it is appropriate to speak not of a contrast between heaven and earth, but rather of a 'complementation' between them.[111]

Moltmann goes on to develop his view of what heaven might mean for us today. Underlying his argument is the concept, derived from Bloch, of creation as 'open system'. Moltmann suggests that the earth represents the determined side of this system, and heaven the undetermined side, which is open to God: 'earth means the reality of the world which is knowable because it is real, and definable because it is definitive; whereas heaven means God's potentiality *for* the earth, which is unknowable and indefinable but defining'.[112]

Heaven is 'the kingdom of potentialities'. By this Moltmann does not simply mean the potential of the earth *per se*, but rather its potential as determined by God.[113] Heaven is already present in the life of the church as the *coelum gratiae*, perceived in God's initiative towards the redemption and liberation of the world in the Christ event, framed by the incarnation and the ascension. It is yet to be manifested in the *coelum gloriae*, the coming of the triune God and the creation of a new heaven and new earth. In discussing the nature of the *coelum gratiae*, Moltmann stresses the cosmic significance of the Christ event, drawing on such passages as the angels' proclamation to the shepherds in Luke 2:9–15, and the opening of heaven at the baptism of Jesus (Matt. 3:16 and pars.), together with Ephesians 1:3ff. and Colossians 1:15–20, which explicitly set Christ in a cosmic context:

> The risen One rules, not only over the church, but over heaven and earth as well. The Creator has given him the lordship over his world. That is why he fills heaven and earth with the glory of his resurrection life and will renew the universe . . . the movement of God in the raising of Christ and his ascension into heaven sets the whole universe on the move towards the coming kingdom of glory.[114]

---

[111] Moltmann (1985), p. 162.   [111] Moltmann (1985), p. 165.

[113] In a passage which clearly shows Moltmann's debt to both Bloch and process theology, he argues that all processes involve connections between reality and potential. These are encompassed by *creative* potentialities, which surpass in quality the actual making-possible of the potentialities inherent in the processes themselves. These creative potentialities constitute heaven, and they are determined by God in order to seek to bring constructive, rather than destructive results. Perversions of these creative potentialities, which result in destruction, may arise because God does not impose his will autocratically. Such perversions represent what might be called the demonic or the Satanic (Moltmann, 1985, pp. 168–9).

[114] Moltmann (1985), p. 172.

Reflections in the light of the Book of Revelation

Moltmann's discussion of the relationship of heaven and earth offers a stimulating comparison with the spatial dimension of the Book of Revelation. His reinterpretation of heaven as the realm of creative potentialities has affinities with the process of judgement, preservation and vindication set out in chs. 6–19 of the text. I have argued that this section of the text represents a series of divine initiatives designed to bring about the possibility of the consummation of the union between heaven and earth in the New Jerusalem. To that extent, Moltmann's view of heaven as creative potentiality encountering the historical present bears some similarity to the way in which the relationship between heaven and earth is conceived of in Revelation.

However, in my analysis of the spatial dimension of the Book of Revelation, I argued that heaven represents a wider, deeper reality within which present, earthly reality is to be seen. To that extent, heaven is not merely a kingdom of potentialities: for the seer, there is a powerful *stability* as well as dynamism about the vision of heaven.[115] Moreover, although I would argue, following L. L. Thompson, that there certainly is an element of 'complementation'[116] between heaven and earth in the structure of the text (I have firmly ruled out a dualistic interpretation of the text in my analysis), there is nonetheless a clear sense of contrast between heaven and earth in the text. This seems to go beyond Moltmann's model of reality/creative potentiality. Chs. 1–4 of the text establish a dissonance between 'what is' and 'what appears to be', part of which stems from the apparent mismatch between the eternal rule of God as manifest in heaven and the ambiguity of the earthly present. It is therefore important for the seer's scheme that heaven is seen as representing an ultimate reality which is already present (albeit hidden), and not merely a potentiality which becomes reality only in the ultimate future.

Conclusion

In this section I have sought to explain that while there are similarities in the approaches of Pannenberg and Moltmann to a theological understanding of the dynamic of history, there are important differences. Pannenberg stresses in particular the unity of history: the picture he paints is of an

---

[115] See for example the very striking wide-ranging temporal references stretching across ultimate temporal horizons in the vision of heaven in ch. 4, such as: the activity of the living creatures: ἀνάπαυσιν οὐκ ἔχουσιν ἡμέρας καὶ νυκτός (4:8); the description of God as ὁ ἦν καὶ ὁ ὢν καὶ ὁ ἐρχόμενός (4:8); and the one who lives εἰς τοὺς αἰῶνας τῶν αἰώνων (4:10).

[116] Moltmann's term (1985, p. 162).

unfolding panorama, as yet glimpsed only partially, which will be fully seen at the eschaton. Moltmann, on the other hand, criticizes Pannenberg for presenting a picture which is too ordered and stable, and which – despite Pannenberg's aim – subtly undermines the openness of the future.[117] Moltmann's charge is that Pannenberg has 'cosmologized' the historical process at the expense of eschatology. I have suggested that Pannenberg's use of the idea of retroactive ontology and his commitment to the sovereign freedom of God make Moltmann's criticism appear less than totally convincing.

In several contexts in this section I have had cause to note that in the ontological frameworks adopted by both Pannenberg and Moltmann God is seen as coming to the present from the future. This offers an explanation of the apparent present hiddenness of divine sovereignty within a framework which nevertheless foresees eschatological transformation by the intervention of God. John of Patmos was concerned to account for exactly the same issue, and did so in an apocalyptic framework, expressing present ambiguity by spatial distinctions between heaven and earth. The temporal progression of the text resolves this dichotomy, ultimately with the descent of the New Jerusalem from heaven. The solutions offered by Pannenberg and Moltmann in the context of modern theological debate clearly have strong similarities to the theology of Revelation.[118] Yet their reinterpretations of apocalyptic in ways which do not depend on the traditional three-decker universe are achieved at the cost of reducing the sense of the hidden *presence* of God's power, which is such an important theme in Revelation.

6.4   Prolepsis: the transformation of the apocalyptic framework

Pannenberg: proleptic revelation in Christ

In considering the extent to which the concept of universal history might receive exegetical support, I have generally turned to those features of the Book of Revelation which underline its *continuity* with Jewish

---

[117] One way of conceptualizing the differences between Pannenberg and Moltmann on this subject is to return to the influence which Hegel has exerted on them. Perhaps Pannenberg is reflecting particularly the ultimate unity (synthesis) underlying Hegelian dialectic, whereas Moltmann is reflecting more the contradiction between thesis and antithesis within the dialectical process. See my discussion of Pannenberg, Moltmann and Hegel in chapter 1.

[118] See Hart (1999), a helpful essay on the transformative impact of eschatological hope and imagination. In his discussion of hope in the work of Moltmann, Bloch and George Steiner, Hart draws attention to similarities with the transcendent perspective which Revelation offers its readers to enable them to reinterpret the earthly present.

apocalyptic. In turning to Pannenberg's concept of prolepsis, I shall need to concentrate more on those aspects of the text which *differentiate* it from Jewish apocalyptic, in particular the way in which it reflects the early Christian transformation of the apocalyptic tradition in the light of the Christ event.

Pannenberg defines what he means by prolepsis in the fourth of his dogmatic theses in *Revelation as History*: 'The universal revelation of the deity of God is not yet realized in the history of Israel, but first in the fate of Jesus of Nazareth, insofar as the end of all events is anticipated in his fate.'[119] To assess the significance of this claim, it is necessary first to see how Pannenberg situates the Christ event within the context of apocalyptic expectation. For Pannenberg, the first-century apocalyptic expectation of general resurrection provides the framework within which the significance of Christ's resurrection was understood at the time, and within which it should be understood now. Pannenberg explains this most clearly in a passage which I cite here in full because of its importance:

> Although the apocalyptic concept of the end of the world may be untenable in many details, its fundamental elements, the expectation of a resurrection of the dead in connection with the end of the world and the Final Judgment, can still remain true even for us. At any rate the primitive Christian motivation for faith in Jesus as the Christ of God, in his exaltation, in his identification with the Son of Man, is essentially bound to the apocalyptic expectation for the end of history to such an extent that one must say that if the apocalyptic expectation should be totally excluded from the realm of possibility for us, then the early Christian faith in Christ is also excluded; then, however, the continuity would be broken between that which might still remain as Christianity after such a reduction and Jesus himself, together with the primitive Christian proclamation through Paul's time. One must be clear about the fact that when one discusses the truth of the apocalyptic expectation of a future judgment and a resurrection of the dead, one is dealing directly with the basis of the Christian faith. Why the man Jesus can be the ultimate revelation of God, why in him and only in him God is supposed to have appeared, remains incomprehensible apart from the horizon of the apocalyptic expectation.[120]

---

[119] Pannenberg (1969a), p. 139. Pannenberg's idea of prolepsis has been attacked from within the discipline of systematic theology for compromising the radical nature of his view of the future. See Burhenn (1975), pp. 541–2, and P. Clayton (1988), *passim*.

[120] Pannenberg (1968), pp. 82–3. Pannenberg's claim that the resurrection of Jesus has to be seen in the context of the general resurrection is open to question. For example,

Pannenberg is therefore concerned to place the Christ event within an apocalyptic framework. At the same time, he argues that the Christ event *transforms* the conceptual framework inherited from Jewish apocalyptic: Jesus' teaching is characterized by a sense of the nearness of the end and the presence of salvation. The essentially future orientation of Jewish apocalyptic is replaced with a more complex sense of eschatological tension between the 'now' and the 'not yet'.[121] This feature of Jesus' teaching is widely accepted by New Testament scholars. But Pannenberg presses beyond this to argue that the event of Jesus' resurrection has a similarly transforming impact at the level of ontology: 'with Jesus the end is not only – as in the apocalyptic writings – seen in advance, but it has happened in advance'.[122] The resurrection of Christ is the present, anticipatory disclosure of what will be finally manifested, which will include the general resurrection.[123] Pannenberg cites the reference in Revelation 1:5 to Christ as the ὁ πρωτότοκος τῶν νεκρῶν in support of his argument.[124]

In the context of prolepsis, Pannenberg also addresses the problem of the delay of the parousia, which has constantly dogged attempts to incorporate the world-view of New Testament apocalyptic into modern theology. I have argued in respect of the temporal dimensions of the text that the book is best seen as representing a view which is definitely *temporal*, in the sense that it matters whether events are past, present or future, but that it does not seek to offer a *chronology* of events. Although Pannenberg has not addressed himself to the question of the

Koch, whose view of Pannenberg's use of apocalyptic is generally positive, takes issue with him here, arguing that Jesus' contemporaries appear to have seen his resurrection as a unique event, rather than necessarily the beginning of a wider process. Koch argues that the connection made by Paul in 1 Cor. 15 between the resurrection of Christ and the general resurrection is rare in the New Testament (Koch, 1972, pp. 105–6). Steiger (1967) also questions Pannenberg's assumption of the link between Christ's resurrection and the apocalyptic framework. Indeed, he goes further than Koch, and suggests that not even 1 Cor. 15 can be held to support Pannenberg's contention, since Paul's concern is to argue for a general resurrection of the dead on the basis of Christ's resurrection, whereas Pannenberg is seeking to explicate the significance of Christ's resurrection on the basis of an assumed general resurrection. Steiger's point is simplistic. Paul does not merely argue *from* Christ's resurrection *to* the general resurrection: he surely presupposes the background of apocalyptic expectation in order to be able to construct his argument at all.

[121] See Pannenberg (1998), pp. 544–5.   [122] Pannenberg (1968), p. 61.

[123] See also Pannenberg (1991), pp. 209ff. As such, the resurrection of Christ is an event of fulfilment that has taken place already, but which is not yet complete until the final eschatological consummation, which Pannenberg sees as the work of the Holy Spirit (1998, pp. 550–5).

[124] Pannenberg (1968), p. 67. In chapter 5 (p. 117) I also argued that this phrase reflects the idea of Christ as the pioneer of the general resurrection, over against the view of some commentators that the emphasis is more on the sovereignty of Christ.

delay of the parousia in the specific context of the Book of Revelation, he has done so more generally. Interestingly, his conclusions are, I think, consistent with what I have suggested. His basic argument is that the relationship between the proleptic revelation of the Christ event and the ultimate consummation is a formal one, not a chronological one, so that the relationship between anticipation and consummation is preserved and still accessible to us, despite the apparent delay of the parousia and consequent loss of a feeling of imminence.[125] Moreover, attempts to calculate the future timing of God's intervention are denials of divine freedom.[126]

Moltmann: the Christ event as anticipation and contradiction

Moltmann shares Pannenberg's conviction that the resurrection of Christ anticipates the universal eschatological horizon, and that his resurrection is inextricably linked to the general resurrection.[127] He also agrees that the Christ event transforms the apocalyptic framework, as its note of present fulfilment bursts open the scheme of two ages in the Jewish apocalyptic tradition.[128] In particular, however, Moltmann emphasizes the way in which the Jewish apocalyptic expectation of the vindication of the righteous is transformed into the divine offer of grace for the lost.[129]

> The qualitative difference between a past determined by sin, law and death, and the future determined by grace, love and eternal life, is stressed so emphatically that there is no continuity between one and the other. The difference between this and the apocalyptic understanding of time lies solely in the fact that with Christ and in the fellowship of his people this qualitatively new future has already begun, in the very midst of this present age.[130]

---

[125] Pannenberg (1970), p. 179, n. 44. See also Pannenberg (1968), pp. 106ff., 242–3.

[126] Pannenberg (1970), p. 37.

[127] Moltmann (1967), p. 142, and especially p. 162: 'Jesus' resurrection from the dead by God was never regarded as a private and isolated miracle for his authentication, but as the beginning of the general resurrection of the dead, i.e. as the beginning of the end of history in the midst of history.'

[128] Moltmann (1974), pp. 170–1.

[129] Moltmann (1974), pp. 128ff. Moltmann argues that God's raising of Christ, despite his status as a blasphemer, transforms the means of salvation from obedience to the law, as in Jewish apocalyptic, to grace. See also Moltmann (1990), pp. 223–4.

[130] Moltmann (1985), p. 122. See further discussion on this point below, in section 6.5, on continuity and discontinuity in eschatological consummation.

Hence, it is once again evident that Moltmann's approach is coloured in particular by his emphasis on discontinuity between the new age inaugurated by the Christ event on the one hand and the present age on the other. This is reflected in his critique of Pannenberg's analysis of the relationship between the Christ event and the eschatological future. For Moltmann, Pannenberg devotes too much attention to *formal* questions about the anticipation of the general resurrection in the resurrection of Christ, and too little attention to the *content* of the future of Christ and his followers in the light of Christ's resurrection; too much attention to Christ as the first fruits of the general resurrection and too little attention to him as the source of risen life.[131] In other words, Pannenberg's attention has been distracted by the formal structures of universal history and the proleptic revelation of the eschaton in the resurrection of Christ, at the expense of the implications of the resurrection of the crucified Jesus for the present life of the believer. For Moltmann, Pannenberg has neglected the extent to which the believer's new life in Christ involves a contradiction of this present age.

In this context Moltmann turns to his distinction between *Futur* and *Zukunft*.[132] He argues that in the Christ event the future (*Zukunft*) of God affects history in such a way as to trigger its own future (*Futur*). In other words, the Christ event comes from the future of God, contradicting the present age; in turn, its impact on the present initiates a new future which grows out of that present impact. As Moltmann argues:

> the starting-point is the anticipation, the prolepsis, the sending ahead of God's future, or *Zukunft*, in the passion and resurrection of Christ... If this future or *Zukunft* is made present in Christ, then, and because of that, the present determined by him

---

[131] Moltmann (1967), p. 82. Moltmann argues that this perspective has profound effects on the life of the individual believer, who lives in the context of the old age, but also in the reality of what Moltmann terms 'messianic time': 'the present time of the believer is no longer determined by the past. It takes its definition from the future. The believer's present is free from the past and open for the future of the Messiah. It is the present of the One who is to come' (1985, p. 123). In a related argument Moltmann suggests that Pannenberg fails to distinguish between resurrection *from* the dead (as at the millennium in 20:4ff.) and the general resurrection *of* the dead. Resurrection *from* the dead is characterized by 1 Cor. 15, where the resurrection of the believer is seen as sharing in the new life of Christ. Resurrection *of* the dead, however, subordinates Christology to apocalyptic eschatology. For Moltmann, Revelation uses the model of resurrection *of* the dead, of which he disapproves. He then (confusingly!) cites Rev. 21:5 as support for the model of resurrection *from* the dead (1996, pp. 194–6).

[132] See my above discussion of retroaction, pp. 171–6, in which I explained the distinction which Moltmann makes between *Zukunft*, as that which comes from the future, and *Futur*, as the future which develops out of the present.

becomes the germ of what is to come and gains a *Futur* which corresponds to this *Zukunft*...The soteriological 'descent' from the presence of salvation to the consummating future... is comprehended and enclosed by the converse theological 'descent' from the eschatological sole lordship of God to the provisional lordship of Christ.[133]

Moltmann's treatment of the timing of the parousia is complex. He asserts strongly the importance of the parousia, without which the Christ event would remain 'incomprehensible fragments'.[134] He dismisses the approaches of Bultmann, Barth and Althaus, which seem to reduce the parousia to a timeless sense of expectation, in which the parousia is not expected in time, but instead is somehow super-temporal.[135] On the other hand, Moltmann finds it unhelpful to consider the parousia as a temporal event, since that would suggest it was merely another event in the general flow of time and, as such, marked by transience. Rather, the parousia is qualitatively different from other events: 'What *will come* according to the Christian expectation of the parousia brings the end of time and the beginning of eternal creation... As the end of time, the parousia comes to all times simultaneously in a single instant. For the future of Christ also brings the end of becoming and the end of passing away.'[136] Once again, Moltmann's approach is influenced by his commitment to the idea of the Christ event (and hence the parousia) as contradiction of the present. The parousia will bring worldly time to an end, transforming historical time into eternal time.[137]

---

[133] Moltmann (1979), pp. 30–1.   [134] Moltmann (1990), p. 316.
[135] Moltmann (1990), p. 317–18.   [136] Moltmann (1990), p. 317.
[137] Moltmann cites Revelation 10:6 in support of his argument (1990, p. 327), suggesting that χρόνος οὐκέτι ἔσται should be translated as 'there shall be no more time'. He has since repeated this interpretation of the verse (1996, p. 280). Most modern commentators would disagree with this, preferring to translate χρόνος as 'delay'. In a fascinating exchange, Bauckham has taken Moltmann to task for this questionable exegesis (Bauckham, 1999, pp. 179–80). Moltmann responds: 'If we take the "hermeneutical bridge" as model, then the disciplined exegesis tells us what the text meant for the author and the people he was addressing in his own time; but the theological reflection is supposed to say what it means today, if we place it in the context of *our* own time... I am a theological partner in dialogue with the texts which I cite, not their exegete' (1999, pp. 230, 231). Unfortunately, this response begs all kinds of questions about the relationship between exegesis and systematic theology (see chapter 2 above). In relation to Rev. 10:6, Moltmann engages in a defence which is highly questionable. He argues that even if 10:6 means there will be no more delay before the completion of God's purposes, the verse can still by implication be taken to mean that 'the end of time has come' because the end of time is an inevitable consequence of the eschaton (1999, pp. 231–2). That time will really end is arguable, but is in no way a justification for citing this verse as evidence.

Reflections in the light of the Book of Revelation

How far might the Book of Revelation provide exegetical support for the theological idea of prolepsis? I began this section by suggesting that the exegetical underpinning for this idea would come from those elements of early Christian apocalyptic which *differentiate* it from Jewish apocalyptic, rather than from those elements which represent continuity between the two. In this respect, the Book of Revelation may be seen as the paradigmatic instance of the transformation of apocalyptic by early Christianity. While the text offers easily the most sustained piece of apocalyptic writing in the New Testament, it also implies the most exalted role for Christ, with the possible exception of the Fourth Gospel. At the same time, its stress on the impact of the death and resurrection of the Lamb breaks open the traditional two-ages scheme of Jewish apocalyptic: there is a definite *present* dimension to salvation.[138]

There are also more specific ways in which the Book of Revelation might be used to support the idea of prolepsis in the relationship between the Christ event and the ultimate consummation of history. The evidence in the text has not been used by either Pannenberg or Moltmann in detail at all, but I believe it is there. What follows is drawn out of my analyses of the spatial and temporal dimensions of the text.

First, the text closely associates the figure of Christ, and the symbol of the Lamb which represents him, with the ultimate rule of God. Thus, expressions of ultimate sovereignty are associated with Christ as well as with God: for example, the description of Christ as ὁ πρῶτος καὶ ὁ ἔσχατος in 1:17; the ascription to him of eternal worship in 1:6 and 5:13; and doxological statements referring to his sovereignty in 11:15 and 12:10.[139] So, in terms of the temporal categories with which I have analysed the text, the Lamb is associated with the ultimate future. Yet he is also seen in a specific historical context, with symbolic references to the Christ event appearing in 1:5, 18; 5:5, 6, 10, 12; 11:8; 12:5, 8. It can therefore be argued that the appearance of Christ in history is seen by the seer as an anticipatory revelation of the ultimate future. The Lamb is, with God the Father (1:6; 21:22; 22:1ff.), responsible for the ultimate future, yet his historical appearance has not yet resulted in the unambiguous manifestation of divine sovereignty which is awaited. This framework might be said to correspond to Moltmann's idea of the 'theological descent

[138] See my discussion of the genre of Revelation, and particularly the argument that it should be seen as both apocalypse and prophecy (section 3.4).

[139] These references can also take spatial form, notably for example the association of the Lamb with the throne of God in 3:21; 5:13; 22:1, 3.

from the eschatological sole lordship of God to the provisional lordship of Christ'.[140]

Second, the appearance of the Lamb on the plane of earthly history has in turn triggered a process in which a new future grows out of the present, in a way analogous to Moltmann's 'soteriological descent from the presence of salvation to the consummating future'.[141] Thus, as I have suggested in my analysis of the spatial and temporal dimensions of the text, the appearance of the Lamb in 5:6ff. has pivotal implications for the whole process of the subsequent resolution of the dissonance between the earthly present and the ultimate future.[142]

Third, the Lamb is seen as the centre of the eschatological community in a proleptic sense. His sacrifice is the basis on which the community of his followers is constituted (1:5–6; 5:9; 7:14; 12:11). He is at the centre of the community (7:17; 14:1; 21:22; 22:1, 3). Of these passages, those in chs. 1, 5, 7, 12 and 14 are clearly set in proleptic contexts, looking forward to the consummation.

6.5   Eschatological consummation

Having examined the ways in which Pannenberg and Moltmann have considered the question of the overall coherence of history, and the place of the historical Christ event within it, I turn now to the ways in which they conceive of the consummation of that process. There are similarities between their approaches but, as before, while Pannenberg is inclined to stress in particular the unitive nature of reality, and therefore the sense in which the eschaton is to be conceived of as a consummation, Moltmann emphasizes the way in which the eschaton might be conceived of as a contradiction of present reality.

Pannenberg: consummation as completion

Pannenberg has recently produced a stimulating discussion of the spatial and temporal implications of the eschatological process, in which he makes considerable use of Hegelian dialectic. His starting point is a distinction, drawing on Hegel, between the finite and the infinite. The infinite must be conceived of as the antithesis of the finite. This means that the infinite is not merely that which is not finite: if it *were*, it would by definition exclude the finite, and therefore no longer be infinite, but merely

---

[140] Moltmann (1979), p. 31.   [141] Moltmann (1979), p. 30.
[142] See especially the discussion on pp. 123–4.

represent another finite reality. Rather, the infinite must both contradict and include the finite.

On the spatial plane, Pannenberg applies this basic idea to the relationship between the holiness of God and the profanity of the world. In the Old Testament tradition, the power of the holy threatens the world, and therefore the holy has to be kept separate from the profane; yet God in his mercy also elects Israel to participate in his holiness.[143] In the post-exilic period, the promise of salvation beyond judgement is extended to cover the whole of secular reality, so that 'the holiness of God both opposes the profane world and embraces it, bringing it into fellowship with the holy God'.[144]

On the temporal plane Pannenberg discusses the relationship between time and the eternity of God. In the Old Testament tradition God is from everlasting to everlasting (Ps. 90:2). Yet, argues Pannenberg, this is not merely an expression of an infinitely long linear period. From Psalm 90:4 he derives the thought that all times are simultaneously present to God, and links this to the tradition in apocalyptic literature that heaven (the dwelling of God) offers a vantage point from which the whole of history, from the primordial past (*1 En.* 32:6) to the end-times, may be seen. In this connection, he mentions the use of the phrase ὁ πρῶτος καὶ ὁ ἔσχατος in Revelation 1:17; 2:8; 21:6; and 22:13. The juxtaposition of this phrase in 1:17–18 with Christ's self-description as ὁ ζῶν leads Pannenberg to suggest that its meaning is that Christ 'shares the life of the Father which embraces all ages'.[145] Pannenberg argues that the influence of the Platonic tradition in early Christianity led to a concentration on the *enduring* nature of the eternity of God, over against the transience of the created order, missing the importance of the way in which 'God as always the same embraces all time and has all temporal things present to him ... God's eternity includes the time of creatures in its full range, from the beginning of creation to its eschatological consummation.'[146]

Pannenberg brings together spatial and temporal aspects of the eschatological consummation using the infinite-finite model I mentioned earlier. He argues, on the one hand, that the consummation will mean that historical time is *contradicted* by eternity, so that the separation between moments is abolished, reflecting the way in which the whole of time is present to God. On the other hand, he argues that historical time will be

[143] Pannenberg (1991), pp. 398–9.
[144] Pannenberg (1991), p. 399. Pannenberg cites as evidence Num. 14:21 and Zech. 14:20–1.
[145] Pannenberg (1991), p. 402.
[146] Pannenberg (1991), pp. 403, 405–6. See also Pannenberg (1998), p. 606.

embraced by eternity, so that distinctions between moments in time are preserved, reflecting the way in which eternity is not simply atemporal, but includes time.[147]

Moltmann: consummation as radical transformation

Moltmann's view of the eschatological process is also influenced by Hegel to an extent. As in other areas, however, whereas Pannenberg chooses to emphasize the unifying features of Hegelian dialectic, Moltmann stresses contradiction. Moltmann argues that the parousia will bring world time to an end: '[the Day of the Lord] lies athwart all the days and times. It will not come merely "from ahead", as it were, but also "from above". It will happen not only *in* time but also *to* time.'[148]

Therefore, although for Moltmann the eschaton should be seen as an event and not merely a timeless reality, he is concerned to distinguish it from events which occupy transient moments within time. The eschaton also irrevocably changes the whole nature of the temporal plane by bringing worldly time to an end; it therefore must be seen as standing over against, as well as within, time.[149] In order to explain more fully his contention that the eschaton stands both within and beyond time, Moltmann draws a parallel with the moment of creation. The conception which he uses of the moment of creation distinguishes between two different elements: first, a primordial moment, in which God voluntarily restricts his presence in order to make space for creation, and second, a moment of inception, which marks the start of created time. Moltmann suggests

---

[147] 'With the completion of God's plan for history in his kingdom, time itself will end (Rev. 10:6–7) in the sense that God will overcome the separation of the past from the present and the future and therefore the separation of the present from the past and the future that is a feature of cosmic time in distinction from eternity. In the eschatological consummation we do not expect a disappearance of the distinctions that occur in cosmic time, but the separation will cease when creation participates in the eternity of God' (Pannenberg, 1994, p. 95; this use of Rev. 10:6 is today widely discredited, whatever the merits of Pannenberg's general arguments here. Moltmann also interprets 10:6 in this highly questionable way; see n. 137 above). On this point, see also Pannenberg's comments on 'the coming of eternity into time' (1998, pp. 595–607). This aspect of the eschatological consummation also has social implications: 'Distinction no longer means separation because individuals are no longer seeking to "be as God" but living out their own finitude in its relation to the individuality of others.' The new society which results will therefore be characterized by mutual acceptance, not self-assertion (1998, pp. 629–30).

[148] Moltmann (1990), p. 327.

[149] Hence Moltmann's criticism of Cullmann (whom he sees as imprisoning eschatology within time) and of Bultmann (whom he sees as allowing history to be swallowed up by eschatology). Neither allows the eschaton to stand *both* within *and* over against time (1996, pp. 6–22).

that the eschaton be seen in a similar fashion, again with two distinct elements. First, in what Moltmann terms the 'eschatological moment', God voluntarily de-restricts himself in a movement paralleling the primordial moment; and second, the transfigured creation enters the kingdom of glory. The eschaton is thus two-sided, partly marking an end to earthly time and partly ushering in a new time.

> God de-restricts himself and manifests his glory so that in the transfigured creation he may be 'all in all'. Created time ends and 'the time of creation' passes away. The created spaces will be dissolved and 'the space of creation' passes away. Heaven and earth find their final, transfigured form in God's unrestricted omnipresence itself. The original divine self-limitation which made the time and space of creation possible gives way to God's all-embracing, all-pervading derestriction of himself.[150]

Thus, for Moltmann, the eschaton is connected to history, but also transforms history itself into something qualitatively new. He expresses this in another way by comparing and contrasting eschatology and millenarianism:

> Millenarianism is the special, this-worldly side of eschatology, the side turned towards experienced history; eschatology is the general side of history, the side turned to what is beyond history. Millenarianism looks towards future history, the history of the end; eschatology looks towards the future of history, the end of history. Consequently the two sides of eschatology belong together as a goal and end, history's consummation and its rupture.[151]

For Moltmann, eschatological consummation is therefore both new (*novum*) and a gathering together of the old (*anamnesis*).[152]

Moltmann's unremitting commitment to God as future leads him to reject any sense that the eschatological consummation will represent a mere 'completion' with no further openness to creative process. Such a

---

[150] Moltmann (1990), p. 329. Moltmann finds support for this twofold model in Rev. 21:3–4. 21:4 (τὰ πρῶτα ἀπῆλθαν) 'defines the space that is open for the positive reality that is to come' (or in Hegelian terms, represents the negation of the negative) while 21:3 offers the picture of God permeating the whole of reality with his glory (Moltmann, 1979, p. 124ff.). See also now Moltmann (1996), pp. 280–1, and p. 296, where he links the flight of heaven and earth from God's presence (Rev. 20:11) to divine de-restriction.

[151] Moltmann (1996), p. 197.

[152] See Moltmann (1996), p. 265. Note the parallels here with Pannenberg's account of consummation. Both accounts show the influence of Hegelian dialectic.

'completion' would mean for Moltmann the end of human freedom and God's potentialities. Rather,

> It will be permissible for us to assume that there will be time and history, future and possibility in the kingdom of glory as well, and that they will be present in unimpeded measure and in a way that is no longer ambivalent. Instead of timeless eternity, we would therefore do better to talk about eternal time, and instead of the end of history of the end of pre-history and the beginning of the eternal history of God, man and nature. We must then think of change without transience, time without the past, and life without death.[153]

Moltmann has returned to this argument recently, to suggest that with the eschaton, 'irreversible historical time' will cease. It will be replaced by 'aeonic time', a reflection of God's eternity, which may be conceived of as cyclical, rather than linear.[154] Moltmann's consistently future orientation also leads him to reject the idea that the eschatological state represents a return to a primordial, Edenic state. He argues that the original creation was contingent and perfectible, rather than perfect, contrasting therefore with the perfection of the New Jerusalem. He cites the absence from the new creation of sea (21:1) and night (22:5), the forces of chaos, and the absence of the sun and moon (21:23), which marked the temporal process of the old creation, as support for his case.[155]

Reflections in the light of the Book of Revelation

Although there are similarities between Pannenberg and Moltmann in their treatment of eschatological consummation, Moltmann's scheme at this point stresses a radical continuing future orientation, whereas

---

[153] Moltmann (1979), p. 126.

[154] Moltmann (1996), p. 295. He writes: 'In the aeonic cycles of time, creaturely life unremittingly regenerates itself from the omnipresent source of life, from God. An analogy is provided by the regenerating cycles of nature, and the rhythms of the body, which already sustain life here. The purposeful time of history is fulfilled in the cyclical movements of life's eternal joy in the unceasing praise of the omnipresent God.' Bauckham (1999, pp. 183–6) questions whether Moltmann's idea of cyclical time is sufficiently coherent or adequate. In particular, Moltmann appears to be ruling out the possibility of new things ever happening after the eschaton. Bauckham accepts that transience will be absent, but 'It is not clear that, in the attempt to conceive a kind of time without transience, we need exclude any kind of novelty. What is required is that the new must be added to the already without replacing it. Nothing is any longer lost, but more may be added' (p. 184). See my comments below on the apparently cramped imagination of Pannenberg's view of the possibilities in eternity.

[155] Pannenberg also resists the idea of a return to Eden, partly because of his commitment to an Irenaean model of the fall (1973, pp. 58ff.; 1985, pp. 57–8).

Pannenberg requires a strong element of 'completion' to permit the framework of universal history to be complete and events to be seen in their final context and ultimate significance. Each of these proposals resonates with the text of Revelation in different ways.

The descent of the New Jerusalem from heaven and the creation of the new heaven and new earth most certainly mark a point of consummation, to which the rest of the text has looked forward. The descent of the New Jerusalem is the culmination of a descent pattern which runs throughout the text, as I argued in chapter 4. The descent motif represents the extension of divine power from the heavenly to the earthly plane, and takes in key points in the text, notably the reference to the Christ event (5:5ff.), which begins the whole dynamic of judgement and salvation from 6:1 onwards, the descent of the strong angel with the scroll, now opened (10:1ff.), and the casting down of Babylon (18:21). The New Jerusalem also marks the fulfilment of the eschatological promises given to the churches in 2:1–3:22. The promises are given to those who overcome, who are faithful during the tribulation of 6:1–19:21. And it also marks the culmination of the sequence of pictures of the followers of the Lamb rejoicing in his presence, which runs through chs. 7, 14 and 21 of the text.[156]

The resolution of spatial and temporal dissonance does not come merely through continuity with what has gone before, however, but also through contradiction. The symbol of the New Jerusalem is of course contrasted with that of Babylon in the text. For example, the New Jerusalem is the bride of the Lamb (21:9), the dwelling place of God (21:3, 22) and the home of those whose names are written in the book of life (21:27). Babylon is the great whore (17:1), the dwelling place of demons and unclean spirits (18:2), held in esteem by those whose names are not written in the book of life (17:8). Deutsch gives a useful summary of these contrasts.[157] Moltmann himself makes the point (not in Deutsch's list) that whereas the New Jerusalem descends from God, Babylon is associated with the ancient story of Babel, the tower by means of which humanity sought to reach heaven.[158]

---

[156] In this connection, see Pannenberg's comments on the kingdom of God as the fulfilment of human society (1998, pp. 580ff.).

[157] Deutsch (1987), pp. 122–4. Deutsch also brings out the important *parallels* between the two cities, such as that they are both bedecked with jewels, introduced to John by an angel, and so on. The combination of parallels and clear contrasts serves to underline the distinction between the two cities – one is the antithesis of the other. It also serves an ironic purpose, suggesting the apparent attractiveness of Babylon (cf. the apparent parallels between the beast and the Lamb; see chapter 3, pp. 69–71).

[158] Moltmann (1996), p. 312.

The spatial and temporal resolution effected with the descent of the New Jerusalem therefore stems partly from culmination, partly from contradiction. In both senses, the city is linked fundamentally with the character of the preceding history, and represents the ultimate context within which earthly history is to be viewed. This might be seen as lending support to Pannenberg's ideas of an ultimate perspective from which all else must finally be seen.

On the other hand, the vision of the New Jerusalem is not a static one. It is full of life, as shown in the references to the water of life in 21:6 and 22:1, and to the tree of life with its healing properties in 22:2.[159] Moreover, future events still seem to be envisaged after the descent of the New Jerusalem: the kings of the earth are to bring their glory into the city (21:24), and the implication is that the nations are to be healed (22:2). And at a more implicit level, commentators have detected in the imagery of this passage suggestions that God's redeeming purposes do not end with the descent of the city. For example, it is possible to interpret the connections between the precious stones of 21:18–21 and the priestly breastplate of Exodus 28:17 as implying that the followers of the Lamb are to act as priests to the rest of humanity. Fiorenza argues that the relationship between the relatively short length of the wall in 21:17 and the huge size of the cubic city in 21:16 represents the relationship between the number of the initial followers of the Lamb and ultimate universal salvation.[160]

It therefore seems that the picture of the eschaton offered at the end of the text fits completely into neither of the schemes offered by Pannenberg and Moltmann. It represents a definite moment of consummation, which is marked both by transformation and continuity with what has gone before. This has affinities with Pannenberg's requirement for an ultimate point of reference from which the significance of universal history can be seen, while the sense of completion seems at odds with Moltmann's more dynamic vision. However, the suggestions in the text of further salvific activity by God tend to call into question the more static nature

[159] Although both Moltmann and Pannenberg reject the idea that eschatological consummation marks a return to an Edenic state, it is clear that this motif is present in Revelation, through such imagery as the tree of life; see Deutsch (1987), pp. 117, 126, and Levenson (1985), pp. 127, 141, for a discussion of the motif in relation to Jewish tradition, and Bauckham and Hart (1999), pp. 147–53, for an assessment of the theological importance of the links between Eden and the new creation.

[160] Fiorenza (1991), p. 112. Fiorenza's argument here is endorsed by Moltmann (1996, p. 314). Pannenberg, in contrast, refuses to adopt a fully universalist position, on the grounds that the possibility of damnation is such a clear feature of the New Testament witness. So he argues for the possibility of eternal damnation as what he calls a 'borderline case' (1998, p. 620).

of Pannenberg's eschatological reference point, and appear more closely related to Moltmann's idea that time – albeit transformed time – continues after the eschaton.[161] It may be that discrepancies of this kind are always likely, given the symbolic, allusive (and sometimes elusive) nature of apocalyptic literature on the one hand, and the ordered, comprehensive approach of systematic theology on the other.

I have argued at length in chapters 3–5 that the culmination of the text in the symbol of the New Jerusalem should be seen not merely as resolution, but also as an intensification of dissonance which focuses back to the earthly present of the reader. Thus the New Jerusalem is not only a resolution: it is also a starting point from which life in the present is to be lived. As should by now be clear, Pannenberg and Moltmann are also both deeply occupied with the implications of eschatology for the present, and I now turn back to this issue in the final section of this chapter.

6.6   The present in eschatological context

Provisionality

We have seen how one of the crucial elements of Pannenberg's theology is the anticipation of an ultimate consummation, at which point the nature of the whole of reality will be manifest. An obvious implication of this for the present is that all judgements made before the eschaton are necessarily provisional.[162] For Pannenberg, this is especially important in his desire to maintain the openness of the future over against what he sees as the more closed scheme offered by Hegel.

> The Hegelian conception of history is not in fact the only pos-
> sible one, because the end of history can also be understood as
> something which is itself only *provisionally* known, and in re-
> flecting upon this provisional character of our knowledge of the

---

[161] Pannenberg's treatment of eschatological consummation at the end of his *Systematic Theology* leaves a curiously disappointing impression in this regard. His emphasis on completion and fulfilment (1998, pp. 586ff.), rather than the dynamism of life in the kingdom of God, somehow fails to fire the imagination, despite his reference to 'new and higher stages of creaturely participation in the eternal life of God' (p. 601).

[162] This provisionality extends to the most fundamental elements of Christian belief: 'Like any other concept, even the Christian concept of God is only an anticipation of the reality whose concept it claims to be' (1998, p. 631). That Pannenberg sees the apologetic implications of this position is clear from the fact that in the closing pages of his *Systematic Theology* he returns not only to the revelation of the love of God in the consummation of creation, but also to the problem of theodicy (1998, pp. 632ff.).

> end of history, the horizon of the future could be held open and
> the finitude of human experience preserved.[163]

How far is the concept of provisionality reflected in the Book of Revelation? At one level, it clearly is. In my analysis of the spatial and temporal
dimensions of the text I showed how the structure of the text entails the establishment of a dissonance between 'what is' and 'what appears to be'.
The cry of the martyrs under the altar, 'how long . . . ?' (6:10), reflects
the tension and pain of a world out of joint. But the regular glimpses of
ultimate reality on both the spatial and temporal planes underline the provisionality of 'what appears to be'. God's ultimate victory is assured. The
apparent victories of his enemies are illusory. On the other hand, the
visions granted to the seer must in a sense remain provisional, until
the manifestation of divine power they anticipate is actually achieved
in history.

However, at a deeper level, the seer does not appear to regard his message as provisional. It may as yet be revealed only in *anticipation* of
the ultimate manifestation of God's rule, and be 'provisional' to that extent. But there is no suggestion in the text that its basic premises, that
God will restore justice and vindicate his elect, are provisional in the
sense that they may or may not turn out to be true. For John, there is
no question of this; and indeed, it is partly *because* these basic premises
are held to be definitely true that the whole problem of the dissonance
between 'what appears to be' and 'what is' arises in the first place. In
other words, for John, 'what appears to be' is provisional; 'what is' is
non-negotiable. Interestingly, although this non-negotiability would appear on the surface to distance the structure of John's thought from that
of both Pannenberg and Moltmann, it may be that at a deeper level the
distance is less than might be supposed. Certainly, in Pannenberg's case,
his motivation for seeking to defend an open future, and hence the provisionality of judgement in the present, is to avoid impinging upon the
sovereign freedom of God. The non-negotiability of the coming reign
of God in Revelation is similarly a statement about the sovereign freedom of God to intervene and transform the world. Pannenberg needs to
assert the openness of the future to preserve divine freedom from the
kind of evolutionary system typified by Hegelian dialectic, in which the
past organically determines the future. John was operating in a totally
different intellectual environment, in which elements of determinism
could be seen more readily as the outworking of God's will, rather
than as constraints upon the will of God. Therefore, amid the obvious

---

[163] Pannenberg (1970), p. 135; (1973), p. 177.

differences, there may be at least one common core element: the concern to preserve the sovereign freedom of God in both the present and the future.

The ultimacy of divine justice

Another implication of seeing the present in the light of the future consummation is that the power of human institutions is relativized in the light of the anticipated ultimate manifestation of God's sovereignty. 'An understanding of reality that is inspired not by the past nor by external structures but by the power of the future confronting the present cannot result in a conservative desire to maintain the established order.'[164] In his discussion of Pannenberg's eschatological ethics, Ted Peters sets the implications out clearly:

> 'The futurity of God's rule actually serves to open up possibilities for ethical action while still denying any human institution the glory of perfection which might warrant its making an absolute claim on us for obedience. The kingdom of God, just because it is eschatological, draws us beyond the present state of being and prohibits the claim to totalitarian rule by any temporal dictator.'[165]

Peters goes on to argue that the setting of Pannenberg's theology in a universal eschatological context lends itself to a stress upon universal peace and justice, rather than special-interest agendas, although he also puts forward the suggestion that Pannenberg's theology may hold within it the possibility of accommodating liberationist approaches. Nonetheless, Pannenberg is open to attack from a liberationist perspective, on the grounds that a universalizing viewpoint will tend to mask the specific injustices suffered by the marginalized, and underplay the importance of political action to combat injustice.[166]

Moltmann, in contrast, urges positive engagement with the world in order to change it. This feature of Moltmann's theology is brought out by Bauckham:

> Authentic Christian hope is not that purely other-worldly expectation which is resigned to the inalterability of affairs in this world. Rather, because it is hope for the future of this world, its

---

[164] Pannenberg (1969b), p. 116.   [165] Peters (1988), p. 243.
[166] Thus Cobb says of Pannenberg: 'He listens respectfully only to those who accept the disciplines honed over generations of scholarship and contribute to their advance. It is evident that one who interprets God's work in history in this way will not be attuned to liberationist voices' (1988, p. 72).

effect is to show present reality to be *not yet* what it can be and
will be. The world is seen as transformable in the direction of
the promised future. In this way believers are liberated from ac-
commodation to the *status quo* and set critically against it. They
suffer the contradiction between what is and what is promised.
But this critical distance also enables them to seek and to acti-
vate those present possibilities of world history which lead in the
direction of the eschatological future. Thus, by arousing *active*
hope the promise creates anticipations of the future kingdom
within history.[167]

The role of Christian anticipation is to 'encourage everything in history
which ministers to life, and strive against everything that disseminates
death'.[168] The revelation of the end-time (Moltmann refers explicitly to
John's term ἀποκάλυψις from 1:1) reveals the instability of the powers
and encourages resistance.[169] Thus, the power of oppressive institutions
is relativized. Moltmann argues that, for this reason, apocalyptic writers
felt able to narrate the anticipated fall of unjust powers as 'an anticipation
of something that has not yet happened, but it is an anticipation in the
mode of the narrated past of what must pass away'.[170] Moltmann also
underlines the importance of divine justice being reflected ultimately on
earth, in his discussion of the millennium.[171] For Moltmann, the millennium in Revelation is primarily a hope for the martyrs. He argues that
the vindication of the martyrs must take place in history. 'It would be
a confutation of their martyrdom if God were not to show his power
at the very point where, for him and with him, they suffered in his

[167] Bauckham (1995), p. 10. See also Thiselton's discussion of Moltmann in this context
(1995, pp. 145ff.).

[168] Moltmann (1977), p. 196. This activist view of the role of Christian faith leads
Moltmann to argue that 'the theologian is not concerned merely to supply a different *interpretation* of the world of history and of human nature, but to *transform* them in expectation
of a divine transformation' (1967, p. 84). This is a conscious echo of Marx's eleventh thesis
on Feuerbach: 'The philosophers have only *interpreted* the world, in various ways; the
point, however, is to change it.'

[169] Moltmann (1996), p. 137.

[170] Moltmann (1996), p. 140. This pattern can be seen operating in Rev. 18, with the use
of the past tense to describe the anticipated future judgement upon Babylon. The use of the
aorist in the repeated cry of ἔπεσεν ἔπεσεν Βαβυλὼν ἡ μεγάλη at 14:8 and 18:2 makes the
point particularly vividly.

[171] See Bauckham (1999), pp. 123–47, for a critique of Moltmann's commitment in
The Coming of God to the idea of the millennium as a transitional eschatological state,
and Moltmann's brief reply (Moltmann 1999, pp. 149–54). Bauckham's argument is that
in the context of contemporary theology, the millennium should be seen not as a discrete
transitional state, but rather as emphasizing the immanent and this-worldly aspect of eschatological consummation; see also Bauckham and Hart (1999), pp. 132–39. I have myself
argued on similar lines (Gilbertson, 1997).

helplessness, and if God were not to assert his rights in the very situation in which they were executed.'[172] The conviction of the ultimate manifestation of divine justice in history, in this world, leads, for Moltmann, to a clear consequential praxis of resistance 'against the godless kingdoms of this world'.[173] Moltmann is therefore highly critical of theologies of rapture, characteristic of much modern pre-millennialism.[174] The idea of the rapture in fact implies a 'rupture' in history, in which God's vindication of his people takes place not in history, but outside it, thus depriving Christian hope of its ethical imperative to seek to change this world.[175] He is similarly critical of what he terms political or ecclesiastical millenarianism, which identifies the outworking of divine justice in the millennium with the success of particular human institutions, such as the United States, or the institutional church.[176] Moltmann's criticism of both rapture theology (an escape from history) and political millenarianism (dissolving the millennium into mere history) mirrors his more general concern to see the eschaton as both within time and beyond it.[177]

In the case of both Moltmann and Pannenberg there is a strong sense in which ethical action is driven from the future. Christian praxis in the present is to be shaped by eschatology. In my analysis of the text of Revelation I drew attention to the way in which the focus of the text is brought back from the ultimate horizons, represented by the descent of the New Jerusalem, to the earthly present of the reader. This is shown especially in the epilogue.[178] But it is also shown more generally in

---

[172] Moltmann (1996), p. 152.   [173] Moltmann (1996), p. 152.

[174] 'Revelation was not written for "rapturists" fleeing from the world, who tell the world "goodbye" and want to go to heaven; it was meant for resistance fighters, struggling against the godless powers on this earth' (1996, p. 153).

[175] Moltmann (1996), p. 193.

[176] See Moltmann (1996), pp. 159–84. Moltmann characterizes political or ecclesiastical millenarianism as 'historical millenarianism', as opposed to 'eschatological millenarianism', which resists the identification of the millennium merely with historical developments. Moltmann's points here are well made. Apart from anything else, they serve to indicate that the text of Revelation has within it the resources to transcend the difficulties suggested by Fiorenza, to the effect that it cannot be justly appropriated by the powerful (see chapter 3, pp. 60–1). Reading the symbol of the millennium in a way which *relativizes* the power of human institutions, and undermines their claims to ultimacy, surely helps to meet Fiorenza's concerns.

[177] Pannenberg has warned that Moltmann's approach could lead to the subordination of Christian faith to political goals. His argument is that Moltmann has given insufficiently rigorous attention to exactly how the general desire for transformation reflected in prophetic and apocalyptic literature might be made concrete in contemporary circumstances, with the result that Moltmann resorts too quickly to a neo-Marxian programme which is not distinctively Christian (Pannenberg, 1984a). See also Otto's rather more vituperative version of the same criticism (1991, ch. 2).

[178] See above, pp. 106–8 and 136–40.

recent interpretation of the text in its rhetorical context. In chapter 3 I undertook a threefold analysis of views of the seer's interest in history, of the rhetorical impact of the symbolism of the text, and of the genre of the text. My conclusion in each case was that the rhetorical impact of the text – calling for the avoidance of compromise, in warning of coming persecution, and in promising ultimate vindication – derives from its ultimate context of the just action of God in judgement, salvation and vindication. Just as in Pannenberg and Moltmann, the ethical imperative comes from the eschatological context.

The interesting thing about the Book of Revelation in this context is that it manages to combine *both* a universal perspective, which relativizes all human institutions, *and* a view of history from below, reflecting the concerns of the oppressed. As an example, we might take the account of the fall of Babylon in 18:1–24. Although the primary reference is clearly to Rome, this is overlaid with echoes of Old Testament references to other cities.[179] The symbol of Babylon thus takes on a universal quality in terms of both time and location: Rome 'summed up in itself and surpassed the wickedness of the tyrant powers of the past'.[180] The fall of the great city becomes a symbol for the relativization of all human tyranny in the face of the manifestation of divine justice.[181] At the same time, the symbol is not only universal, but also particular. The complex of images of the great city, of which ch. 18 forms a part, consists partly of clear references to Rome and Jerusalem which had specific relevance to the communities to which John wrote.[182] This combination of the relativization of human

---

[179] The key Old Testament texts underlying the description of the destruction of Babylon in ch. 18 are Isa. 13 and Jer. 51, in relation to the fall of Babylon itself, and Ezek. 26–8, the oracle against Tyre. The latter passage is especially noteworthy given its combination of a description of the city as a finely adorned woman, a list of the cargoes she traded, the desolation predicted for her, and mourning for her by kings, merchants and seafarers, all of which appear in Rev. 18. In addition, there are echoes of two further passages, the prophecy against Edom in Isa. 34, with its picture of the desolate land as a haunt of wild animals, and the condemnation of Nineveh in Nahum 3:1ff., with its description of the city as a harlot responsible for massive bloodshed. Kraybill (1996) draws attention to the similarities in the list of jewels adorning the New Jerusalem in 21:19–20 and those worn by the king of Tyre in Ezek. 28:13. He argues that the jewels are to be 'restored to the mountain of God in a community of economic justice' (p. 209).

[180] Beasley-Murray (1974), p. 264.

[181] This is suggested by the use of the wide-ranging term οἱ βασιλεῖς τῆς γῆς in 18:3, 9 to describe the rulers who have collaborated with Rome. The term occurs regularly in Revelation, apart from the references in ch. 18. The kings of the earth collaborate with Babylon (17:2, 18) and rebel against God (16:14 (the slightly different term βασιλεῖς τῆς οἰκουμένης ὅλης); 19:19). They suffer judgement (6:15). Ultimately they are subject to God (1:5; 21:24).

[182] For example, 11:8 refers to the great city as the place where Christ was crucified, clearly a reference to Jerusalem, and to Christ as the pioneer of the sufferings undergone

power in the face of God's universal sovereignty and the judgement upon Rome due to its specific oppression of the saints is illustrated graphically in 18:24: καὶ ἐν αὐτῇ αἷμα προφητῶν καὶ ἁγίων εὑρέθη καὶ πάντων τῶν ἐσφαγμένων ἐπὶ τῆς γῆς.[183] At the conclusion of the passage Babylon is thus simultaneously accused of the *specific* crime of killing prophets and saints, and held responsible *generally* for the blood of all those who have ever been killed.

6.7   Conclusions

In this chapter I have sought to explain the respective positions of Pannenberg and Moltmann on the theology of history, bringing out both the similarities and the differences between them. I have also compared and contrasted their positions with my reading of the Book of Revelation. As I hope has become clear, there is considerable scope for dialogue between my analysis of the spatial and temporal dimensions of Revelation and the views of Pannenberg and Moltmann on the theology of history, although the conceptual worlds of John of Patmos and twentieth-century German theology are of course very different. In both cases, there is a concern to articulate at a fundamental level the relationship between divine reality and human history. In chapters 3–5 we saw how Revelation sets the reader's experience within ultimate spatial and temporal horizons, and focuses attention back onto the earthly present in the light of those ultimate perspectives. A similar dynamic is at work in different ways in the work of both Pannenberg and Moltmann. Both have developed a theology whose orientation is to the ultimate future but which also has a critical impact on the present in the light of that ultimate future.

The analysis in this chapter has yielded interesting and fruitful results. I began with Pannenberg's idea of revelation as history. I established that the model of revelation he has now developed, giving a clearer role to verbal revelation within an overall context of God's self-revelation in events, shows interesting affinities with the Book of Revelation. I then considered the question of the appropriation of revelation by the believer. Here the

---

by the community. The city of ch. 18 is also clearly linked to the beasts of ch. 13, which are widely interpreted as relating to the political power of Rome and the imperial cult in Asia Minor. In a highly suggestive article, Minear (1966) brings out the interplay of the universal and the particular in the imagery of the city in Revelation.

[183] Howard-Brook and Gwyther (1999) juxtapose a series of contrasts in what they see as a 'war of myths' between Revelation and Rome. For example, 'the empire of our God' is set against the Roman myth of empire; 'Babylon the shedder of blood' against the Pax Romana; the victory of the Lamb and his followers against the Roman 'Victoria' myth (pp. 223–35).

position, at least on the surface, was more problematic, but I suggested that there was possibly continuity between the text and Pannenberg's position at a deeper level. In the eschatological future of Pannenberg's scheme, the meaning of all events becomes manifest and, moreover, such meaning will be seen to have been true all along. Hence, for example, if a martyr's death – an apparent defeat – is seen to be a victory in the ultimate future, then it will in fact have been a victory all along, although not perceived as such at the time.

I then considered the views of Pannenberg and Moltmann on the dynamics of history. The Book of Revelation certainly operates with a unified view of history, in which events taken together have a coherent meaning. The process envisaged in the text is one in which the rule of God, which is universal but not yet publicly manifest on the earthly plane, extends downward from heaven to embrace the whole of the cosmos. For both Pannenberg and Moltmann, however, God's rule is hidden in the present not because of spatial distinctions between heaven and earth, but because God's rule comes from the future. This is a stimulating reinterpretation of the apocalyptic world-view. But the reinterpretation is achieved at the cost of diminishing the sense of the present – albeit hidden – reality of the rule of God so eloquently expressed in Revelation.

The twofold dynamic of the expansive outward vision to ultimate horizons coupled with a sharp inward focus on the earthly present, which has formed such a central part of my analysis of the text, is clearly present in both Pannenberg and Moltmann. The sharp inward focus of the text back to the present of the reader is paralleled in the ways Pannenberg and Moltmann both place Christian ethics in an eschatological framework, so that the present is to be seen and lived in the light of the future.

In section 2.4 I argued that Revelation contains 'hints, markers and signposts', on the basis of which theological assertions may be made. In this chapter I have demonstrated that the text can be used in making judgements about proposals advanced by two contemporary theologians. In some cases I have identified clear continuities between the text and these proposals; in other cases there is discontinuity; and in yet other cases there is continuity at deeper levels despite apparent discontinuity. I shall now summarize these findings in slightly more detail in my concluding chapter.

7

CONCLUSIONS

The aim of this study has been to examine the extent to which the reading of one New Testament text – the Book of Revelation – can be used to support or question the contemporary theologies of history proposed by Wolfhart Pannenberg and Jürgen Moltmann.

I began in chapter 1 by setting the contributions of Pannenberg and Moltmann in their context, comparing and contrasting their proposals with other influential ideas about the relationship between faith and history. In chapter 2 I proceeded to explore some of the methodological issues which arise from the consideration of the relationship between theology and scripture. I argued against attempts to see the relationship between exegesis and systematics as a 'two-stage' process, in which the results of biblical interpretation are first determined, then transmitted wholesale to an entirely separate discipline, which seeks to apply them to contemporary questions. Rather, I suggested that it was both legitimate and important for the two disciplines to interrelate.[1] Similarly, I argued for the relationship between scripture and theological formulation to be seen as dialectical.[2] Scripture is a starting point for the generation of conceptual frameworks in theology. These frameworks then need to be reassessed continually, to determine their adequacy as elaborations of scripture. At the same time, new light may be shed on scripture itself by reading it through the lenses provided by such conceptual frameworks. Chapter 2 therefore constitutes a defence of one of the key assumptions underlying this study: that it is legitimate, not to say desirable, to consider scripture and theology together, as I have done in chapters 3–6.

In chapter 2 I also questioned the adequacy of models which emphasize the *function* of scripture at the expense of its *content*. The danger inherent in many functionalist approaches is that truth-claims can become relativized. Such approaches may emphasize the *effect* which scripture has (for example on the building up of a community); meanwhile, the question

---

[1] See section 2.2.   [2] See section 2.3.

of the relationship between scriptural affirmation and reality can become secondary. I have argued that it is misleading to dilute the importance of the content of scripture in this way. The relationship between reality and scriptural affirmation is critically important. This becomes clear in my analysis of Revelation, in which I conclude that the rhetorical function of the text depends precisely upon the truth-claims it makes about ultimate reality.

In chapter 3 I turned to the text, considering three debates among interpreters: firstly, the significance of the text for the historical process; secondly, the rhetorical situation and rhetorical impact of the text; thirdly, the definition of the genre of apocalypse. I concluded that all three debates suggested that Revelation can appropriately be read as a text which seeks *both* to expand the spatial and temporal horizons of its readers, so that their present context is understood in an ultimate framework, *and* to focus back on the earthly present to induce a response by the reader in the light of those ultimate horizons. In chapters 4 and 5 I worked through the text in detail, demonstrating how this dual dynamic of outward expansion and inward focus is developed in the spatial and temporal dimensions of the text. Chapter 6 returned to the arguments of Pannenberg and Moltmann, and the twentieth-century debate with which I began. I considered different elements of the views of Pannenberg and Moltmann on the theology of history, seeking to bring out both the similarities and the differences in their approaches. I went on to compare and contrast their positions with my reading of the text, suggesting ways in which Revelation might support or question their ideas.

In chapters 3–6 I have sought therefore to examine a biblical text and some contemporary theological proposals together, in the light of my conclusions in chapter 2. Of course, the genres of a first-century Christian apocalypse and works of contemporary systematic theology are very different. One employs highly symbolic language in an allusive and poetic way. The other builds precisely reasoned arguments on the basis of propositions drawn from a wide range of disciplines.[3] However, for all the manifest differences in context and approach between Revelation and contemporary theology (which I would not seek to minimize) there are clear affinities between the text and the work of both Pannenberg and Moltmann, as well as points of contrast. As I made clear in chapter 2, the

---

[3] A detailed comparison of twentieth-century systematic theology and first-century apocalyptic writing *as literary forms* is beyond the scope of this study. Such a study might yield interesting results, however. For example, it would be stimulating to compare the different rhetorical approaches of the two genres in the light of their contrasting social settings.

purpose of comparing and contrasting contemporary theological proposals with a biblical text is not to provide a comprehensive judgement on the
adequacy or otherwise of such proposals. I have considered only one text
in detail. Parallel exercises with other biblical texts would yield different
results. Moreover, scripture is only one of the resources upon which systematic theology might legitimately draw: others include church tradition,
experience, and engagement with other disciplines, such as philosophy
and the social sciences. Nonetheless, theological judgements need to show
some identifiable continuity with scripture if they are to be regarded as
authentic expressions of Christian understanding.

The scope of this project has enabled detailed engagement both with
the proposals of two contemporary systematicians and with current New
Testament scholarship relating to a particular text. Both Pannenberg and
Moltmann have of course been explicitly influenced by apocalyptic, so
this study has in effect been a sustained worked example of how that
influence might be assessed in relation to one scriptural text. Earlier assessments by biblical specialists of the use to which Pannenberg and
Moltmann put apocalyptic tradition were often lukewarm at best.[4] This
was largely because it was assumed that apocalypticists maintained a
negative, deterministic view of human history, at odds with the claims
of Pannenberg and Moltmann relating to divine action in history and the
openness of the future. My review of more recent work on apocalyptic,
and on Revelation specifically, suggests that this negative reaction needs
reassessment three decades after the original debate sparked by Pannenberg and Moltmann. The work of Christopher Rowland, in particular, has
underlined a strong interest in the present on the part of apocalyptic writers: this age is not simply an evil aeon with no ultimate worth.[5] Richard
Bauckham and Leonard Thompson have emphasized the way in which
Revelation reveals layers of reality within which the earthly present is
to be seen, rather than offering a deterministic, dualistic framework of
understanding. In chapters 3–6 I have presented a view of the text which
takes account of these findings, and which suggests considerable affinity
between the text and the positions of Pannenberg and Moltmann.

In some cases my analysis of Revelation has provided support for arguments which Pannenberg and Moltmann have explicitly based upon
interpretations of apocalyptic literature. Most obviously, the basic find-
ing of chapters 3–5, that the text functions by expanding the reader's
perspective to ultimate horizons then refocusing back onto the present
in the light of that ultimate perspective, is paralleled strikingly in the

---

[4] See Murdock (1967), Laws (1975), J. Barr (1975). [5] Rowland (1982).

work of both Pannenberg and Moltmann. Their shared concern to place present experience in a context which takes seriously the past and the future of human history has clear similarities to Revelation. The expansion of perspectives outward to ultimate horizons is shown in Pannenberg's fundamental argument about the unity and coherence of the historical process as the self-revelation of God; in Moltmann's account of the justice of God confronting and contradicting the present; and in the key connection which both Pannenberg and Moltmann make between the eschaton and its proleptic revelation in the Christ event.[6] The other element of the dynamic of the text, refocusing back inwards to the earthly present of the reader, is echoed in the determination of both Pannenberg and Moltmann to see ethics in an eschatological perspective, using the ultimate future as a motor to drive ethical response in the present.[7] In all of these areas Pannenberg and Moltmann show emphases distinct from each other, as I explained in chapter 6, but there are overall similarities between their approaches and the theology of the text.

I have also suggested that the proposals of Pannenberg and Moltmann show limited or partial continuity with the text on the question of the nature of eschatological consummation. In Revelation, eschatological consummation, symbolised by the descent of the New Jerusalem, represents *both* transformation *and* completion of that which precedes it. Arguably, this can be seen as transcending the distinction between Pannenberg's emphasis on the eschaton as culmination and ultimate reference point, and Moltmann's emphasis on the eschaton as contradiction. It may be that Pannenberg and Moltmann might each helpfully take closer account of the emphasis which the other has placed on the interpretation of the eschaton, so that full justice is done to the eschaton as both culmination and transformation. The symbol of the New Jerusalem and the role it plays in Revelation would provide a good starting point.

The study has therefore established important continuities between Revelation and the proposals made by Pannenberg and Moltmann. At the same time, I have suggested ways in which a reading of Revelation might question their proposals. For example, in Revelation there is a clear sense of the present (albeit as yet hidden) reality of God's ultimate sovereignty; this is expressed partly in spatial terms, using the framework of the three-decker universe. In the proposals of both Pannenberg and Moltmann this spatial dimension is diminished, in favour of the idea that the rule of God comes from the future. But the paradoxical sense of ultimate *present* security for the people of God, despite appearances

---

[6] See pp. 164–71 and 179–86.   [7] See pp. 195–9.

to the contrary (such an important part of the message of Revelation), becomes more indirect and arguably less accessible when the power of God is radically characterized as 'from the future'.[8] A critique of the position of Pannenberg or Moltmann, using the text along these lines, acquires more force than it would otherwise possess, precisely because of continuities elsewhere between the text and the thought of Pannenberg and Moltmann, such as the concern to see the present in the light of the ultimate future.

As well as identifying areas where my reading of the text clearly supports or questions proposals made by Pannenberg or Moltmann, I have suggested other instances of apparent discontinuity between Revelation and Pannenberg and Moltmann which perhaps hide similarities of thought at a deeper level. I mentioned in the previous paragraph the variance between the strong sense in Revelation of God's present (though hidden) sovereignty, which John conveys via spatial distinctions between heaven and earth, and the way in which both Pannenberg and Moltmann express the relationship between human history and the rule of God in more radically temporal terms, so that God's rule comes from the future. This is an important discontinuity between text and theology. Yet at a deeper level, there are elements of continuity between the two models. The radically temporal view espoused by the two modern theologians is an alternative way of dealing with the same problem confronting John of Patmos: how can the sovereignty of God be reconciled with its apparent hiddenness in the present? Or, to put it another way, how might the realized and unrealized elements of eschatology most effectively be expressed? Both Revelation and the models proposed by Pannenberg and Moltmann offer a vision in which the power of God will ultimately shape events decisively, but in which that power is for the moment not publicly manifest.[9]

Another example of less obvious continuity between text and theology came in my discussion of Pannenberg's idea of revelation as history. At first sight, an ἀποκάλυψις of hidden layers of reality may appear to have little in common with the idea of the self-revelation of God in historical events. Yet, as I suggested, Pannenberg's refinement of his position to include verbal revelation within an overall framework of revelation as history does in fact open up parallels with the pattern of proclamation and fulfilment in the text.[10] Similarly, at first sight, Pannenberg's emphasis on the role of reason in the appropriation of revelation appears at odds with an ἀποκάλυψις, which by definition reveals things which are not

[8] See pp. 171–8.   [9] See pp. 171–6.
[10] See pp. 149–54.

clearly visible. Yet, as I argued in chapter 6 (pp. 171–6), Pannenberg's use of the idea of retroactive ontology enables links to be made between his thought and the central apocalyptic conviction that things currently hidden will be revealed.

A final example of an area of less obvious continuity between Revelation and the proposals of Pannenberg or Moltmann is the question of the extent to which the future is open or determined. Both Pannenberg and Moltmann are committed to the notion of an open future, although some of Pannenberg's critics, including Moltmann, have detected a deterministic streak in his thought.[11] I argued that while Moltmann's criticism of Pannenberg in this area was not particularly well-founded, some tensions nonetheless remained in Pannenberg's thought, stemming from the difficulty of reconciling his commitment to an open future with his concern to defend the sovereign freedom of God. In this respect, the intellectual landscape of Revelation is of course very different. While there are elements of contingency in the text, the overall shape of things to come is clear. I suggested that, despite obvious differences, there may be continuity at a fundamental level, at least between Revelation and Pannenberg's proposals. John seeks to affirm the sovereignty of God by revealing the broad shape of divine action to come. Pannenberg is similarly seeking to affirm the freedom of God. But he is developing (and reacting against) an intellectual tradition inspired by Hegelian dialectic, and is thus highly sensitive to determinism. For Pannenberg, therefore, divine sovereignty is affirmed through postulating an open future. Thus there are crucial differences between Revelation and Pannenberg here, but perhaps also some fundamental strands of continuity.

An exercise of this kind is inevitably limited in scope. I have stressed more than once that merely comparing theological judgements with one biblical text cannot be regarded as an overall assessment of their adequacy. So the ground covered in this study represents a small part of a much wider inquiry which would be needed to do full justice to the relationship between the theologies of Pannenberg and Moltmann and scripture. Reference would need to be made to other apocalyptic texts, both canonical and extra-canonical, and to alternative scriptural models for conceiving the nature of history, such as the salvation-history model of Luke–Acts. More detailed comparisons would need to be made between Pannenberg, Moltmann and other movements in contemporary theology, notably process theology. A fuller examination of the hermeneutical strategies employed by Pannenberg and Moltmann, especially with

[11] See pp. 166–70.

reference to the history of interpretation of apocalyptic texts, would be useful.

However, although this has been a limited exercise, my hope is that it has illustrated how bridges may be built between New Testament interpretation and systematic theology in ways which do justice to both.

BIBLIOGRAPHY

Allison, Dale C. 1987, *The End of the Ages Has Come: An Early Interpretation of the Passion and Resurrection of Jesus*. Edinburgh: T. & T. Clark.

Anderson, Hugh 1976, 'A Future for Apocalyptic?', in Johnston R. McKay and James F. Miller (eds.), *Biblical Studies: Essays in Honour of William Barclay* (London: Collins), pp. 56–71.

Aune, David E. 1972, *The Cultic Setting of Realized Eschatology in Early Christianity*. NovTSup 28. Leiden: E. J. Brill.

    1986, 'The Apocalypse of John and the Problem of Genre', *Semeia* 36, pp. 65–96.

    1988, *The New Testament in Its Literary Environment*. Cambridge: James Clarke & Co.

    1990, 'The Form and Function of the Proclamations to the Seven Churches (Revelation 2–3)', *NTS* 36, pp. 182–204.

    1997, *Revelation 1–5*, WBC 52a. Dallas: Word Books.

    1998a, *Revelation 6–16*, WBC 52b. Dallas: Word Books.

    1998b, *Revelation 17–22*, WBC 52c. Dallas: Word Books.

Barr, David L. 1984, 'The Apocalypse as a Symbolic Transformation of the World: A Literary Analysis', *Int* 38, pp. 39–50.

Barr, James 1962, *Biblical Words for Time*. London: SCM Press.

    1975, 'Jewish Apocalyptic in Recent Scholarly Study', *BJRL* 58, pp. 9–35.

    1988, 'The Theological Case against Biblical Theology', in Gene M. Tucker, David L. Petersen and Robert R. Wilson (eds.), *Canon, Theology and Old Testament Interpretation: Essays in Honour of Brevard Childs* (Philadelphia: Fortress), pp. 3–19.

    1999, *The Concept of Biblical Theology: An Old Testament Perspective*. London: SCM Press.

Barrett, Cyril 1990, 'The Language of Ecstasy and the Ecstasy of Language', in Martin Warner (ed.), *The Bible as Rhetoric: Studies in Biblical Persuasion and Credibility* (London and New York: Routledge), pp. 205–21.

Bartels, K. H. 1975, 'πρωτότοκος', *NIDNTT* I, pp. 667–70.

Barth, Karl 1972, *Protestant Theology in the Nineteenth Century*. Eng. trans. London: SCM Press.

Bauckham, Richard 1987, *Moltmann: Messianic Theology in the Making*. Basingstoke: Marshall Pickering.

    1993a, *The Climax of Prophecy: Studies on the Book of Revelation*. Edinburgh: T. & T. Clark.

1993b, *The Theology of the Book of Revelation*. Cambridge: Cambridge University Press.

1995, *The Theology of Jürgen Moltmann*. Edinburgh: T. & T. Clark.

1999, 'The Millennium' (pp. 123–47) and 'Time and Eternity' (pp. 155–226) in R. Bauckham (ed.), *God Will Be All in All: The Eschatology of Jürgen Moltmann*. Edinburgh: T. & T. Clark.

Bauckham, Richard, and Hart, Trevor 1999, *Hope against Hope: Christian Eschatology in Contemporary Context*. London: Darton, Longman and Todd.

Bauer, W., Arndt, W. F. and Gingrich, F. W. 1979, *A Greek–English Lexicon of the New Testament and Other Early Christian Literature* (2nd edition, revised by F. W. Gingrich and F. W. Danker). Chicago and London: Chicago University Press.

Bauernfeind, O. 1967, 'νικάω, νίκη, νῖκος, ὑπερνικάω', *TDNT* IV, pp. 942–5.

Beagley, Alan James 1987, *The 'Sitz im Leben' of the Apocalypse with Particular Reference to the Role of the Church's Enemies*. BZNW 50. Berlin and New York: de Gruyter.

Beale, G. K. 1999, *The Book of Revelation*. NIGTC. Grand Rapids: Eerdmans; Carlisle: Paternoster.

Beasley-Murray, G. R. 1974, 'How Christian Is the Book of Revelation?', in R. Banks (ed.), *Reconciliation and Hope: New Testament Essays on Atonement and Eschatology* (Exeter: Paternoster), pp. 275–84.

1978, *The Book of Revelation* (revised edition). NCB. Grand Rapids: Eerdmans; London: Marshall, Morgan, and Scott.

Bebbington, David 1979, *Patterns in History*. Leicester: Inter-Varsity Press.

Behm, J. 1965, 'καινός, καινότης, ἀνακαινίζω, ἀνακαινόω, ἀνακαίνωσις, ἐγκαινίζω', *TDNT* III, pp. 447–54.

Berger, Peter L., and Luckmann, Thomas 1967, *The Social Construction of Reality*. London: Allen Lane.

Betz, Hans-Dieter 1969, 'The Concept of Apocalyptic in the Theology of the Pannenberg Group', *JTC* 6, pp. 192–207.

Blass, F., and Debrunner, A. 1961, *A Greek Grammar of the New Testament and Other Early Christian Literature* (tr. and revised by R. W. Funk). Chicago and London: University of Chicago Press.

Bloch, Ernst 1986, *The Principle of Hope* (Eng. trans.). Oxford: Blackwell.

Böcher, Otto 1983, *Kirche in Zeit und Endzeit*. Neukirchen: Neukirchener Verlag.

Boesak, Allan A. 1987, *Comfort and Protest*. Edinburgh: St Andrew Press.

Boman, Thorleif 1960, *Hebrew Thought Compared with Greek*. London: SCM Press.

Boring, M. Eugene 1989, *Revelation*. IBC. Louisville: John Knox Press.

1992, 'Narrative Christology in the Apocalypse', *CBQ* 54, pp. 702–23.

Bornemann, R. 1991, 'Toward a Biblical Theology', in J. Reumann (ed.), *The Promise and Practice of Biblical Theology* (Minneapolis: Augsburg Fortress), pp. 117–28.

Bornkamm, G. 1967, 'μυστήριον, μυέω', *TDNT* IV, pp. 802–28.

Bourdieu, Pierre 1963, 'The Attitude of the Algerian Peasant toward Time', in J. Pitt-Rivers (ed.), *Mediterranean Countrymen: Essays in the Social Anthropology of the Mediterranean* (Paris: Recherches Méditerranéennes, Etudes I), pp. 55–72.

Boyer, Paul 1992, *When Time Shall Be No More: Prophecy Belief in Modern American Culture*. Cambridge, Mass.: Harvard University Press.

Braaten, Carl E. 1968, *History and Hermeneutics*. London: Lutterworth.

1971, 'The Significance of Apocalypticism for Systematic Theology', *Int* 25, pp. 480–99.

1983, 'The Kingdom of God and Life Everlasting', in Peter C. Hodgson and Robert King (eds.), *Christian Theology: An Introduction to Its Traditions and Tasks* (London: SPCK), pp. 274–98.

Braaten, Carl E., and Clayton, Philip (eds.) 1988, *The Theology of Wolfhart Pannenberg: Twelve American Critiques with an Autobiographical Essay and Response*. Minneapolis: Augsburg.

Brown, Colin 1988, *History and Faith: A Personal Exploration*. Leicester: Inter-Varsity Press.

Bruce, F. F. 1973, 'The Spirit in the Apocalypse', in B. Lindars and S. S. Smalley (eds.), *Christ and Spirit in the New Testament* (Cambridge: Cambridge University Press), pp. 333–44.

Brueggemann, W. 1978, *The Land*. London: SPCK.

Bultmann, Rudolf 1957, *History and Eschatology*. Edinburgh: Edinburgh University Press.

1969, *Faith and Understanding*. Eng. trans. London: SCM Press.

1985, *New Testament and Mythology and Other Basic Writings* (ed. S. M. Ogden). London: SCM Press.

Burhenn, Herbert 1975, 'Pannenberg's Doctrine of God', *SJT* 28, pp. 535–49.

Burridge, K. O. L. 1967, 'Lévi-Strauss and Myth', in Edmund Leach (ed.), *The Structural Study of Myth and Totemism* (London: Tavistock), pp. 91–115.

1971, *New Heaven, New Earth: A Study of Millenarian Activities*. Oxford: Blackwell.

Butterfield, Herbert 1957, *Christianity and History*. London: Fontana.

Caird, G. B. 1980, *The Language and Imagery of the Bible*. London: Duckworth.

1984, *The Revelation of St John the Divine* (2nd edition). BNTC. London: A. & C. Black.

Cairns, David 1968, Review of Van A. Harvey, *The Historian and the Believer*, *SJT* 21, pp. 221–3.

Carnegie, David R. 1982, 'Worthy Is the Lamb: The Hymns in Revelation', in H. H. Rowdon (ed.), *Christ the Lord: Studies in Christology Presented to Donald Guthrie* (Leicester: Inter-Varsity Press), pp. 243–56.

Carnley, Peter 1972, 'The Poverty of Historical Scepticism', in S. W. Sykes and J. P. Clayton (eds.), *Christ, Faith and History* (Cambridge: Cambridge University Press), pp. 165–89.

1987, *The Structure of Resurrection Belief*. Oxford: Clarendon Press.

Charles, R. H. 1920, *A Critical and Exegetical Commentary on the Revelation of St John* (2 vols.). ICC. Edinburgh: T. & T. Clark.

Charlesworth, James H. (ed.) 1983, *The Old Testament Pseudepigrapha*, vol. I. New York: Doubleday.

(ed.) 1985, *The Old Testament Pseudepigrapha*, vol. II. New York: Doubleday.

Childs, Brevard S. 1992, *Biblical Theology of the Old and New Testaments*. London: SCM Press.

Clayton, John Powell (ed.) 1976, *Ernst Troeltsch and the Future of Theology*. Cambridge: Cambridge University Press.

Clayton, Philip 1988, 'Anticipation and Theological Method', in Carl E. Braaten and Philip Clayton (eds.), *The Theology of Wolfhart Pannenberg: Twelve American Critiques with an Autobiographical Essay and Response* (Minneapolis: Augsburg), pp. 122–50.

Clifford, R. J. 1972, *The Cosmic Mountain in Canaan and the Old Testament*. Cambridge, Mass.: Harvard University Press.

Clouse, Robert G. (ed.) 1977, *The Meaning of the Millennium: Four Views*. Downers Grove: Inter-Varsity Press.

Coakley, Sarah 1988, *Christ without Absolutes*. Oxford: Oxford University Press.

Cobb, John B. 1988, 'Pannenberg and Process Theology', in Carl E. Braaten and Philip Clayton (eds.), *The Theology of Wolfhart Pannenberg: Twelve American Critiques with an Autobiographical Essay and Response* (Minneapolis: Augsburg), pp. 54–74.

Cody, Aelred 1979, 'The New Testament', *Concilium* 123, pp. 34–42.

Cohn, Norman 1970, *The Pursuit of the Millennium*. London: Paladin.

Cohn, Robert L. 1981, *The Shape of Sacred Space: Four Biblical Studies*. Chico: Scholars Press.

Collingwood, R. G. 1994, *The Idea of History* (revised edition, ed. Jan van der Dussen). Oxford: Oxford University Press.

Collins, John J. 1977, 'Pseudonymity, Historical Reviews and the Genre of the Revelation of John', *CBQ* 39, pp. 329–43.

   1979, 'Introduction: Towards the Morphology of a Genre', and 'The Jewish Apocalypses' in *Semeia* 14, pp. 1–19 and 21–59.

   1983a, 'Apocalyptic Eschatology as the Transcendence of Death', in P. D. Hanson (ed.), *Visionaries and Their Apocalypses* (London: SPCK), pp. 61–84.

   1983b, 'New Testament Cosmology', *Concilium* 166, pp. 3–7.

   1984, *The Apocalyptic Imagination: An Introduction to the Jewish Matrix of Christianity*. New York: Crossroad.

   1990, 'Is a Critical Biblical Theology Possible?', in W. H. Propp, B. Halpern and D. N. Freedman (eds.), *The Hebrew Bible and Its Interpreters* (Winona Lake, Ind.: Eisenbrauns), pp. 1–17.

Court, John M. 1979, *Myth and History in the Book of Revelation*. Atlanta: John Knox Press.

   1994, *Revelation*. Sheffield: JSOT Press.

Culler, Jonathan 1988, *Saussure* (revised edition). London: Fontana.

Cullmann, Oscar 1951, *Christ and Time*. Eng. trans. London: SCM Press.

   1967, *Salvation in History*. Eng. trans. London: SCM Press.

Cunningham, Adrian (ed.) 1973, *The Theory of Myth*. London: Sheed and Ward.

Davies, G. I. 1978, 'Apocalyptic and Historiography', *JSOT* 5, pp. 15–28.

Davis, R. Dean 1992, *The Heavenly Court Judgment of Revelation 4–5*. Lanham, Md. and London: University Press of America.

Despland, Michel 1973, *Kant on History and Religion*. Montreal and London: McGill-Queen's University Press.

Deutsch, Celia 1987, 'Transformation of Symbols: The New Jerusalem in Revelation 21:1–22:5', *ZNW* 78, pp. 106–26.

Dickey, Laurence 1987, *Hegel: Religion, Economics and the Politics of Spirit*. Cambridge: Cambridge University Press.

Douglas, Mary 1967, 'The Meaning of Myth, with Special Reference to La Geste d'Asdiwal', in Edmund Leach (ed.), *The Structural Study of Myth and Totemism* (London: Tavistock), pp. 49–70.

1978, 'Cultural Bias'. London: Royal Anthropological Institute of Great Britain and Ireland, Occasional Paper 35.

Dray, W. H. 1964, *Philosophy of History*. Englewood Cliffs: Prentice-Hall.

Drescher, Hans-Georg 1992, *Ernst Troeltsch: His Life and Work*. Eng. trans. London: SCM Press.

Dulles, Avery 1988, 'Pannenberg on Revelation and Faith', in Carl E. Braaten and Philip Clayton (eds.), *The Theology of Wolfhart Pannenberg: Twelve American Critiques with an Autobiographical Essay and Response* (Minneapolis: Augsburg), pp. 169–87.

Dunn, J. D. G., and Mackey, J. P. 1987, *New Testament Theology in Dialogue*. London: SPCK.

Ebeling, G. 1969, 'The Ground of Christian Theology', *JTC* 6, pp. 47–68.

Edwards, Douglas R. 1991, 'Surviving the Web of Power: Religion and Politics in the Acts of the Apostles, Josephus, and Chariton's Chaereas and Callirhoe', in Loveday Alexander (ed.), *Images of Empire* (JSOTSup 122; Sheffield: JSOT), pp. 179–201.

Eliade, Mircea 1965, *The Myth of the Eternal Return* (2nd edition). Princeton: Princeton University Press.

Ellul, J. 1970, *The Meaning of the City*. Eng. trans. Grand Rapids: Eerdmans.

1977, *Apocalypse: The Book of Revelation*. Eng. trans. New York: Seabury Press.

Enroth, Anne-Marit 1990, 'The Hearing Formula in the Book of Revelation', *NTS* 36, pp. 598–608.

Fackenheim, Emil 1967, *The Religious Dimension in Hegel's Thought*. Bloomington and London: Indiana University Press.

Fackre, Gabriel 1990, 'Eschatology and Systematics', *Ex Auditu* 6, pp. 101–17.

Falkenroth, U., and Brown, C. 1976, 'ὑπομένω', *NIDNTT* II, pp. 772–6.

Farley, Edward, and Hodgson, Peter C. 1983, 'Scripture and Tradition', in Peter C. Hodgson and Robert King (eds.), *Christian Theology: An Introduction to Its Traditions and Tasks* (London: SPCK), pp. 35–61.

Farrer, Austin 1949, *A Rebirth of Images*. Westminster: Dacre Press.

1964, *The Revelation of St John the Divine*. Oxford: Clarendon Press.

Ferguson, John 1970, *The Religions of the Roman Empire*. London: Thames and Hudson.

Fergusson, David 1992, *Bultmann*. Collegeville, Minn.: Michael Glazier, The Liturgical Press.

Feuer, Lewis S. (ed.) 1969, *Marx and Engels: Basic Writings on Politics and Philosophy*. Glasgow: Fontana.

Finger, Thomas 1991, 'Biblical and Systematic Theology in Interaction: A Case Study on the Atonement', in B. C. Ollenburger (ed.), *So Wide a Sea: Essays on Biblical and Systematic Theology* (Elkhart, Ind.: Institute of Mennonite Studies), pp. 1–17.

Fiorenza, Elisabeth Schüssler 1983, 'The Phenomenon of Early Christian Apocalyptic: Some Reflections on Method', in D. Hellholm (ed.), *Apocalypticism in the Mediterranean World and the Near East* (Tübingen: J. C. B. Mohr), pp. 295–316.

1985, *The Book of Revelation: Justice and Judgment*. Philadelphia: Fortress.

1986, 'The Followers of the Lamb: Visionary Rhetoric and Socio-Political Situation', *Semeia* 36, pp. 123–46.

1991, *Revelation: Vision of a Just World*. Minneapolis: Fortress.

Ford, J. Massyngberde 1975, *Revelation*. AB. Garden City, New York: Doubleday.

Fowl, Stephen E., and Jones, L. Gregory 1991, *Reading in Communion: Scripture and Ethics in Christian Life*. London: SPCK.

Fuchs, E. 1969, 'On the Task of a Christian Theology', *JTC* 6, pp. 69–98.

Fuller, Daniel 1968, *Easter Faith and History*. London: Tyndale Press.

Funk, R. W. 1969, 'Apocalyptic as an Historical and Theological Problem in Current New Testament Scholarship', *JTC* 6, pp. 175–91.

Gager, John G. 1983, 'The Attainment of Millennial Bliss through Myth: The Book of Revelation', in P. D. Hanson (ed.), *Visionaries and Their Apocalypses* (London: SPCK), pp. 146–55.

Galloway, Allan 1973, *Wolfhart Pannenberg*. London: Allen & Unwin.

Geertz, Clifford 1973, *The Interpretation of Cultures*. New York: Basic Books.

Gell, Alfred 1992, *The Anthropology of Time: Cultural Constructions of Temporal Maps and Images*. Oxford and Providence: Berg.

Geyl, Pieter 1955, *Use and Abuse of History*. New Haven: Yale University Press.

Giblin, Charles Homer 1974, 'Structural and Thematic Correlations in the Theology of Revelation 16–22', *Bib* 55, pp. 487–504.

1991, *The Book of Revelation: The Open Book of Prophecy*. Collegeville, Minn.: Liturgical Press.

Giet, Stanislas 1957, *L'Apocalypse et l'histoire*. Paris: Presses Universitaires de France.

Gilbertson, Michael R. 1997, *The Meaning of the Millennium: Revelation 20 and Millennial Expectation*. Cambridge: Grove Books.

Golden, Leon 1976, 'The Clarification Theory of Catharsis', *Hermes* 104, pp. 437–52.

Goodman, Martin 1991, 'Opponents of Rome: Jews and Others', in Loveday Alexander (ed.), *Images of Empire* (JSOTSup 122; Sheffield: JSOT Press), pp. 222–38.

Goulder, M. D. 1981, 'The Apocalypse as an Annual Cycle of Prophecies', *NTS* 27, pp. 342–67.

Gowan, Donald E. 1985, 'The Fall and Redemption of the Material World in Apocalyptic Literature', *HBT* 7/2, pp. 83–103.

Green, Joel B. 2000, 'Scripture and Theology: Uniting the Two So Long Divided', in Joel B. Green and Max Turner (eds.), *Between Two Horizons: Spanning New Testament Studies and Systematic Theology* (Grand Rapids and Cambridge: Eerdmans), pp. 23–43.

Grenz, Stanley J. 1990, *Reason for Hope: The Systematic Theology of Wolfhart Pannenberg*. New York and Oxford: Oxford University Press.

Gruenwald, Ithamar 1980, *Apocalyptic and Merkavah Mysticism*. Leiden and Cologne: E. J. Brill.

1988, *From Apocalypticism to Gnosticism*. Frankfurt: Verlag Peter Lang.

Gundry, Robert H. 1987, 'The New Jerusalem: People as Place, Not Place for People', *NovT* 29, pp. 254–64.

Hall, Robert G. 1991, *Revealed Histories: Techniques for Ancient Jewish and Christian Historiography*. JSPSup 6. Sheffield: JSOT Press.

Halloran, B. M. 1987, 'The Apocalypse of John: A Hermeneutical Study'. Unpublished MPhil thesis, University of St Andrews.

Hamerton-Kelly, R. G. 1973, *Pre-Existence, Wisdom, and the Son of Man: A Study of the Idea of Pre-Existence in the New Testament*. Cambridge: Cambridge University Press.

Hanson, P. D. 1979, *The Dawn of Apocalyptic: The Historical and Sociological Roots of Jewish Apocalyptic Eschatology* (revised edition). Philadelphia: Fortress.

   1980, 'The Responsibility of Biblical Theology to Communities of Faith', *TToday* 37, pp. 39–50.

   1984a, 'The Future of Biblical Theology', *HBT* 6/1, pp. 13–24.

   1984b, 'The Apocalyptic Consciousness', *Quarterly Review* 1984/4, pp. 23–39.

   1985, 'Biblical Apocalypticism: The Theological Dimension', *HBT* 7/2, pp. 1–20.

Harder, Helmut G., and Stevenson, W. Taylor 1971, 'The Continuity of History and Faith in the Theology of Wolfhart Pannenberg: Toward an Erotics of History', *JR* 51, pp. 34–56.

Harrington, Wilfrid 1993, *Revelation*. Collegeville, Minn.: The Liturgical Press.

Hart, Trevor 1999, 'Imagination for the Kingdom of God?: Hope, Promise and the Transformative Power of an Imagined Future', in R. Bauckham (ed.), *God Will Be All in All: The Eschatology of Jürgen Moltmann* (Edinburgh: T. & T. Clark), pp. 49–76.

Harvey, Van A. 1967, *The Historian and the Believer: The Morality of Historical Knowledge and Christian Belief*. London: SCM Press.

Hauck, F. 1967, 'μένω, ἐμ-, παρα-, περι-, προσμένω, μονή, ὑπομένω, ὑπομονή', *TDNT* IV, pp. 574–88.

Hegel, G. W. F. 1975, *Lectures on the Philosophy of World History: Introduction*. Eng. trans. Cambridge: Cambridge University Press.

   1984, *Lectures on the Philosophy of Religion*, vol. I (ed. P. C. Hodgson). Berkeley: University of California Press.

Helgeland, John 1980, 'Time and Space: Christian and Roman', *ANRW* 23.2, Berlin: de Gruyter, pp. 1285–305.

Hellholm, David 1986, 'The Problem of Apocalyptic Genre and the Apocalypse of John', *Semeia* 36, pp. 13–64.

Hemer, C. J. 1986, *The Letters to the Seven Churches of Asia in Their Local Setting*. JSNTSup 11. Sheffield: JSOT Press.

Hill, David 1972, 'Prophecy and Prophets in the Revelation of St John', *NTS* 18, pp. 401–18.

Holtz, Traugott 1962, *Die Christologie der Apokalypse des Johannes*. Berlin: Acadamie-Verlag.

Holwerda, D. 1983, 'Faith, Reason, and the Resurrection in the Theology of Wolfhart Pannenberg', in A. Plantinga and N. Wolterstorff (eds.), *Faith and Rationality* (Notre Dame: University of Notre Dame Press), pp. 265–316.

Howard-Brook, Wes, and Gwyther, Anthony 1999, *Unveiling Empire: Reading Revelation Then and Now*. Maryknoll: Orbis.

Hudson, Wayne 1982, *The Marxist Philosophy of Ernst Bloch*. London: Macmillan.

Hurtado, L. W. 1985, 'Revelation 4–5 in the Light of Jewish Apocalyptic Analogies', *JSNT* 25, pp. 105–24.

1988, *One God, One Lord: Early Christian Devotion and Ancient Jewish Monotheism.* London: SCM Press.

Jeanrond, Werner 1991, *Theological Hermeneutics: Development and Significance.* Basingstoke and London: Macmillan.

Jeske, Richard L. 1985, 'Spirit and Community in the Johannine Apocalypse', *NTS* 31, pp. 452–66.

Johnson, Alfred M., Jr 1979, *Structuralism and Biblical Hermeneutics.* Pittsburgh: Pickwick Press.

Jörns, Klaus-Peter 1971, *Das hymnische Evangelium: Untersuchungen zu Aufbau, Funktion und Herkunft der hymnischen Stücke in der Johannesoffenbarung.* SNT 5. Gütersloh: Mohn.

Judge, E. A. 1960, *The Social Pattern of the Christian Groups in the First Century.* London: Tyndale Press.

Kanagaraj, J. J. 1995, '"Mysticism" in the Gospel of John: An Inquiry into the Background of John in Jewish Mysticism'. Unpublished PhD thesis, University of Durham.

Karrer, Martin 1986, *Die Johannesoffenbarung als Brief.* Forschungen zur Religion und Literatur des Alten und Neuen Testaments 140. Göttingen: Vandenhoeck & Ruprecht.

Käsemann, E. 1969, 'The Beginnings of Christian Theology', and 'On the Topic of Primitive Christian Apocalyptic', *JTC* 6, pp. 17–46 and 99–133.

1984, *The Wandering People of God: An Investigation of the Letter to the Hebrews.* Eng. trans. Minneapolis: Augsburg.

Kaufman, Gordon D. 1991, 'Critical Theology and the Bible: A Response to A. James Reimer', in B. C. Ollenburger (ed.), *So Wide a Sea: Essays on Biblical and Systematic Theology* (Elkhart, Ind.: Institute of Mennonite Studies), pp. 59–64.

Kelsey, David 1975, *The Uses of Scripture in Recent Theology.* London: SCM Press.

Koch, Klaus 1972, *The Rediscovery of Apocalyptic.* Eng. trans. SBT Second Series 22. London: SCM Press.

Kraybill, J. Nelson 1996, *Imperial Cult and Commerce in John's Apocalypse.* JSNTSup 132. Sheffield: Sheffield Academic Press.

Kvanvig, Helge S. 1989, 'The Relevance of the Biblical Visions of the End Time: Hermeneutical Guidelines to the Apocalyptical Literature', *HBT* 11/1, pp. 35–58.

Ladd, George Eldon 1972, *A Commentary on the Revelation of John.* Grand Rapids: Eerdmans.

1974, 'Apocalyptic and New Testament Theology', in R. Banks (ed.), *Reconciliation and Hope: New Testament Essays on Atonement and Eschatology* (Exeter: Paternoster), pp. 285–96.

Lambrecht, Jan 1980, 'A Structuration of Revelation 4:1–22:5', in J. Lambrecht (ed.), *L'apocalypse johannique et l'apocalyptique dans le Nouveau Testament* (Leuven: Leuven University Press), pp. 77–104.

Lash, Nicholas 1986, *Theology on the Way to Emmaus.* London: SCM Press.

Lauer, Robert H. 1981, *Temporal Man: The Meaning and Uses of Social Time.* New York: Praeger.

Laws, Sophie 1975, 'Can Apocalyptic Be Relevant?', in Morna Hooker and Colin Hickling (eds.), *What about the New Testament?: Essays in Honour of Christopher Evans* (London: SCM Press), pp. 89–103.

1989, *In the Light of the Lamb: Imagery, Parody and Theology in the Apocalypse of John*. Wilmington, Del.: Michael Glazier.

Leach, Edmund 1970, *Lévi-Strauss*. London: Fontana/Collins.

1976, *Culture and Communication: The Logic by which Symbols are Connected*. Cambridge: Cambridge University Press.

Leach, Edmund, and Aycock, D. Alan 1983, *Structuralist Interpretations of Biblical Myth*. Cambridge: Cambridge University Press.

Le Grys, Alan 1992, 'Conflict and Vengeance in the Book of Revelation', *ExpTim* 104, pp. 76–80.

Lessing, G. E. 1956, *Theological Writings* (ed. H. Chadwick). London: Black.

Levenson, Jon D. 1985, *Sinai and Zion*. Minneapolis: Winston Press.

1990, 'Theological Consensus or Historicist Evasion? Jews and Christians in Biblical Studies', in R. Brooks and J. J. Collins (eds.), *Hebrew Bible or Old Testament?* (Notre Dame: Notre Dame University Press), pp. 109–45.

Lévi-Strauss, Claude 1966, *The Savage Mind*. Eng. trans. London: Weidenfeld & Nicolson.

1972, *Structural Anthropology*. Eng. trans. London: Penguin.

Lévi-Strauss, Claude, and Ricoeur, Paul 1970, 'A Confrontation', in *New Left Review* 62, pp. 57–74.

Lewis, C. S. 1977, 'Historicism', reprinted in C. T. McIntire (ed.), *God, History and Historians: Modern Christian Views of History* (New York: Oxford University Press), pp. 224–38.

Lincoln, A. T. 1981, *Paradise Now and Not Yet*. Cambridge: Cambridge University Press.

Lindbeck, George A. 1984, *The Nature of Doctrine: Religion and Theology in a Postliberal Age*. London: SPCK.

Lohmeyer, E. 1926, *Die Offenbarung des Johannes*. Tübingen: J. C. B. Mohr.

Lonergan, Bernard 1971, *Method in Theology*. London: Darton, Longman and Todd.

Löwith, Karl 1949, *Meaning in History*. Chicago and London: University of Chicago Press.

McCullagh, C. B. 1971, 'The Possibility of an Historical Basis for Christian Theology', *Theol* 74, pp. 513–22.

McGrath, Alister E. 1990, *The Genesis of Doctrine*. Oxford: Blackwell.

1994, *The Making of Modern German Christology* (2nd edition). Leicester: Apollos.

Macro, Anthony D. 1980, 'The Cities of Asia Minor under the Roman Imperium', *ANRW* 7.2, Berlin: de Gruyter, pp. 658–97.

Magie, David 1950, *Roman Rule in Asia Minor*. Princeton: Princeton University Press.

Malbon, Elizabeth Struthers 1984, 'The Text and Time: Lévi-Strauss and New Testament Studies', in Robert L. Moore and Frank E. Reynolds (eds.), *Anthropology and the Study of Religion* (Chicago: Center for the Scientific Study of Religion), pp. 177–91.

1986, *Narrative Space and Mythic Meaning in Mark*. San Francisco: Harper & Row.

Malina, Bruce J. 1989, 'Christ and Time: Swiss or Mediterranean?', *CBQ* 51, pp. 1–31.
1995, *On the Genre and Message of Revelation: Star Visions and Sky Journeys.* Peabody, Mass.: Hendrickson.
Maritain, Jacques 1959, *On the Philosophy of History.* London: Geoffrey Bles.
Martens, Elmer A. 1991, 'Biblical Theology and Normativity', in B. C. Ollenburger (ed.), *So Wide a Sea: Essays on Biblical and Systematic Theology* (Elkhart, Ind.: Institute of Mennonite Studies), pp. 19–35.
Martin, R. P. 1974, *Worship in the Early Church.* Grand Rapids: Eerdmans.
Marwick, Arthur 1989, *The Nature of History* (3rd edition). Basingstoke: Macmillan.
Maurer, C. 1971, 'σύνοιδα, συνείδησις', *TDNT* VII, pp. 898–919.
Mauser, Ulrich W. 1987, '"Heaven" in the World of the New Testament', *HBT* 9/2, pp. 31–51.
Mazzaferri, Frederick David 1989, *The Genre of the Book of Revelation from a Source-Critical Perspective.* BZNW 54. Berlin: de Gruyter.
Mealy, J. Webb 1992, *After the Thousand Years: Resurrection and Judgement in Revelation 20.* JSNTSup 70. Sheffield: JSOT Press.
Meeks, M. D. 1974, *Origins of the Theology of Hope.* Philadelphia: Fortress.
Meeks, W. A. 1983, 'Social Functions of Apocalyptic Language in Pauline Christianity', in D. Hellholm (ed.), *Apocalypticism in the Mediterranean World and the Near East* (Tübingen: J. C. B. Mohr), pp. 687–705.
Michaelis, W. 1965, 'παντοκράτωρ', *TDNT* III, pp. 914–15.
Michaels, J. Ramsey 1997, *Revelation.* Downers Grove and Leicester: Inter-Varsity Press.
Michalson, G. E., Jr 1980, 'Pannenberg on the Resurrection and Historical Method', *SJT* 33, pp. 345–59.
1983, 'Theology, Historical Knowledge and the Contingency–Necessity Distinction', *IJPR* 14, pp. 87–98.
1985, *Lessing's 'Ugly Ditch': A Study of Theology and History.* University Park and London: Pennsylvania State University Press.
Minear, Paul 1962, 'The Cosmology of the Apocalypse', in W. F. Klassen and G. F. Snyder (eds.), *Current Issues in New Testament Interpretation* (London: SCM Press), pp. 23–37.
1966, 'Ontology and Ecclesiology in the Apocalypse', *NTS* 13, pp. 89–105.
1979, 'Some Archetypal Origins of Apocalyptic Predictions', *HBT* 1, pp. 105–35.
1981, *New Testament Apocalyptic.* Nashville: Abingdon Press.
Moltmann, Jürgen 1967, *Theology of Hope.* Eng. trans. London: SCM Press.
1969, *Religion, Revolution and the Future.* Eng. trans. New York: Charles Scribner's Sons.
1974, *The Crucified God.* Eng. trans. London: SCM Press.
1977, *The Church in the Power of the Spirit.* Eng. trans. London: SCM Press.
1979, *The Future of Creation.* Eng. trans. London: SCM Press.
1985, *God in Creation.* Eng. trans. London: SCM Press.
1990, *The Way of Jesus Christ: Christology in Messianic Dimensions.* Eng. trans. London: SCM Press.
1991, *History and the Triune God.* Eng. trans. London: SCM Press.

1992, *The Spirit of Life: A Universal Affirmation*. Eng. trans. Minneapolis: Fortress.

1994, *Jesus Christ for Today's World*. Eng. trans. London: SCM Press.

1996, *The Coming of God: Christian Eschatology*. Eng. trans. London: SCM Press.

1999, 'The World in God or God in the World?' (pp. 35–41); 'The Hope of Israel and the Anabaptist Alternative' (pp. 149–54); 'The Bible, the Exegete and the Theologian' (pp. 227–32); all in R. Bauckham (ed.), *God Will Be All in All: The Eschatology of Jürgen Moltmann*. Edinburgh: T. & T. Clark.

Moore, Hamilton 1990, 'Revelation as an "Apocalypse" in the Context of Jewish and Christian Apocalyptic Thought'. Unpublished PhD thesis, Queen's University, Belfast.

Morgan, Robert 1976, 'Ernst Troeltsch and the Dialectical Theology', in John Powell Clayton (ed.), *Ernst Troeltsch and the Future of Theology* (Cambridge: Cambridge University Press), pp. 33–77.

Morgan, Robert, with Barton, John 1988, *Biblical Interpretation*. Oxford: Oxford University Press.

Moulton, W. F., and Geden, A. S. 1978, *A Concordance to the Greek Testament* (5th edition, revised by H. K. Moulton). Edinburgh: T. & T. Clark.

Mounce, Robert H. 1977, *The Book of Revelation*. NICNT. Grand Rapids: Eerdmans.

Mowry, Lucetta 1952, 'Revelation 4–5 and Early Christian Liturgical Usage', *JBL* 71, pp. 75–84.

Moyise, Steve 1992, 'Intertextuality and the Book of Revelation', *ExpTim* 104, pp. 295–8.

1995, *The Old Testament in the Book of Revelation*. JSNTSup 115. Sheffield: Sheffield Academic Press.

Murdock, W. R. 1967, 'History and Revelation in Jewish Apocalypticism', *Int* 21, pp. 167–87.

Navone, John J. 1966, *History and Faith in the Thought of Alan Richardson*. London: SCM Press.

Neill, Stephen, and Wright, Tom 1988, *The Interpretation of the New Testament* (2nd edition). Oxford: Oxford University Press.

Nickelsburg, George W. E. 1991, 'The Apocalyptic Construction of Reality in 1 Enoch', in John J. Collins (ed.), *Mysteries and Revelations: Apocalyptic Studies since the Uppsala Colloquium* (JSPSup 9; Sheffield: Sheffield Academic Press), pp. 51–64.

Nicol, Iain G. 1976, 'Facts and Meanings: Wolfhart Pannenberg's Theology as History and the Role of the Historical-Critical Method', *RelS* 12, pp. 129–39.

Niebuhr, H. Reinhold 1949, *Faith and History*. London: Nisbet & Co.

Niethammer, Lutz 1992, *Posthistoire: Has History Come to an End?* Eng. trans. London: Verso.

Nineham, D. E. (ed.) 1963, *The Church's Use of the Bible*. London: SPCK.

1976, *The Use and Abuse of the Bible*. London: Macmillan.

Obayashi, Hiroshi 1970, 'Pannenberg and Troeltsch: History and Religion', *JAAR* 38, pp. 401–19.

O'Collins, G. 1968, 'The Principle and Theology of Hope', *SJT* 21, pp. 129–44.

O'Donovan, Oliver 1986, 'The Political Thought of the Book of Revelation', *TynBul* 37, pp. 61–94.

Ogden, Schubert M. 1976, 'The Authority of Scripture for Theology', *Int* 30, pp. 242–61.

O'Leary, Stephen D. 1994, *Arguing the Apocalypse: A Theory of Millennial Rhetoric*. New York and Oxford: Oxford University Press.

Ollenburger, B. C. 1985, 'Biblical Theology: Situating the Discipline', in J. T. Butler, E. W. Conrad and B. C. Ollenburger (eds.), *Understanding the Word* (JSOTSup 37; Sheffield: JSOT Press), pp. 37–62.

— 1986, 'What Krister Stendahl "Meant" – A Normative Critique of "Descriptive Biblical Theology"', *HBT* 8/1, pp. 61–98.

— 1987, *Zion the City of the Great King: A Theological Symbol of the Jerusalem Cult*. JSOTSup 41. Sheffield: JSOT Press.

— 1991, 'Biblical and Systematic Theology: Constructing a Relationship', in B. C. Ollenburger (ed.), *So Wide a Sea: Essays on Biblical and Systematic Theology* (Elkhart, Ind.: Institute of Mennonite Studies), pp. 111–45.

O'Rourke, J. J. 1968, 'The Hymns of the Apocalypse', *CBQ* 30, pp. 399–409.

Otto, Randall E. 1991, *The God of Hope: The Trinitarian Vision of Jürgen Moltmann*. Lanham, New York and London: University Press of America.

Pailin, David 1975, 'Lessing's Ditch Revisited: The Problem of Faith and History', in Ronald H. Preston (ed.), *Theology and Change: Essays in Memory of Alan Richardson* (London: SCM Press), pp. 78–103.

Pannenberg, Wolfhart 1967, 'Response to the Discussion', in J. M. Robinson and J. B. Cobb, Jr (eds.), *New Frontiers in Theology*, vol. III: *Theology as History* (New York, Evanston and London: Harper & Row), pp. 221–76.

— 1968, *Jesus – God and Man*. Eng. trans. London: SCM Press.

— (ed.) 1969a, *Revelation as History*. Eng. trans. London: Sheed and Ward.

— 1969b, *Theology and the Kingdom of God*. Eng. trans. Philadelphia: Westminster Press.

— 1970, *Basic Questions in Theology*, vol. I. Eng. trans. London: SCM Press.

— 1971, *Basic Questions in Theology*, vol. II. Eng. trans. London: SCM Press.

— 1973, *Basic Questions in Theology*, vol. III. Eng. trans. London: SCM Press.

— 1976, *Theology and the Philosophy of Science*. Eng. trans. London: Darton, Longman and Todd.

— 1977, *Human Nature, Election and History*. Eng. trans. Philadelphia: Westminster Press.

— 1984a, *Christian Spirituality and Sacramental Community*. Eng. trans. London: Darton, Longman and Todd.

— 1984b, 'Constructive and Critical Functions of Christian Eschatology', *HTR* 77, pp. 119–39.

— 1985, *Anthropology in Theological Perspective*. Eng. trans. Edinburgh: T. & T. Clark and Philadelphia: Westminster Press.

— 1991, *Systematic Theology*, vol. I. Eng. trans. Edinburgh: T. & T. Clark.

— 1994, *Systematic Theology*, vol. II. Eng. trans. Edinburgh: T. & T. Clark.

— 1998, *Systematic Theology*, vol. III. Eng. trans. Edinburgh: T. & T. Clark.

Perrin, Norman 1976, *Jesus and the Language of the Kingdom*. London: SCM Press.

Peters, Ted 1975, 'Truth in History: Gadamer's Hermeneutics and Pannenberg's Apologetic Method', *JR* 55, pp. 36–56.

1988, 'Pannenberg's Eschatological Ethics', in Carl E. Braaten and Philip Clayton (eds.), *The Theology of Wolfhart Pannenberg: Twelve American Critiques with an Autobiographical Essay and Response* (Minneapolis: Augsburg), pp. 239–65.

Pippin, Tina 1994, 'Peering into the Abyss: A Postmodern Reading of the Biblical Bottomless Pit', in E. Struthers Malbon and Edgar V. McKnight (eds.), *The New Literary Criticism and the New Testament*, (JSNTSup 109; Sheffield: Sheffield Academic Press), pp. 251–67.

Plant, Raymond 1983, *Hegel: An Introduction* (2nd edition). Oxford: Blackwell.

Polk, David P. 1988, 'The All-Determining God and the Peril of Determinism', in Carl E. Braaten and Philip Clayton (eds.), *The Theology of Wolfhart Pannenberg: Twelve American Critiques with an Autobiographical Essay and Response* (Minneapolis: Augsburg), pp. 152–68.

Popper, K. R. 1961, *The Poverty of Historicism*. London: Routledge.

Price, C. P. 1990, 'Revelation as our Knowledge of God: An Essay in Biblical Theology', in John T. Carroll, Charles H. Cosgrove and E. Elizabeth Johnson (eds.), *Faith and History: Essays in Honor of Paul W. Meyer* (Atlanta: Scholars Press), pp. 313–34.

Price, S. R. F. 1984, *Rituals and Power: The Roman Imperial Cult in Asia Minor*. Cambridge: Cambridge University Press.

Prigent, P. 1980, 'Le Temps et le royaume dans l'Apocalypse', in J. Lambrecht (ed.), *L'Apocalypse johannique et l'apocalyptique dans le Nouveau Testament* (Leuven: Leuven University Press), pp. 231–45.

Rahner, Karl 1966, 'The Hermeneutics of Eschatological Assertions', in *Theological Investigations*, vol. IV (London: Darton, Longman and Todd), pp. 323–46.

Räisänen, Heikki 1990, *Beyond New Testament Theology*. London: SCM Press.

Rayner, Steve 1982, 'The Perceptions of Time and Space in Egalitarian Sects: A Millenarian Cosmology', in Mary Douglas (ed.), *Essays in the Sociology of Perception* (London: Routledge and Kegan Paul), pp. 247–74.

Reimer, A. James 1991, 'Biblical and Systematic Theology as Functional Specialities: Their Distinction and Relation', in B. C. Ollenburger (ed.), *So Wide a Sea: Essays on Biblical and Systematic Theology* (Elkhart, Ind.: Institute of Mennonite Studies), pp. 37–58.

Richardson, Alan 1947, *Christian Apologetics*. London: SCM Press.

1964, *History Sacred and Profane*. London: SCM Press.

Ricoeur, Paul 1974, *The Conflict of Interpretations: Essays in Hermeneutics* (ed. D. Ihde). Evanston: Northwestern University Press.

Rissi, Mathias 1966, *Time and History: A Study on the Revelation*. Eng. trans. Richmond: John Knox Press.

1972, *The Future of the World*. Eng. trans. London: SCM Press.

Roberts, Robert, C. 1977, *Rudolf Bultmann's Theology: A Critical Interpretation*. London: SPCK.

Robinson, J. M., and Cobb, J. B., Jr (eds.) 1967, *New Frontiers in Theology*, vol. III: *Theology as History*. New York, Evanston and London: Harper & Row.

Roloff, Jürgen 1993, *The Revelation of John*. Eng. trans. Minneapolis: Fortress.

Rössler, Dietrich 1960, *Gesetz und Geschichte: Untersuchungen zur Theologie der jüdischen Apokalyptik und der pharisäischen Orthodoxie*. WMANT 3. Neukirchen: Neukirchener Verlag.

Rowland, Christopher 1982, *The Open Heaven*. London: SPCK.

1988, *Radical Christianity*. Cambridge: Polity Press.

1993, *Revelation*. London: Epworth.

Rowley, H. H. 1957, *The Relevance of Apocalyptic* (2nd edition). London: Lutterworth Press.

Russell, D. S. 1964, *The Method and Message of Jewish Apocalyptic*. London: SCM Press.

Schlier, Heinrich 1956, *Die Zeit der Kirche*. Freiburg: Herder.

Schmithals, Walter 1975, *The Apocalyptic Movement*. Eng. trans. Nashville and New York: Abingdon Press.

Schnackenburg, Rudolf 1964, 'The Dogmatic Evaluation of the New Testament', in H. Vorgrimler (ed.), *Dogmatic vs Biblical Theology* (London: Burns & Oates), pp. 147–72.

Schneemelcher, W. 1992, *New Testament Apocrypha*, vol. II. Eng. trans. Cambridge: James Clarke & Co. Ltd.

Schneiders, Sandra M. 1991, *The Revelatory Text: Interpreting the New Testament as Sacred Scripture*. San Francisco: HarperCollins.

Scholes, Robert 1982, *Semiotics and Interpretation*. New Haven and London: Yale University Press.

Schwöbel, Christoph 1996, 'Rational Theology in Trinitarian Perspective: Wolfhart Pannenberg's *Systematic Theology*', *JTS* 47, pp. 498–527.

Scobie, C. H. H. 1991, 'The Challenge of Biblical Theology' and 'The Structure of Biblical Theology', *TynBul* 42, pp. 31–61 and 163–94.

Scott, James C. 1990, *Domination and the Arts of Resistance: Hidden Transcripts*. New Haven and London: Yale University Press.

Scruton, Roger 1982, *Kant*. Oxford: Oxford University Press.

Segal, Alan F. 1980, 'Heavenly Ascent in Hellenistic Judaism, Early Christianity and Their Environment', *ANRW* 23.2, Berlin: de Gruyter, pp. 1333–94.

Smalley, Stephen S. 1994, *Thunder and Love: John's Revelation and John's Community*. Milton Keynes: Word Books.

Snyder, Graydon F. 1969, 'The Literalization of the Apocalyptic Form in the New Testament Church', *BR* 14, pp. 5–18.

Sperber, Dan 1975, *Rethinking Symbolism*. Eng. trans. Cambridge: Cambridge University Press.

Stauffer, Ethelbert 1955, *Christ and the Caesars*. Eng. trans. London: SCM Press.

Steiger, Lothar 1967, 'Revelation-History and Theological Reason: A Critique of the Theology of Wolfhart Pannenberg', in R. W. Funk (ed.), *History and Hermeneutic* (New York: Harper and Row), pp. 82–106.

Stendahl, K. 1962, 'Biblical Theology, Contemporary', *Interpreter's Dictionary of the Bible*, New York: Abingdon Press. Vol. I, pp. 418–31.

Stuckenbruck, Loren T. 1995, *Angel Veneration and Christology*. WUNT 2.70. Tübingen: J. C. B. Mohr.

Stuhlmacher, Peter 1979, *Historical Criticism and Theological Interpretation of Scripture: Towards a Hermeneutics of Consent*. London: SPCK.

Sweet, John 1979, *Revelation*. London: SCM Press.

Swete, H. B. 1906, *The Apocalypse of St John*. London: Macmillan.

Talbert, Charles H. 1994, *The Apocalypse: A Reading of the Revelation of John*. Louisville, KY: Westminster/John Knox Press.

Talmon, Shemanyahu 1971, 'The Biblical Concept of Jerusalem', *JES* 8, pp. 300–16.

Thiselton, Anthony C. 1977, 'Semantics and New Testament Interpretation', in I. H. Marshall (ed.), *New Testament Interpretation* (Exeter: Paternoster), pp. 75–104.

 1980, *The Two Horizons: New Testament Hermeneutics and Philosophical Description with Special Reference to Heidegger, Bultmann, Gadamer, and Wittgenstein*. Grand Rapids: Eerdmans; Exeter: Paternoster.

 1992, *New Horizons in Hermeneutics: The Theory and Practice of Transforming Biblical Reading*. London: HarperCollins.

 1995, *Interpreting God and the Postmodern Self: On Meaning, Manipulation and Promise*. Edinburgh: T. & T. Clark.

Thompson, Leonard L. 1986, 'A Sociological Analysis of Tribulation in the Apocalypse of John', *Semeia* 36, pp. 147–74.

 1990, *The Book of Revelation: Apocalypse and Empire*. New York and Oxford: Oxford University Press.

Thompson, Marianne M. 1992, 'Worship in the Book of Revelation', *Ex Auditu* 8, pp. 45–54.

Travis, Stephen H. 1980, *Christian Hope and the Future of Man*. Leicester: Inter-Varsity Press.

Troeltsch, Ernst 1972, *The Absoluteness of Christianity*. Eng. trans. London: SCM Press.

 1977, *Writings on Theology and Religion* (tr. and ed. R. Morgan and M. Pye). London: Duckworth.

 1991, *Religion in History*. Eng. trans. Edinburgh: T. & T. Clark.

Tupper, E. F. 1974, *The Theology of Wolfhart Pannenberg*. London: SCM Press.

Turner, Victor 1974, *Dramas, Fields and Metaphors*. Ithaca and London: Cornell University Press.

Turner, V. and Turner, E. 1978, *Image and Pilgrimage in Christian Culture*. New York: Columbia University Press.

VanderKam, James C. 1986, 'The Prophetic-Sapiential Origins of Apocalyptic Thought', in James D. Martin and Philip R. Davies (eds.), *A Word in Season: Essays in Honour of William McKane* (Sheffield: JSOT Press), pp. 163–76.

Walsh, W. H. 1951, *An Introduction to the Philosophy of History*. London: Hutchinson.

Watson, Francis 1994, *Text, Church and World: Biblical Interpretation in Theological Perspective*. Edinburgh: T. & T. Clark.

 1997, *Text and Truth: Redefining Biblical Theology*. Edinburgh: T. & T. Clark.

Welch, Claude 1972, *Protestant Thought in the Nineteenth Century*, vol. I. New Haven and London: Yale University Press.

Wengst, Klaus 1987, *Pax Romana and the Peace of Jesus Christ*. London: SCM Press.

Wheelwright, Philip 1962, *Metaphor and Reality*. Bloomington: Indiana University Press.

 1968, *The Burning Fountain* (revised edition). Bloomington: Indiana University Press.

Wilcox, Max 1980, 'Tradition and Redaction of Revelation 21:9–22:5', in J. Lambrecht (ed.), *L'Apocalypse johannique et l'apocalyptique dans le Nouveau Testament* (Leuven: Leuven University Press), pp. 205–15.

Wilder, Amos N. 1982, *Jesus' Parables and the War of Myths*. London: SPCK.

Williams, Rowan 1991, 'The Literal Sense of Scripture', *MTheol* 7, pp. 121–34.

Wright, N. T. 1992, *The New Testament and the People of God*. London: SPCK.

Yamauchi, Edwin 1980, *The Archaeology of New Testament Cities in Western Asia Minor*. Glasgow: Pickering and Inglis.

Yarbro Collins, Adela 1977, 'The Political Perspective of the Revelation to John', *JBL* 96, pp. 241–56.

1979, 'Early Christian Apocalypses', *Semeia* 14, pp. 61–121.

1980, 'Revelation 18: Taunt-Song or Dirge?', in J. Lambrecht (ed.), *L'Apocalypse johannique et l'apocalyptique dans le Nouveau Testament* (Leuven: Leuven University Press), pp. 185–204.

1984, *Crisis and Catharsis: The Power of the Apocalypse*. Philadelphia: Westminster Press.

1986, 'Early Christian Apocalypticism', *Semeia* 36, pp. 1–11.

1990, 'Eschatology in the Book of Revelation', *Ex Auditu* 6, pp. 63–72.

Young, F. 1990, *The Art of Performance: Towards a Theology of Holy Scripture*. London: Darton, Longman and Todd.

Young, F., and Ford, D. F. 1987, *Meaning and Truth in 2 Corinthians*. London: SPCK.

Yovel, Yirmiahu 1980, *Kant and the Philosophy of History*. Princeton: Princeton University Press.

INDEX OF PASSAGES CITED

**Other ancient Jewish
literature**

**Other ancient Christian
literature**

INDEX OF MODERN AUTHORS

INDEX OF SUBJECTS